THREE'S A CROWD

THREE'S A CROWD

The Dynamic of Third Parties,
Ross Perot, &
Republican Resurgence

Ronald B. Rapoport
& Walter J. Stone

With a New Afterword

THE UNIVERSITY OF MICHIGAN PRESS *Ann Arbor*

First paperback edition 2008
Copyright © by the University of Michigan 2005
All rights reserved
Published in the United States of America by
The University of Michigan Press
Manufactured in the United States of America
∞ Printed on acid-free paper

2011   2010   2009   2008   6   5   4   3

A CIP catalog record for this book is available from the British Library.

Library of Congress Cataloging-in-Publication Data

Rapoport, Ronald.
    Three's a crowd : the dynamic of third parties, Ross Perot, and
Republican resurgence / Ronald B. Rapoport and Walter J. Stone.
        p.   cm.
    Includes bibliographical references and index.
    ISBN-13: 978-0-472-11453-5 (cloth : alk. paper)
    ISBN-10: 0-472-11453-0 (cloth : alk. paper)
        1. Political parties—United States.   2. Perot, H. Ross, 1930–
3. Republican Party (U.S. : 1854–   )   I. Stone, Walter, 1947–
II. Title.

JK2265.R176   2005
324.273'8—dc22   2005020758

ISBN-13: 978-0-472-03099-6 (pbk. : alk. paper)
ISBN-10: 0-472-03099-X (pbk. : alk. paper)

To our parents:
Audre Rapoport & Bernard Rapoport
Olga W. Stone & Kenneth F. Stone (1911–1999)

Contents

✐

Acknowledgments

⁂

ACKNOWLEDGING THE MANY DEBTS we have accumulated during the years we have worked on this project is a pleasure, not only because writing these words of thanks means we no longer have to endure questions about when the "Perot book" will be finished. This project has taken many twists and turns since we began in the summer of 1992 with a national survey of potential volunteers in the emerging Perot movement. Throughout the project we have been fortunate to have the assistance and support of an ever increasing set of friends, colleagues, family members, and party leaders and officials in completing this book.

Without the willingness of individuals in our samples of potential Perot activists and party contributors to participate in repeated waves of surveys between 1992–2000, our research would not have been possible. Brad Harris, our first contact in the Perot campaign, deserves credit for suggesting we sample from the hundreds of thousands of callers to the toll-free number set up by the Perot campaign in 1992. Clay Mulford, who was involved from the campaign's inception and was campaign chair when Perot reentered the race in October 1992, helped us to secure the 1992 sample as well as a 1996 sample of Reform Party contributors. We owe a debt of thanks also to the Democratic and Republican national committees (and particularly to Janice Knopp and Albert Mitchler at the RNC and Don Fowler and Faith Brown of the DNC) for supplying us with parallel national samples of major-party contributors.

As the project proceeded, we conducted in-depth interviews with relevant participants. Clay Mulford increased our indebtedness to him by agreeing to be the first to provide crucial information about the 1992 Perot campaign. Jack Gargan, Perot's first volunteer and the last chair of the Reform Party before Pat Buchanan's campaign in 2000, was also a great resource.

Others were also generous with their time and information. Dave Sackett, of Lance Tarrance Associates; Joe Gaylord, one of the architects of the Contract with America; Congressman Bill Paxon and Maria Cino, respectively former chair and executive director of the National Republican Congressional Committee; and Bill McClintock of William McClintock Associates aided our understanding of the 1994 election campaign and its outcome. Nancy Rodriguez, treasurer of Virginians for Perot in 1992; Orson Swindle, the first chair of United We Stand America and an advisor to the McCain campaign; Rick Davis, John McCain's campaign manager; Cliff Arnebeck, former chair, Coalition to End the Permanent Congress; and Bill McInturff, McCain's pollster, gave us important insights linking the Perot and McCain campaigns.

Our ability to conduct the surveys would not have been possible without the generous assistance of the National Science Foundation, which awarded us three research grants in support of this project along with several supplemental and Research Experience for Undergraduates (REU) awards (SES-9211432; SBR-9410869; SES-9987446). Data Recognition Corporation provided excellent service with our surveys under the watchful eyes of Deanna Hudella, Carmen Wilson, and Julie Roles, whose professionalism, care, and good humor we probably took too much for granted.

We also had generous support from the College of William and Mary, the University of Colorado, and the University of California, Davis. We are grateful to the Institute of Behavioral Science at the University of Colorado for providing us and our graduate students office space and facilitating our collaboration over seven years when the Rapoport family summered in Boulder. Walt Stone is also grateful to Stanford University's Department of Political Science and the Hoover Institution at Stanford for support and space during an extended leave.

We were blessed with a dedicated group of graduate and undergraduate students, from and with whom we learned a great deal. Colorado students who worked on this project were Lonna Atkeson, Paul Gentile, Patricia Jaramillo, Jennifer Koester, Jay McCann, Randall Partin, David Ungemah, and Lori Weber. On the William and Mary side Brian Berg, Will Blake, Karen Bruner, Mark Burton, Stephanie Caucutt, Brent Colburn, Lauren Fasler, Rachel Fitzgerald, Will Gomaa, Jonathan Kajeckas, John Kauffman, Elizabeth Leon, Doug McNamara, Kris Miler, Richard Perry, Jonathan Pierpan, Jon Rodger, Brian Spang and Andy Tomlinson provided important assistance. Greg Pastor has the distinction of being the only student at both Colorado and William and Mary. Other student assistance came from Lydia Tolles (Stanford) and Ryan Claassen, Monique Schneider, and Jennifer Soares (UC Davis). Although not a student, Patricia Rapoport spent copious hours opening, stuffing, and organizing mailings. There may be others we have failed to mention—if so, we are no less grateful to them.

Several scholars generously provided us with data, including Patrick Brandt, Christian Collet, Gary Jacobson, and Gerald Wright. Richard Winger, of *Ballot Access News*, gave us assistance and information on a number of matters related to third parties in U.S. politics.

Our intellectual debts are acknowledged in our citations to the extensive scholarly literature on which we draw and to which we hope to contribute. In addition we have benefited from comments, suggestions, advice, and support on every aspect of this project from friends and colleagues: Alan Abramowitz, Lonna Atkeson, David Brady, Richard Cook, Larry Evans, Fritz Gaenslen, John Geer, John Green, Ed Greenberg, Bob Jackman, Mary Jackman, Dave Lewis, Jani Little, Zeke Little, Cherie Maestas, Sandy Maisel, Tom Mann, Jay McCann, John McGlennon, John McIver, Kelly Metcalf-Meese, Joel Schwartz, Karen Schwartz, Pat Seyd, Pev Squire, Mike Tierney, Lori Weber, Herb Weisberg, Paul Whiteley, Marshall Wittman, and Gerald Wright. Two anonymous reviewers read the manuscript for the University of Michigan Press and offered many helpful suggestions.

Ron Rapoport would also like to thank Ken Sherrill, who introduced him to political science as a freshman at Oberlin, and Paul Dawson and Jere Bruner who nurtured that interest and delivered him to the University of Michigan, where he had the good fortune of working first with Kenneth Langton and then Kent Jennings. Much of what he brought to this project is attributable to the generous tutelage provided by these mentors.

While working on this book, we have been fortunate in having the advice of several editors whose commitment and interest aided our progress. Nancy Davidson, now retired from Brookings, provided lunches and architectural tours of Washington, DC, along with encouragement and support early in the project. Jim Reische at the University of Michigan Press has been supportive, enthusiastic, and patient in guiding our work into print. His understanding of and appreciation for our project— not to mention his taste in restaurants—make him the ideal editor. Thanks as well to Kevin Rennells and other staff members at The University of Michigan Press for the care they took in editing and producing our work.

Our wives and children tolerated our absences and distractions with grace and humor. Patricia Rapoport and Ann Cassidy-Stone contributed beyond all reckoning; we lack the means to express adequately our gratitude to them. Our children, Abby and Emily Rapoport, and Ken, Jenny, and BJ Stone, grew up hearing about this project and generously lent their time to a variety of tasks. If, in spite of all the able assistance we have received, errors of fact, omission, or interpretation remain, we plan to blame each other.

We dedicate this book to our parents, who first introduced us to the wonders and excitement of politics.

Williamsburg, VA, and Davis, CA, June 2005

I. The Perot Movement & Third-Party Politics in America

I

Introduction

THE DYNAMIC OF THIRD PARTIES

$\mathcal{Op}$

Americans are ambivalent about political parties. Better than 85 percent of American citizens identify more or less strongly with one of the two major parties, most vote consistently with their party identification, and most people think the American two-party system is a good thing. At the same time, however, dissatisfaction with the parties' nominees in presidential elections is common, as many wish they had more choice in elections or would like to see a third party emerge in national politics (Black and Black 1994). Reforms that weaken the parties, such as open primaries and nonpartisan elections, enjoy broad support.

Insurgent candidates have sometimes appeared to benefit from this ambivalence about the major parties, at least to a point. When dissatisfaction with the major parties is high, a third-party or independent candidate is more likely to emerge and attract significant electoral support.[1] The interest in and support for such candidacies can be high, it seems, because they challenge the two-party system and "politics as usual." However, such candidates are also victimized by the attraction most people feel to the major parties. Thus, even though early summer polls showed John Anderson attracting more than 25 percent of prospective

---

1. We follow standard practice and use the expressions *third-party candidate, minor-party candidate,* and *independent candidate* interchangeably to mean a candidate who runs as other than a nominee of the Democratic or Republican parties.

voters' support in 1980 and Ross Perot ahead of the 1992 Democratic and Republican nominees in trial-heat matchups, the inevitable decline set in quickly as voters' loyalties to the major parties kicked in with the onset of their respective campaigns (Zaller and Hunt 1994, 1995). Indeed, formidable barriers to third parties usually deter potential candidates, some of whom are quite prominent, from running outside the two-party system. In fact, of course, "successful" third-party candidacies are rare, and even they require a redefinition of "success." No third party has emerged to form an enduring national political party capable of electing its candidates to multiple offices in the American system of government since the Republican Party appeared in the pre–Civil War turmoil of the 1850s. So, if we mean by "success" a party's ability regularly to elect its candidates to office, including to the presidency, we have no examples in over 150 years. However, most scholars follow Walter Dean Burnham, who defined "successful" third parties as those that attract at least 5 percent of the vote (Burnham 1970, 28).

By the Burnham standard, Ross Perot's electoral movement in 1992 and his Reform candidacy in 1996 were extraordinarily successful. As an independent candidate in 1992, Perot attracted 18.9 percent of the popular vote. As the 1996 nominee of the newly created Reform Party, his popular vote was still comfortably above 5 percent, though it dropped from the 1992 mark to 8.4 percent. Perot's popular-vote total in 1992 was second only to ex-president Theodore Roosevelt's 27.5 percent among all twentieth-century third-party candidates. Perot's was the first third-party movement to attract more than 5 percent of the vote in two successive presidential elections since the Republican Party emerged to supplant the Whigs as the major-party alternative to the Democrats.

As important as the Perot movement is in the history of third parties, this is not a book primarily about Ross Perot as an individual, nor is its principal focus the Perot movement per se. We begin with a simple insight recognized by virtually every close observer of third-party politics in the United States: third parties are creatures of the American two-party system. A typical third party derives its support because in some way the Democratic and Republican parties have failed, and its most important impact on the two major parties typically occurs after the third party disappears. Our study of the Perot movement is primarily a study of a process of major-party change rooted in the emergence, success, and demise of "major" or "successful" third parties of the sort that Burnham discussed. Indeed, Burnham was interested in these parties because he saw them as harbingers of significant major-party change, in the form of a "realignment." While we do not employ a realignment framework for our analysis, we agree with Burnham that enduring shifts in the coalitional makeup of the two major parties are among the most important events in U.S. politics and that the appearance of a popular third party often signals notable change in the two-party system.

STING LIKE A BEE: THE DYNAMIC OF THIRD PARTIES

Burnham is not alone in pointing to the importance of third parties in effecting major-party change. James Sundquist's (1983) treatise on partisan realignment in the United States posits a leading role for third parties. In both the realignment and the third-party literatures, third parties signal deep discontent with the major parties. Third parties instigate change by stimulating a response from the major parties. The key to understanding how third parties produce change is another widely observed regularity: successful third parties do not last long. In fact, the historian Richard Hofstadter (1955, 97) put it succinctly, "Third parties are like bees; once they have stung, they die." He might have said, "*because* they sting, they die." The sting and subsequent demise of the party is what we label the "dynamic of third parties." The dynamic applies to "successful" third parties—candidates and movements that have sufficient electoral clout to "sting" the political system. Change occurs because the successful third party presents the major parties with an opportunity to appeal to the third party's constituency in subsequent elections. One or both major parties changes its positions to bid for the third party's constituency, and former third-party supporters migrate into the party that makes the successful appeal. The third party then dies because its constituency has been co-opted by a major party and because it can no longer attract significant support. "Three's a crowd," then, because the two major parties have such a strong incentive to crowd out the third-party movement in subsequent elections by appealing to its constituency.

Our description of how third parties produce change is not new, although no one, to our knowledge, has called the process the "dynamic of third parties." The process itself has been apparent to students of third parties, as any inspection of their work illustrates. The authors of the most systematic and ambitious analysis of third-party politics in the scholarly literature open their book by pointing to the dynamic of third parties (Rosenstone, Behr, and Lazarus 1996, 8):

> Thus the power of third parties lies in their capacity to affect the content and range of political discourse, and ultimately public policy, by raising issues and options that the two major parties have ignored. In so doing, they not only promote their cause but affect the very character of the two-party system. When a third party compels a major party to adopt policies it otherwise may not have, it stimulates a redrawing of the political battle lines and a reshuffling of the major party coalitions.

J. David Gillespie (1993, 13) succinctly describes the relationship between a third party's level of support and its viability as a party.

> It seems almost to be a natural law: the more formidable a third party's challenge to the central place of the major parties, the more likely it is that the third party's life will be transient and short.

Daniel Mazmanian (1974, 143) likewise points to the regularity of the dynamic of third parties.

> Usually after a strong showing by a minor party, at least one of the major parties shifts its position, adopting the third party's rhetoric if not the core of its programs. Consequently, by the following election the third-party constituency . . . has a major party more sympathetic to its demands.

Some scholars have questioned how much of an impact third parties have. Paul Beck (1997), in a leading textbook on American parties, questions the effect of third parties because very few come close to winning a presidential election or are able to win significant numbers of electoral votes. For instance, as impressive as Ross Perot's popular-vote showing was, he managed to win not a single electoral vote. Occasionally, a third party's vote may be greater than the vote differential between the major parties, but questions can always be raised about whether the election would have been different had the third party not run at all. Likewise, Beck (49–50) raises interesting questions about the influence of third parties on subsequent change in the two major parties. For instance, had a minor party or independent candidate not come forward in a particular election, perhaps interest groups or major-party candidates would have championed issues taken on by the third party. Implicit in Beck's analysis is an assumption that the two-party system is inherently responsive and that it does not require occasional prompting from insurgent electoral movements to detect and respond to change.

The sorts of counterfactuals that would have to be posed in order to address Beck's critique—for example, whether the same level of discontent would have been as effectively communicated in the absence of a successful third-party movement in a given election—are beyond our purpose in this book. We cannot definitively prove that the appearance of a successful third party elevates the chances of major-party response in a way that is different from what would have happened had the third party not appeared, since we do not have the luxury of rerunning elections with and without strong third-party challenges. Nonetheless, the expression *dynamic of third parties* describes a process most scholars agree regularly occurs, which results in an impact of third parties on the major-party system.

If there is nothing new in the dynamic of third parties, why do we need another book on a commonplace observation? We have two answers to that question, one specific to the Perot phenomenon and one more general.

The specific answer is that almost without exception, scholars and other close observers of contemporary electoral politics missed the significance of H. Ross Perot's independent campaign for the presidency in 1992. Our thesis is that the Perot movement fits the dynamic of third parties almost perfectly. That Perot was successful by historic standards in attracting votes is beyond dispute. However, no one has considered the aftermath of the 1992 election through the lens of the dynamic of third parties. Two years after Perot's first campaign, the Republican Party captured majority control of the House of Representatives after forty years as the minority party. Only a few scholars have suggested there might be a link between Perot and the Republican victory (Klinkner 1996; Wattenberg 1996). Indeed, as we shall see in chapter 8, most scholarly accounts of the Republican win in 1994 dismiss or ignore a Perot connection. In fact, just as the dynamic of third parties predicts, a major party made a bid for the Perot constituency, and the Republican Party's victories in succeeding elections can be explained as a direct consequence of the success of that bid.

Why would the scholarly community fail to consider the possibility of a connection between the Republican victory and the Perot movement, especially if the dynamic of third parties is part of the conventional wisdom of political science? One possible answer is suggested by Perot himself. His candidacy was not one calculated to appeal to the academic community. His folksy, straight-talk style struck many academics as simplistic, bordering on demagogic. He stressed a can-do, anti-Washington approach to politics that ignored many of the complexities of governance familiar to close observers. Moreover, he had money—lots of money—and was willing to invest millions of his own money in his campaign. As a consequence, there was a ready-made explanation for Perot's historic success in 1992, which encouraged scholars to ignore the consequences of the Perot movement for major-party change.

In the second edition of their pathbreaking and justifiably influential analysis of third parties, Rosenstone and his coauthors added a chapter on Ross Perot's 1992 campaign. They start by suggesting that Perot did not fit the standard profile of a third-party candidate (Rosenstone, Behr, and Lazarus 1996, 238): "Perot's campaign was anything but a typical third party run for the presidency." While acknowledging that Perot attracted legions of volunteer activists, the authors stress that "it was Perot himself who paid for and controlled the 'grass-roots' movement" (238–39). They dismiss many of the "conventional" explanations for Perot's success, as "myths" that do not withstand scrutiny. Perot's emergence and electoral success cannot be explained because the major parties were in decline or because they aroused unusually high levels of voter dissatisfaction. Voters in 1992 were not especially alienated from conventional politics compared with other recent elections in which no third-party candidate emerged, nor did economic fears, Perot's personal magnetism, or vast untapped potential supporters of a third-party challenge in the electorate explain his extraordinary vote share. The explanation is money, pure and simple (Rosenstone, Behr, and Lazarus 1996, 271).

> The lesson of 1992 . . . is not that the pool of potential third party supporters has expanded. The lesson of 1992 is that *Ross Perot had the resources to tap into that pool.* . . . Perot's success in 1992 does not so much signal a further eroding of the two-party system or a greater willingness of Americans to support third party candidates as it does an even more familiar theme in American politics: money buys votes.

Our point is not to disagree with all of the details of the argument set forth by Rosenstone and his colleagues. Indeed, we agree with them that 1992 was not dramatically different in some respects from years in which no third-party candidate emerged (Gold 1995). We also agree that Perot's money did not hurt. However, we hold that Perot's legitimacy, visibility, and success as a candidate rested more heavily on his ability to mobilize hundreds of thousands of volunteer activists who collected petition signatures to enable him to get his name on the ballot. These activists were crucial in attracting voters to the Perot banner, and we will argue in various ways that his success in recruiting volunteer activists was ultimately more important to his success than was the money he spent on advertising and related expenditures. Moreover, we will show that Perot did not "buy" his activist supporters in the spring and summer of 1992, when the movement took off and gained unprecedented national popularity.

A big problem with the "money explanation" is that it effectively removes from consideration the question of whether the Perot case fits the dynamic of third parties. If Perot "bought votes," why should the major parties alter their message to appeal to his followers? If money is the explanation, the lesson is that the major parties and their candidates need only raise and spend more money (which they certainly have been successful in doing!), not respond to a discontented constituency whose agenda was identified by Perot and whose concerns would have to be recognized by a party bidding for their support. Were money the whole story, the dynamic of third parties would not apply to the Perot case: his constituency would not have been motivated by a coherent issue agenda, and there would have been no basis for a subsequent major-party appeal, with the ensuing change a successful appeal produces.

So one reason we need a book on the dynamic of third parties as it relates to the Perot movement is to set the record straight about the nature of Perot's support, especially the impact of his insurgent campaign on subsequent major-party politics. Our claim, advertised in the subtitle of this book, is that the long-awaited "resurgence" of the Republican Party would not have occurred when it did nor in the manner it did without the intervention and electoral success of H. Ross Perot. This claim is not the least bit conventional. It challenges the dominant scholarly views both of the Perot movement and of the electoral successes enjoyed by the Republican Party following the 1992 election.

Our second, more general answer to the question about why another book on this dynamic is necessary is that ours is not a book primarily about a third party. For the reasons already suggested, it is really a book about the major parties and how they change. To make the argument and present our evidence, we employ a careful study of the Perot movement. That will take us into some of the particulars of Perot's campaigns, and it depends heavily on our analysis of why his supporters did what they did in 1992 and in the elections that followed. In that sense, of course, this is "another book on third parties." However, unlike much of the literature on third parties, we are less concerned with explaining why a third-party candidate chose to run or not to run than we are with explaining the impact of the movement on major-party change. Thus, to make our argument, we utilize the entirely conventional observations we have summarized as the dynamic of third parties, and we apply this framework to our analysis of Perot. In addition, whereas other studies of third parties have had to rely on limited information, we can make use of the most comprehensive data ever collected on a major third party and its supporters. As a result, we can examine the dynamic of third parties in more detail and from a broader variety of perspectives than heretofore has been possible.

In order to make our case, we must be able to move from the specifics of the Perot movement and its aftermath to a general case about third parties and major-party change. That is a difficult task, since we are not studying all third parties that might fit with the expectations of the dynamic.

Three conditions must be met in our analysis of the Perot movement, if the dynamic of third parties is to provide a credible account of this case.

Condition 1: *The Perot movement had a large, identifiable issue constituency.*

We know that Perot's vote in 1992 was, by historical standards, large—almost 19 percent of the popular vote. The 8.4 percent he received in 1996 also easily meets Burnham's 5 percent standard. The more interesting question is whether there was an "issue constituency" behind Perot to which the major parties might reasonably appeal in subsequent elections. In order for the dynamic of third parties to anticipate major-party change as a result of the Perot movement, we must demonstrate that he attracted a significant issue constituency. This is not a foregone conclusion in Perot's case, as many observers criticized Perot for not raising clear issue alternatives, especially in the heady days of the spring and summer of 1992, when his potential independent candidacy attracted its greatest support in trial-heat polls against Clinton and Bush. Typical of this point of view was *Washington Post* columnist E. J. Dionne's observation that "Perot's vote suggests his supporters were bound together only by anger over the nation's economy and a rejection of the two major party nominees."[2] Additionally, of course, if the "money explanation" for Perot's support is right, one implication could be that there was not much substance to his candidacy or to the reasons people supported him.

Condition 2: *Following the election in which Perot first appeared, one or both parties bid for his constituency's support based on the issues that motivated them to support him in the first place.*

In order for such a movement as Perot's to have a lasting impact on the two-party system, its policy agenda must attract the attention of one or both parties. This is the signaling function of third parties alluded to by such scholars as Mazmanian, Burnham, and Sundquist. The general logic is simple: the third party succeeds by tapping a constituency motivated by

---

2. E. J. Dionne, "Anger at the Economy Was the Glue Binding Supporters to Perot," *Washington Post,* November 12, 1992, A10.

concerns that the major parties are not representing. By its success, it signals to the major parties the availability of the constituency in future elections. The major party that is best able to make a credible appeal to the constituency (or the party—perhaps the minority party—with the strongest incentive to make the appeal) actively bids for the third-party backers' support in the interelection period.

We have every reason to believe that a major-party bid can work even in a candidate-centered age when the national party organizations have limited control over the recruitment of candidates or the appeals they make. The bid may be in the form of a coordinated policy shift, reflected in the party's platform or in other official pronouncements from party leaders. However, political parties in U.S. politics are not clearly bounded and hierarchical organizations (Eldersveld 1964), so the bid may also result from uncoordinated but consistent efforts by individual candidates seeking an advantage in their own personal efforts to win office. Candidates for the presidential nomination in their party have powerful incentives to attract new constituencies, sometimes even when those constituencies run contrary to dominant interests in the party (Pastor, Stone, and Rapoport 1999; Stone and Rapoport 1998). In addition, individual candidates for the House of Representatives may see an opportunity in their district, signaled by the success of a third-party candidacy, such as Perot's. In this study, we look for evidence of both coordinated and uncoordinated bids from the two major parties in response to the 1992 Perot campaign.

> **Condition 3:** *Perot supporters responded to a major-party bid by shifting their support to the bidding party. In doing so, they not only improved the electoral prospects of the party; by bringing with them the interests that motivated their support of the third party in the first place, they changed the composition of the major party's supporters, thereby altering the issue commitments of the major party that attracted them.*

Despite the antipathy toward the two major parties that helped generate the opportunity for the third party in the first place, we expect to find third-party backers moving into the major-party system after the initial election. Politics is a dynamic process of bargaining, exchanging support for policy commitments, and responding to changed conditions.

The emergence and death of a third party is no different, and we should not let the vitriolic rhetoric that typically accompanies a third-party campaign blind us to the accommodations and responses that may occur in subsequent elections. The two-party system is highly permeable, with candidates' and officeholders' fortunes fluctuating dramatically with changing events and opportunities. Condition 2 emphasizes that party leaders and candidates are opportunistic, but so are citizens and activists, including those who are attracted to a third party's cause.

As third-party supporters move into one of the major parties, two consequences potentially follow. First, the balance of power between the two major parties may shift. This, after all, is the point of making the bid in the first place. The bidding party seeks to improve its electoral prospects by attracting new supporters to its cause. If the bid is successful, this is what happens, unless core partisans, unhappy with the party's shift in policy commitments, defect in large numbers in response to their party's altered positions as it bids for the third party's constituency.

Second, the party changes as the issue concerns that motivated the third party mix with the major party's policy and issue commitments. The extent of change in the major party depends on how different the third party's constituency is from that of the major party and on how large the third party's constituency is. If the bidding party is successful in attracting the third-party constituency, the direct benefit it receives may be a transformation from minority to majority status. The "price" for this transformation may be a significant change in its own makeup or a dilution of the policy commitments favored by the long-term core of the party. It is also possible, as already noted, that the bid could prompt some core supporters to pull out of the party, since the bid might alter or strain previous policy commitments.

The point of specifying these conditions is to provide signposts to the framework suggested by the dynamic of third parties as we apply it to the Perot case. While we are here inevitably tied to the particulars of the Perot example, our central claim is that Perot is best understood as an example of the more general phenomenon described by the dynamic of third parties. Much has been written about Perot's unique personality, his background of success in business, his campaign style, and his public persona (Barta 1993; Germond and Witcover 1993; Posner 1996). These attributes, which, to be sure, were unique to Perot, led most scholars to agree with Rosenstone and his colleagues that Perot's campaign was anything but typical. While we cover some of the particulars associated with Perot and his campaigns, we do so in order to show how Perot fits the broader pattern described by the dynamic of third parties. Much of our case depends on primary evidence we have collected that has heretofore been unavailable about such a successful third-party movement. Balancing the particular events and findings associated with the Perot case against general claims animated by our framework of third parties and major-party change is a major task of this book.

Surely one question is whether the dynamic of third parties can apply to Perot when he succeeded in attracting over 8 percent of the popular vote in the 1996 election. It is easy to see the "sting" in Perot's 1992 vote, but what about the "death" that is supposed to follow immediately after? Far from disappearing after 1992, Perot created an advocacy organization—United We Stand, America—that sought to influence the 1994 elections. He then formed the Reform Party prior to the 1996 elections, ran in its primary-by-mail against former Colorado governor Dick Lamm, and attracted enough votes to place him fifth among all third-party vote totals in the twentieth century.[3] In creating the Reform Party, Perot claimed to be building an enduring alternative force in American politics, although the party failed to sustain itself, imploding over a divisive leadership fight when Perot did not run again in 2000. In that election, the two candidates claiming to carry the Reform Party's banner, Pat Buchanan and John Hagelin, managed to capture only 0.5 percent of the popular vote between them. Ultimately, the bee "stung" and "died" as predicted, although it was four years behind the schedule dictated by the dynamic of third parties.

Although it is possible that Perot's delayed political demise disqualifies his movement from fitting the dynamic of third parties, we reject that as a significant problem. Many of our reasons will be evident as we build our case, but the skeptical reader might consider this: Perot was

---

3. As mentioned earlier, Theodore Roosevelt was first, with 27.5 percent. Perot's vote share in 1992 was second, Robert LaFollette's 16.6 percent in 1924 was third, and George Wallace was fourth with 13.5 percent. A complete listing of third-party vote shares is provided by Bibby and Maisel (2003).

the first third-party candidate to benefit from a Federal Election Commission subsidy available to him in 1996 on the basis of his performance in the 1992 election and his argument that the Reform Party in 1996 was the heir apparent to the 1992 movement he led. Thus, unique institutional support was present in 1996 that may help account for his second run and for the more modest (but still remarkable) success he enjoyed.[4] We recognize that is probably not an adequate explanation to persuade the reader skeptical about the relevance of the dynamic of third parties to Perot, but perhaps it is enough to allow suspension of disbelief. In the conclusion of the book, we will revisit our case for organizing our understanding around the dynamic of third parties, and the reader will have seen our evidence, which fits the dynamic in all other respects remarkably well.

A WORD ON THE EVIDENCE

Our most significant data source is surveys we conducted of a national sample of potential activist volunteers beginning in the 1992 Perot campaign. In the summer of 1992, we were fortunate to receive from the Perot headquarters access to a computer file of over five hundred thousand individuals who had called the Perot toll-free number set up early in the spring of 1992 to receive calls from potential volunteers. In our initial contacts with the Perot organization in the summer of 1992, we were interested in identifying a sample of individuals who would be roughly equivalent to the major-party activists we had surveyed in previous elections. In those studies of Democratic and Republican activists, we had surveyed individuals who attended precinct caucuses or who served as delegates to state party conventions (Rapoport, Abramowitz, and McGlennon 1986; Rapoport and Stone 1994; Stone et al. 1999; Stone, Rapoport, and Schneider 2004). Of course, the Perot movement was much less structured than a national political party, and neither caucus attenders nor convention delegates existed. We decided to survey a random sample of callers to the Perot phone bank as a roughly equivalent group

---

4. Perot also differed from many other third-party candidates because he did not emerge from one of the major parties and thus could not easily return to a party in subsequent elections.

of individuals who were potential campaign activists (Atkeson et al. 1996; McCann, Rapoport, and Stone 1999).

Why did we focus on activists or potential activists rather than ordinary voters? One reason is convenience and accessibility. Activists (e.g., convention delegates, caucus attendees, or those who call a campaign phone bank) identify themselves as unusually interested in the party or movement and as people who will potentially be active in a future or ongoing political campaign. Third-party voters do not identify themselves except in a cross-section survey of the entire population of citizens. Thus, a survey sample of ordinary citizens, even in a year when a third-party candidacy attracts almost 19 percent of the vote, would include a relatively small number of respondents who voted for the third party.[5] If it is necessary to follow third-party voters through subsequent elections, as it is if we are to study implications of the dynamic of third parties, a small baseline sample of voters in the initial election quickly dwindles to meager numbers in subsequent election years.[6]

Other limitations make it difficult for us to rely heavily on voter surveys. In the 1992 election, which was a golden opportunity for the scholarly community to study a third-party movement, Perot himself complicated things dramatically by dropping out of the race between July 16 and October 1, when he redeclared his candidacy. Prior to Perot dropping out of the campaign, the American National Election Study (ANES) staff at the University of Michigan was preparing its interview schedule for the 1992 survey to include a substantial number of questions about Perot and the choice that voters would make in the context of a three-candidate race. However, when Perot dropped out, the ANES greatly reduced the number of questions on its survey pertaining to Perot, and it was unable to reinstate dropped questions after he reentered the race. The result of these limitations is that while we can use the 1992 ANES survey and the 1992–96 ANES panel for some purposes in our analysis, the data are not sufficiently rich to support analysis across the

---

5. For example, the 1992 National Election Study panel survey of the American electorate conducted by the University of Michigan yielded only 128 respondents who reported voting for Ross Perot in the presidential election in that year.

6. The ANES panel included only sixty-one 1992 Perot voters who reported casting a presidential vote in the 1996 election.

full range of questions of interest to us. Several studies of voting for Perot that have been conducted on the 1992 ANES survey do an excellent job of exploring the reasons voters supported or rejected Perot's 1992 candidacy (Abramson et al. 1995; Abramson et al. 2000; Alvarez and Nagler 1995; Gold 1995).[7]

Our surveys of potential Perot activists do not suffer from any of the limitations that restrict our use of general-population surveys. Because we could identify potential Perot activists in advance by sampling from those who called the Perot headquarters, we knew that our sample would yield 100 percent potential activists (by definition) and, we had reason to hope, a large number of actual activist supporters of Perot. In addition, because our study was dedicated to understanding the Perot movement, we devoted our entire survey instrument to questions relevant to a comprehensive analysis of third-party support. We were not deterred from our study when Perot dropped out, although we were concerned for a time that we would not have the opportunity to study an election with a strong third-party candidate.[8] Thus, we have a large sample of potential Perot supporters from our 1992 survey (numbering 1,321 respondents to the August survey), which can form a basis for detailed and confident analysis of the 1992 Perot campaign. This survey also serves as the baseline of a long-term panel study of Perot activist supporters between 1992

---

7. Another source we consulted on voters' response to Perot was exit polls, which yield much larger samples of Perot voters than the ANES surveys, partly because exit polls are based on much larger samples of the national electorate and partly because they only sample individuals who actually voted. The principal limitations of exit polls for our purposes are the small number of questions that can be included and the absence of panel data on respondents. As a result, the identification of Perot voters in 1992 for purposes of studying their behavior in subsequent elections must depend on recall questions, which are notoriously unreliable, especially for general-population surveys about politics. Despite these limitations, we occasionally found it useful to this study to report results from exit polls.

8. Our design called for a preelection survey of Perot callers, which we conducted in September 1992, after Perot dropped out of the campaign. Until he redeclared his candidacy, we thought that our study would end with the postelection survey immediately following the 1992 election, in which we intended to study how supporters of Perot active in the precampaign phase responded to the two-party race between President George H. W. Bush and Bill Clinton. Happily for our study, Perot reentered the campaign, which enabled us to use the August and postelection surveys as a basis for a much more extensive (and, we think, more interesting) study of a major third-party candidacy and its impact on the two-party system.

and 2000. By recontacting our 1992 respondents after the 1994, 1996, and 2000 elections, we were able to follow them through the stages described by the dynamic of third parties, study their reactions to the bids for their support made by the major parties, and track their response to the decline and ultimate demise of the third-party movement they championed in 1992.[9] In short, our design allows us to examine for the first time in great detail the implications of the dynamic of third parties not only as it applies to the behavior of the electorate as a whole but also as it works out in the attitudes and behaviors of core supporters of the third-party movement. To the best of our knowledge, ours is the only large-scale national study ever conducted that is capable of an extensive examination of third-party support and its aftermath.

Our decision to focus the study on activist and potential activist supporters of a third-party movement has other implications as well. In the first place, of course, it means our primary concern is not with voters, even though voters provide the single most visible manifestation of a third party's success or failure. When, as is typical, a minor candidate fails to attract many voters, little attention is paid to the matter. When the occasional "major" third party appears, its success is marked primarily by the size of the vote share it attracts. Likewise, a third-party candidacy, such as Ralph Nader's in 2000, that despite its small vote share is widely seen as affecting the outcome of the election also attracts significant attention. In all cases, the visibility and perceived importance of a third-party movement is closely tied to its ability to attract votes.

Though choosing to study activists rather than voters, we do not disagree with the conventional view that a third party unable to attract significant voter support is of limited interest. For reasons tied to the dynamic of third parties, third parties successful with voters are of enormous potential importance in understanding the shape of our politics. However, our focus on activists does not undermine our ability to understand voters. In the first place, activists are a critically important resource in attracting votes for any electoral movement, whether of a major or third party. Numerous studies have found that activists play a central role in mobilizing ordinary voters, both by leading opinion and by stimulating

---

9. Details about the survey may be found in appendix A.

others to participate (Beck 1974; Eldersveld 1956; Gerber and Green 2000; Katz and Eldersveld 1961; Rosenstone and Hansen 1993). In addition, for a third-party candidate—such as Perot—whose name would not appear on any state's presidential ballot without extensive grassroots efforts in organizing and collecting ballot petition signatures, a serious campaign is impossible without the activists necessary to gain access to the ballot. Activists also extend legitimacy and visibility to a campaign through their personal networks and activity that have an enormous effect on voters' response.

There is another advantage to studying activists, beyond their ecological place in the typical election campaign. Activists are generally better informed about politics and more engaged in the campaign than the average voter, and they are relatively well versed in the choices and issues at stake. As a result, the issue basis of a party or a campaign typically comes into sharper relief by studying activists than by looking exclusively at voters (Kirkpatrick 1975; McClosky, Hoffman, and O'Hara 1960; Miller and Jennings 1986). Of perhaps even greater importance, campaign activists are likely to be especially sensitive to changing opportunities and choices as events unfold (Carmines and Stimson 1989; Jacobson 2000; Miller and Schofield 2003). Third-party activists, for instance, should be more aware of and more responsive than third-party voters to a major-party bid for their support, and a successful bid would almost surely have to appeal to activists as part of its ultimate strategy of attracting voters (Miller and Schofield 2003). Finally, the concept of "political support" takes on a richer meaning in the context of a study of campaign activism than it does when analyzing voting choice. Support as voting is either "on" or "off" in the case of a citizen who votes or fails to vote for a candidate. Campaign activism can be reduced to the same qualitative distinction if we measure whether or not an individual was actively supportive in any way for a campaign, and it will at times be convenient to treat activism as a simple dichotomy of this sort. However, it is also possible to assess the degree of activism, as when we compare individuals who engage in many forms of active support (e.g., contributing money, canvassing for a candidate, and collecting petition signatures) with others who participate in only one or some of these ways. In many instances, comparisons of the amount and type of active support offer a richer basis of analysis than does measuring support by whether or not individuals cast a vote.

Thus, because of the importance of activists in any third-party movement and because their accessibility makes possible the sort of intensive and long-term study that would be difficult or impossible to conduct on ordinary voters, our panel of potential Perot volunteers provides important evidence about why people supported the Texas independent. We also have national samples from 1996 of contributors to the Democratic, Republican, and Reform parties as a second source of activist data, which is especially useful for comparing major-party activists with Reform/Perot activists.[10] Where possible, we supplement our activist surveys with data on the electorate as a whole, typically from the ANES surveys. In addition, we employ other data sources to round out our case, including election-return data, roll-call data, and a variety of other sources, notably in-depth interviews with individuals close to the Perot movement and to the major-party efforts to bid for the Perot constituency after 1992. These other sources of data are especially important to link our study of activists directly to voters, who determine election outcomes, and to members of Congress, who make policy, since third-party activists by themselves do neither of these things directly. These other sources of information provide multiple opportunities to corroborate our theoretical expectations about the impact of a third-party movement well beyond the realm of the activists we surveyed.

THE PLAN OF THIS BOOK

Part 1 sets the context for this book by approaching the question of third-party politics in the United States at the general and specific levels. The general level is described by the framework provided by the dynamic of third parties and, in chapter 2, with a theory of third-party support and major-party change. The dynamic and the theory are both intended to situate our understanding of the Perot movement—as it ap-

---

10. Contributors to all three parties responded to direct-mail solicitations by the parties. The average contribution made was less than fifty dollars, with very few individuals making contributions over two hundred dollars (Stone, Rapoport, and Schneider 2004). Details about these surveys are provided in appendix A in the present study.

peared and garnered support in the 1992 election and in its aftermath through the 2000 election—in the broadest possible context. We seek to identify general insights and propositions that might apply to any successful third-party movement in American history or in the future and to set the analytical agenda for the rest of the book. Chapter 3 shifts to the specifics of the Perot movement by describing the essential facts of his emergence as a candidate, the way he conducted his campaigns, and the ultimate fate of his movement.

Parts 2–4 each address one of the three conditions of the dynamic of third parties spelled out in this chapter. Part 2 develops an explanation for why activists supported Perot, with a special emphasis on the issue basis of that support. We demonstrate that there was indeed a coherent issue component to Perot activism (chaps. 4–5). We also address the decline in support for Perot between the 1992 and 1996 elections as a way of further exploring the basis of Perot's support and its implications for major-party change (chap. 6).

Part 3 concerns the bid the major parties made for the Perot constituency. Although the Clinton administration made an early bid for Perot backers, the Republican Party was much better situated to bid for the Perot constituency. One reason for this was that the Republicans were out of power after the 1992 elections, when the Democrats held the presidency and both houses of Congress. The Perot constituency's dissatisfaction with "politics as usual" and with some parts of the Clinton program gave the Republicans a significant advantage. The Republican bid came in two forms: coordinated moves by the national leadership of the GOP and strategic decisions by individual House and presidential candidates who saw an opportunity to advance their own individual ambitions in the aftermath of the Perot movement. Both the coordinated and the strategic moves by individual candidates add up to a substantial bid by the Republican Party for the support of the Perot constituency.

Part 4 examines the response of the Perot constituency to the Republican bid, a response that produced a "Republican resurgence" beginning with their historic victory in the 1994 elections. We use election-return data to link the 1992 Perot vote to the 1994 Republican victory in the House of Representatives and in the 2000 presidential election. We use our activist panel to demonstrate the effect of participation in the 1992 Perot campaign on the response by Perot activists to the Republican bid. There is an irony to this story: the bitter Perot attack on the major parties in 1992 was especially vitriolic when aimed at the Republican Party and its incumbent nominee President George H. W. Bush, yet the more committed activists were to the Perot campaign in that year, the more likely they were to become engaged in subsequent Republican campaigns. Following the 2002 elections, the Republicans held majorities in all major policy-making branches of the national government, an outcome scarcely to be expected or explained without the appearance and success of Ross Perot in the 1992 election and the logic of the dynamic of third parties in subsequent elections.

II. Understanding the Support for Perot

II

A Theory of Third-Party Support &
Major-Party Change

⁂

IN THIS CHAPTER, WE FRAME OUR analysis of the particulars associated with the Perot movement in 1992 and the ensuing period through
the 2000 election in a broader understanding of how third parties relate
to the two-party system. There are many aspects of the Perot phenomenon that are undoubtedly unique, but our goal in this chapter is to state
our theoretical expectations as broadly and as generally as we can.

In chapter 1, we spelled out three conditions that must be met for the
dynamic of third parties to apply to the Perot movement: an issue-based
constituency for the movement, a major-party bid for the constituency's
support, and a response by the Perot constituency to that bid. These
conditions compel us to address two broad questions in our theory: (1)
why do people support a third-party or independent candidate, and (2)
what is the *effect* of third-party involvement on subsequent political participation, especially participation in major-party campaigns? Understanding why people supported Perot will enable us to assess the extent
to which an issue constituency existed among his backers and the opportunities that constituency created for subsequent major-party appeals. The second question addresses the consequences of the third party
for individuals who supported it and leads us to explore what Perot supporters did in the ensuing elections. The dynamic of third parties raises
specific expectations about major-party bids and third-party supporters'
response, which will structure how we look at the elections between
1992 and 2000.

THE PUSH-PULL MODEL OF
THIRD-PARTY SUPPORT

Virtually any expression of political support is some combination of a positive impulse for an outcome that is favored and a negative reaction against a result that is opposed. A vote in a two-party presidential race may be cast for a candidate or party, for the policy positions of the candidate, or for the candidate because of her positive personal attributes. Explanations of voting choice that emphasize the agreement between the policy stands of the candidate and the individual voter rely on this sort of mechanism (Downs 1957; Merrill and Groffman 1999; Rabinowitz and Macdonald 1989). Voters may also express their dissatisfaction with a candidate or party by their vote for the opposition. In its purest form, rejection of the qualities or performance of one candidate is the sole motivation, with no implication that the voter agrees with the policy stands or other qualities of the candidate for whom she votes (Fiorina 1981; Key 1966; Markus 1988). In reality, combinations of positive and negative motivations influence voters in all elections.

An independent candidate must either attract support that would otherwise go to one of the two major parties or mobilize supporters who previously have not been politically involved. The basis of third-party support involves a combination of attraction and rejection in a slightly different mix than just described for the voter in a two-party contest. The attraction, or "pull," side results from the same sort of factors that can motivate supporters in the two-party case. People support a third-party candidate because they are attracted to him as a positive alternative to the Democratic and Republican candidates.

The premise of the "push" side is that one of two kinds of dissatisfaction with the two-party system must be present. The first kind of discontent arises from a failure of either major party to provide sufficiently attractive alternatives to motivate support. This sort of dissatisfaction will be indicated when the more attractive of the two parties fails to promise a sufficiently desirable outcome. The lower the appeal of the more attractive major-party candidate, the more likely the citizen is to back the independent candidate. This is part of what observers have meant by "major-party failure." Rosenstone, Behr, and Lazarus (1996, 128) succinctly describe this aspect as it applies to voters: "The greater the [policy] distance between the voter and the nearest major party candidate, the more likely it is that the voter will look for a third party alternative . . . [and] the greater the likelihood the voter will cast a third party ballot."

The second "push" ingredient is the amount of choice between the two major parties. The greater the perceived choice between the Democratic and Republican parties is, the more likely the individual is to back the more attractive major-party candidate, even if the dissatisfaction with the favored party/candidate is substantial. The choice between the parties affects the stake the individual has in the outcome of the major-party conflict. A substantial perceived choice gives the individual a stake in the outcome because the loss associated with the less-favored candidate winning is substantial. When George Wallace made his famous claim that there was not a "dime's worth of difference" between the Democratic and Republican parties, he was attempting to persuade potential supporters that they had no stake in the conflict between the major parties. All successful third-party candidates follow Wallace's strategy of emphasizing the absence of a "real choice" between the two major parties.

Figure 2.1 presents the push-pull model of third-party support. The dimension in the figure represents a potential supporter's degree of satisfaction with a political option from least to most attractive. The figure is set up so that the distance between a candidate and the most attractive alternative is the loss represented by the option that candidate presents. In the example illustrated in the figure, the third-party candidate represents an outcome more satisfying to the potential supporter than either of the two major parties. Major-party candidate 1 (**M1**) is substantially less satisfactory than the third-party candidate but is more desirable than major-party candidate 2 (**M2**). Throughout this book, we represent the more satisfactory of the two major parties or candidates as **M1** and the less satisfactory party or candidate as **M2**. The broken lines represent relevant quantities on the satisfaction dimension. Line **A** describes the distance between the independent candidate and the potential supporter's most attractive outcome. In the example illustrated in the figure, the "loss" associated with the third-party candidate's election is small, indicating relatively high satisfaction from that outcome. The more satisfying the candidate is (the lower the loss; the shorter line **A** is), the greater

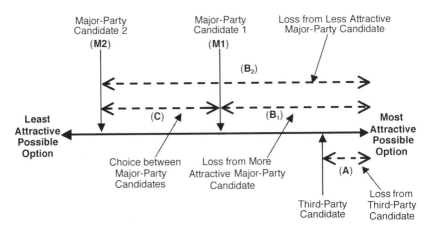

Fig. 2.1.   Push-pull model of third-party support

the pull to the third party is and the more likely the citizen is to back the independent candidate.

Line B_1 represents the loss associated with the more satisfactory major-party candidate. The greater this distance is, the greater the push away from the major party is and the more open the potential supporter is to backing an independent candidate. If there are sufficient numbers of individuals who are disaffected from the two-party system in this way, the potential for a substantial third-party constituency exists. In the absence of a third-party alternative, individuals who are dissatisfied may decide to support the closer major party or to abstain from participation altogether. The distance can create a constituency for the third party if a third party can situate itself in the space between **M1** and its potential supporters (as in fig. 2.1). Of course, the larger the number of individuals who are distant from the major candidates is, the larger the potential third-party constituency is.

The loss associated with the least satisfactory major-party candidate is represented by line B_2. The gap between the two major parties ($B_2 - B_1$ = **C**) represents the degree of choice between them. The smaller **C** is, the less choice there is between the parties, and the greater the push is toward the third party, independent of how close the major parties are to the individual. In the absence of a compelling choice between the major parties, the individual has little stake in the outcome of their conflict. It matters little to the potential supporter whether party 1 or party 2 wins in that event, and a relatively attractive third-party alternative becomes more appealing. On the other hand, the greater the preference is for one major party over the other (the larger **C** is), the less likely the individual is to support the third party, independent of where **M1** is and of where the third party is located.

Dimensions of Evaluation in the Push-Pull Model

Figure 2.1 presents the logic of the push-pull model using an abstract dimension of how attractive different political outcomes are. What dimensions of evaluation are potential supporters likely to use in determining the desirability of political outcomes? Two of the most important are (1) evaluations of the quality of candidates in the election and (2) the policies and issues addressed in the campaign.[1]

CANDIDATE EVALUATIONS

Positive affect toward the candidates may mean that individuals are attracted to candidates seen as having positive traits, such as warmth and trustworthiness, or that they judge candidates especially competent in fulfilling the roles of the office, such as the ability to manage economic and foreign affairs. When candidates are evaluated positively, support is more likely than when they are evaluated negatively. The "pull" side of the model in figure 2.1 is captured by potential supporters' evaluations of the independent candidate, with the expectation that the higher the rating of the candidate is, the more likely the potential supporter is to back the candidate. On the "push" side, the higher the rating of the more favored major-party candidate is, the less likely the potential supporter is to back an independent candidate. Likewise, the greater the difference in affect between the Democratic and Republican candidates is, the lower the support for the third-party candidate is. The conditions most likely

---

1. Much of our emphasis in discussing third-party support is on the candidates rather than on the parties, although we have data on evaluations and perceptions of the parties as well as the candidates. We speak primarily of the candidates because, as a practical matter, candidates are usually more visible and salient referents in the context of the campaign than parties and because the findings when we focus on candidates as opposed to parties tend to be somewhat sharper (although the results in both cases are consistent). We introduce parties explicitly into our analysis when we examine issue priority.

to stimulate support for a third-party candidate, then, are when that candidate is well liked and when both the Democratic and Republican nominees are regarded as unattractive candidates.

ISSUE DISTANCE

We assume that the most attractive policy option occurs when a candidate exactly agrees with the position of the potential supporter. Thus, if an individual takes a moderately favorable position on government-sponsored health insurance, her most attractive outcome is a candidate who takes the same position. A candidate who opposes government-sponsored health insurance or who is more "extreme" in support of government health insurance would be less desirable to the citizen (cf. Rabinowitz and MacDonald 1989). The location of candidates and parties in the "issue space" can then be compared with citizen's own policy preferences, with the purpose of comparing distances between the positions candidates take and the preferences of potential supporters.

When applied to the model in figure 2.1, the issue position that exactly agrees with the position of the potential supporter is the most "extreme" position on the right end of the continuum, labeled "most attractive possible option." The "loss" associated with a candidate's issue position is the distance between the citizen's preferred position and the position of the candidate. The greater that loss is, the less likely the citizen is to support the candidate. However, the logic of the model as it applies to the issue positions of the candidates and potential supporters will be clearer if we depict the positions of the candidates and the potential supporter in the more typical left-right issue space, where the left end of the continuum is the most liberal possible position and the right end is the most conservative possible position. The potential activist in figure 2.2 is slightly right-of-center in her policy preferences; the third-party candidate is $\mathbf{A}$ units to her right; major-party candidate 1 is $\mathbf{B}_1$ units to her right; and major candidate 2 is $\mathbf{B}_2$ units to her left. These all represent exactly the same distances as in figure 2.1. Apart from scale, the difference is that the issue positions in figure 2.2 are relative to the position of the potential activist on a traditional left-right continuum, rather than on a dimension ranging from least to most attractive. We could reconstruct figure 2.1 from figure 2.2 simply by folding the dimension in

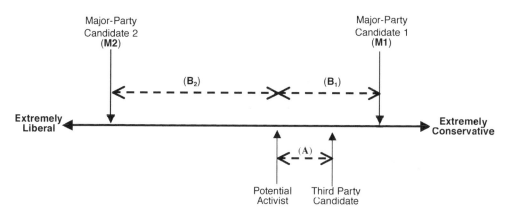

Fig. 2.2. Model of third-party support on liberal-conservative dimension

figure 2.2 at the point of the policy position of the potential activist, since that is her most attractive option.

Just as in figure 2.1, the pull of a third-party candidate is captured by the difference between the candidate's position and that of the citizen. The closer the candidate is to the citizen's own policy preferences on the issue (**A**), the more likely that individual is to support the candidate. It is important to see, however, that on an issue dimension where the candidates can be on the opposite sides of the potential supporter, the choice between the candidates is not equal to the distance between the candidates. Let us assign negative values to represent the number of units **M2** is to the liberal side of the potential activist, and let us assign positive scores to represent the number of units **M1** is to the conservative side of the potential supporter. Then, as figure 2.2 shows, **M2** is three units more liberal than the potential supporter (**B**$_2$ is equal to -3), while **M1** is two units to her right (**B**$_1$ is equal to $+2$). In this example, then, the algebraic difference between **M1** and **M2** is five units, but the choice relative to the potential supporter is one unit. If we imagine moving **M1** one more unit to the right, the difference on the scale between the two candidates would increase to six units, but the choice would drop to zero because both major-party candidates would be equidistant from her position.

The distinction between the distance between the major-party candidates and the choice between them applies to any citizen located between the two major candidates. For a citizen more extreme than both candidates, either on the liberal or the conservative side, the choice and the distance between the major candidates are identical.[2]

Issues have effects comparable to evaluations: (1) the closer potential supporters are to the third-party candidate (the smaller is distance $\mathbf{A}$), the more they support the candidate; (2) the greater the distance between potential supporters and $\mathbf{M1}$, the more they are pushed toward supporting the third-party candidate (distance $\mathbf{B_1}$); and (3) the less choice there is between the major candidates (distance $\mathbf{C}$, or $|\mathbf{B_1} - \mathbf{B_2}|$), the greater the support is for the third-party candidate.

The model in figure 2.2 assumes that there is only one issue and that all that matters is the distance between candidates and the potential supporter. However, a candidate's issue position is not the only political outcome of concern. Potential supporters want their preferred policies to be implemented. Because the American system of government is complex, electing a candidate who takes a favorable position on an issue does not guarantee that position will actually be implemented. Presidents do not make policy by themselves, and they do not succeed in realizing every policy commitment they make. They are usually dependent on the support of their party in Congress. The higher priority of a policy issue on the agenda of the party, the more likely the commitment is to be realized. The lower the policy is among the party's priorities, the more likely it is to fall by the wayside in the give-and-take of the process following the election. Therefore, when we turn to issue priority, we explicitly bring parties into the model, taking account of the dual influences of candidate and party.

Imagine a major-party candidate who adopts a position on an issue that is close to the citizen's own preferences on the issue. In this example, the distance ($\mathbf{B_1}$) between the candidate ($\mathbf{M1}$) and the citizen is small, and it would seem that there is little room for a third-party candidate to emerge and win the citizen's support. However, if the issue has a low

---

2. In the case of a third-party candidate who appeals to extreme voters, as George Wallace did in 1968, the lack of a "dime's worth of difference" between the major candidates (Wallace's claim in his race) equates the distance between the candidates and the choice faced by potential supporters.

priority for the party, the fact that the candidate has taken a pleasing position on it may be of little interest to the citizen, since the likelihood of implementation is small. Especially if the issue is of great importance to the citizen, her interest will be not only in a party's candidate who takes the right position on the issue but also in the party that gives the issue the same high priority that she does. An opportunity for a third-party candidate arises when an issue that is important to many citizens exists and that issue has not been given sufficient attention by the major parties, even if one of the parties routinely takes pleasing positions on it. Citizens who are dissatisfied in this regard are skeptical not about the positions the candidates take on the issue but about whether the issue has a sufficiently high priority so that the positions taken may be implemented. An example of dissatisfaction with a major party's priorities might be the Perot criticism of the Republican Party's commitment to balancing the federal budget. Despite consistent campaign stands in favor of a balanced budget, both Presidents Reagan and Bush presided over record deficits.

Issue priority, therefore, is a dimension on which the parties may be judged, independent of the positions their candidate takes on the policy issue. As such, the "push" and "pull" components apply. Citizens are pulled toward a third party that shares their priorities. Likewise, citizens are pushed away from supporting a major party when the Democratic and Republican parties fail to adopt as their priorities issues of concern to citizens.

The push-pull dimensions so far discussed—candidate evaluations, issue distance, and issue priority—do not exhaust all of the ways that individuals may be pushed or pulled to support a third-party candidate. As we expand the analysis of why people supported Perot, we will accommodate a wider range of factors in our explanation. Nonetheless, the most important dimensions are those related directly to defining the issue constituency of the Perot movement. These issue positions, whether defined by the pull toward the third-party candidate or the push away from the major parties that arises from issue-based dissatisfaction, form the basis for the long-term impact of the third party on the major-party system.

THIRD PARTIES &
MAJOR-PARTY CHANGE

If a successful third party indicates that substantial interests have been left out of the two-party system, its emergence may stimulate significant change because of the response it prompts from one or both of the major parties. According to the dynamic of third parties, successful third parties disappear because they prod the major parties to shift their positions or appeals to capture the constituency of the third party. Such shifts are one way that a third party could stimulate change in the larger party system even as it fades from view. Conditions 2 and 3 of the dynamic of third parties describe this process by emphasizing the major-party bid for the third party's supporters and the subsequent response of these supporters to the change in major-party appeals.

Major-Party Bids for the Third Party's Constituency

Condition 2 of the dynamic of third parties, while crucial to our overall argument, is relatively simple in its implications: either there is evidence that one or both major parties bid for the Perot constituency following the 1992 election, or there is not. We argue that there is ample evidence of a major-party bid, especially by the Republican Party. Our purpose in this chapter is to suggest what a major-party bid might look like, rather than to present the evidence (for which see chap. 7).

How can a political party make policy commitments? Because the American parties are loosely organized, there are many possibilities, all of which we summarize under two broad headings: parties make policy commitments explicitly, through deliberate action taken by an established organizational wing of the party; and parties make commitments implicitly, by building a record of policy-related action as a by-product of uncoordinated individual behavior by officeholders, office seekers, and activists.

The parties make formal policy commitments in a number of ways, some quite visible, others not so visible. We emphasize the most prominent examples of formal party action, including the platforms of the parties' presidential nominating conventions (which make policy commitments) and the party leadership offices in Congress. In this context, the "political parties" are the national party committees and national convention delegates and the party leadership offices in the national government (Budge and Hofferbert 1990; Fishel 1985; Pomper 1973).

The American parties, because of their highly permeable nature, their lack of control over candidate nomination processes, and the fact that they are loose coalitions of state parties (which themselves have limited control and resources), are especially prone to making policy commitments implicitly, through informal and more or less uncoordinated action by officeholders and candidates. One example of this sort of action is in the thousands of roll-call votes cast by members of Congress. These votes may reflect formal policy commitments by the parties, but most often they do not, even when the votes cast reflect sharp party differences.[3] While roll-call votes do not constitute a formal commitment on future policy, they do form a record of policy stands on issues facing government and society. Scholars and other observers of politics examine patterns of roll-call voting in Congress to identify party positions. Political parties are constrained by the record of policy action they establish. In particular, future officeholders and candidates must live with the record established by their forebears. Individual candidates and officeholders are free to disagree with that record or to defend it and extend it as they see fit, but it is likely to affect perceptions of voters, activists, and other officeholders about party policy positions (Cox and McCubbins 1993). Voters, activists, contributors, the press, and other key actors draw inferences from candidates' party affiliation about their positions on a range of issues. Of course, those inferences may be incorrect in the case of any particular issue and candidate, but they are nonetheless important in how the candidate is perceived by potential supporters and political opponents.

Another example of uncoordinated action of particular interest to us

---

3. There is a lively debate in the literature on Congress about how important formal party commitments are in producing party-line voting in Congress. On one side are scholars who argue that party organizations exert at least a marginal influence over roll-call votes (see, e.g., Cox and McCubbins 1993; Rohde 1991). On the other side are those who argue that when party divisions occur on roll-call votes, they are due to the policy preferences of the individual legislators, including the preferences of their constituencies, rather than to any coercive influence or collective action by the national parties (see Brady and Volden 1998; Krehbiel 1998).

concerns individuals deciding to run for national office. While congressional candidates are sometimes actively recruited to run by the national party organizations, the final decision is always an individual one, and the parties most often play only a modest role in candidate emergence. The decision to run is highly strategic, as potential candidates are strongly influenced by their prospects of winning (Black 1972; Jacobson and Kernell 1983; Maisel and Stone 1997; Stone, Maisel, and Maestas 2004). As a result, when potential candidates anticipate favorable conditions in the next election, stronger candidates with office-holding experience and the ability to attract voter support in their districts emerge to run. When conditions are not favorable, strong candidates sit out the election, leaving the field to inexperienced candidates who generally do poorly (Jacobson 1989; Jacobson and Kernell 1983). In other words, when there is an opportunity to build support and run an effective campaign, skilled and experienced candidates emerge to run. If the presence of a successful third party in the previous election signals an opportunity in a particular district, entrepreneurial and strategic prospective candidates may decide to run for Congress and appeal to supporters of the third party. These individual decisions could amount to a "major-party bid" for the third party's constituency if candidates in one party were much more likely to seize the opportunity than candidates in the other major party, even if their decisions were completely uncoordinated by a national party. In the same way, candidates for a major party's presidential nomination might seek the support of the third party's backers, without the approval of the national party.

Of course, if these major-party candidates are successful in their efforts to attract former backers of the third party, the result could easily be change in their party. The party would change because candidates who ran on commitments to attract the third party's constituency would feel compelled to act on those commitments when in office. Even if the candidates were unsuccessful, the party might still change in response to their efforts to mobilize erstwhile third-party supporters. These supporters may remain involved in other major-party campaigns, carrying with them the issue concerns that motivated their involvement for the third party in the first place. In turning to condition 3 of the dynamic of third parties, we consider these possibilities for how third parties change the major parties.

The Response of Third-Party Supporters to a Major-Party Bid

Condition 3 of the dynamic of third parties is a response on the part of third-party supporters to the bid made by a major party to attract them. If there is no response by the third party's constituency, it is difficult to see how the insurgent movement can effect change in the major parties. Supporters might remain outside the two-party system after the third party dies, either withdrawing from involvement altogether or participating in subsequent third-party movements as a roving constituency of discontent. In the Perot case, we expect a bid and the consequent change to occur after 1992, even though Perot ran again in 1996. As a result of the bid, we anticipate a decline in support for Perot between 1992 and 1996—a decline apparent in the drop in his popular vote from almost 19 percent to just over 8 percent. Typically, the decline in a third party's vote can be explained by the simple fact that the third-party candidate does not run a second time.[4] The fact that Perot did run a second time creates a unique opportunity for studying the dynamic, since 1992 Perot supporters had the choice in 1996 of remaining involved for Perot, shifting support to one of the major parties, or dropping out of campaign participation altogether.

Our situation is thus both more complex and more promising than if we were conducting a similar study of Roosevelt activists following the 1912 election or of Wallacites in the aftermath of 1968. It is more complex because, like their predecessors in previous third-party movements, many Perot activists disengaged from their third-party involvement in 1996, but unlike their predecessors in previous third-party movements, they were not forced to drop out by the absence of their candidate in the next election. We cannot say whether Perot's decision to run again meant that the major parties were less successful in bidding for his constituency than they had been in the case of previous third-party movements, but the fact that he ran allows us to weigh the effects of major-party enticements against his continuing appeal. This, of course, suggests

---

4. This is an "explanation" only in the most superficial sense, since it does not explain why the third-party candidate (or a successor nominee) does not run again. The dynamic of third parties, of course, suggests one possible answer: third parties do not mount a second campaign because the major parties have co-opted their constituency.

the relevance of the push-pull model in explaining change. Our situation, therefore, is more promising than if we were studying previous third parties, because we can observe directly the continuing interplay of major- and third-party appeals in our analysis of change through the 1996 election.[5]

The Push-Pull Model as an Explanation of Change in Perot Activism

Declining support for the third-party candidate is a likely consequence of supporters responding to a major-party bid. The push-pull model is designed to account for third-party activism, so it is relatively simple to adopt it to explain declining support for Perot.

If a third-party candidate becomes less attractive to potential activists over time, support for him should decline as a result of reduced pull toward that candidate. He may be less attractive because of changes in issue proximity (which may result from changes in his position or in the positions of potential supporters) or because he is evaluated less positively for other reasons. Similarly, attraction to a third party might decline as a result of changing issue priorities, either of potential supporters or of the candidate or party. Of course, these changes might also occur because a third party nominates a different candidate who is less attractive on one or more of these dimensions than his predecessor. Certainly the major parties experience fluctuations in their support over time as they nominate new candidates who are more or less attractive to voters and potential activists (Kelley and Mirer 1974; Miller, Wattenberg, and Malunchuk 1986; Stokes 1966). In the 1992–96 cycle, Perot ran in both presidential elections. As a result, our expectation is simple: declining activism for Perot should be explained in part by declining attraction to him.

When a major party is successful in adopting issue positions at the core of the third party's constituency, third-party support should decline. According to the push-pull model of support, as the more proximate major party (**M1**) becomes more satisfactory to potential supporters (in-

---

5. Actually, our situation is improved even further because we can study Perot activists' response to the 1994 elections when there was no Perot alternative available on the ballot. Our expectation is that Perot's supporters played a pivotal role in the 1994 elections and the Republicans' historic victory.

dependent of anything the third-party candidate can do), support for the third candidate declines. This hypothesis suggests that the major parties, in bidding for the third party's constituency, may attract its support without any decrease in attraction to the third-party candidate.[6]

Our task in analyzing 1992 and 1996 is to sort out the types of change that occurred among potential Perot supporters and to understand the changing patterns of support for the Texas independent between the two elections. We will now examine change in major-party campaign involvement.

Spillover Effects of Third-Party Activism

One way that American political parties change is by mobilizing new members with different priorities and policy positions (Rapoport and Stone 1994). Examples of how this may occur include the mobilization of the Christian Right into the Republican Party in the 1980s by Ronald Reagan and Pat Robertson or the efforts of Eugene McCarthy and George McGovern to bring antiwar activists into Democratic Party campaigns in the late sixties and early seventies. Both of these examples describe direct mobilization into the affected party. However, we expect to find similar mobilization effects of third-party activism in subsequent major-party campaigns. This is a nonintuitive expectation because it means that the more mobilized individuals were in Perot's antiparty campaign, the more active they were to become in the two-party system Perot sought to discredit.

Our expectation of "spillover effects" from Perot to major-party involvement is grounded in work we have done on the nomination process in the Democratic and Republican parties. In this work, we find regular mobilization effects from nomination campaigns to general election involvement. We expect analogous effects in the case of Perot activism because of significant similarities between the Perot phenomenon and major-party nomination races. These mobilization effects should hold only if there is a major-party bid to attract third-party supporters;

---

6. Increased choice between the parties may also result in reduced push and in a decline in third-party support. A shift in **M1** also increases choice, unless the other party moves toward the citizen as well. As a result, change in the two "push" factors are highly correlated and difficult to separate from one another empirically.

that is, third-party activity stimulates subsequent participation in the major party that successfully bids for their support. We do not expect mobilization effects into a major party that fails to make a bid.

Most observers emphasize that nomination politics encourage a contemporary trend toward candidate-centered politics (Lowi 1985; Wattenberg 1991). Candidates must run for their party's nomination without party assistance, mount their own campaign organization, gather their own resources, and define their own constituency. They cannot rely on the party or its good name in the primary, because their competition is within the party. Likewise, voters cannot distinguish among nomination contenders on partisan grounds, since all candidates are in the same party. As a result, some argue that the "brand loyalty" that candidates generate is based on their qualities and positions as individual candidates, rather than on their position within a broader partisan identity. As politicians build personal followings, political loyalty and conflict turn less on long-term partisan affiliations and more on the performance, name recognition, reputations, and personal following that candidates command.

To many observers, divisiveness in nomination races is harmful to the long-term interests of the political party (Kenney and Rice 1987; Polsby 1983). One reason is because it appears to alienate factions within the party, especially supporters of losing candidates. In its bitterness, the vitriolic rhetoric of nomination contestants attacking each other in their internecine struggle to capture their party's nomination can rival the conflict between Democratic and Republican nominees in the general election. Because of the personal and divisive character of many nomination campaigns, the nomination winner may have difficulty reassembling the party's coalition in the fall. In this view, once the losing nomination candidate is no longer on the ballot, backers of the nomination losers sit out the fall contest, and the "divisive-primary effect" hurts the chances of the party more than they would be hurt without the nasty primary fight.

Early work on this question seemed to confirm these gloomy expectations. Consistent with the divisive-primary hypothesis, several studies found that individuals involved in losing nomination campaigns were significantly less active in their party's subsequent general election effort than those who backed the nomination winner (Johnson and Gibson

1974; Stone 1986). In looking at the effects of nomination activity in more depth, however, we have found consistent evidence of a positive mobilization effect, rather than the demobilization effect we initially expected. Unlike previous studies, we had measures of how much individuals were involved in nomination campaigns, whether for the eventual winner or for one of the losing candidates, rather than measuring only whether or not they were active in the campaign. Because greater activity in a nomination race reflects higher commitment to the candidate, we expected that the more involved individuals were for a nomination loser, the less involved they would be in the general election. This seemed to follow from the personal and divisive nature of nomination contests and was consistent with the conventional view that divisive nomination fights hurt the party's prospects in the general election.

Instead of finding demobilizing effects of participation for nomination losers, however, we discovered positive mobilizing, or spillover, effects of nomination activity (McCann et al. 1996; Stone, Atkeson, and Rapoport 1992). The effects are evident both in campaigns for Congress and, perhaps most surprisingly, in presidential campaigns that experienced divisive nomination fights earlier in the spring. The more mobilized individuals were for losing nomination campaigns, the more active they subsequently became for the winning campaign and for other campaigns in the party.

Figure 2.3 illustrates the sorts of relationship that we have found in our studies of major-party nomination contests since 1984. It is not surprising to see that activity among Republicans in the 1996 Dole nomination campaign is positively related to fall involvement for the Dole-Kemp ticket—the more active Republicans were in the spring for the ultimate winner of the 1996 GOP nomination race, the more active they were for him in the fall. However, the positive relationship between activity for losing nomination candidates in 1996 and general election campaigns for the Republican Party is surprising if nomination contests are seen primarily as candidate-centered and divisive. Rather than a negative association between activity in nomination losers' campaigns and subsequent general election involvement, the more mobilized individuals were for Dole's nomination rivals in 1996, the more active they were for the Dole-Kemp ticket and the more engaged they were for Republican House

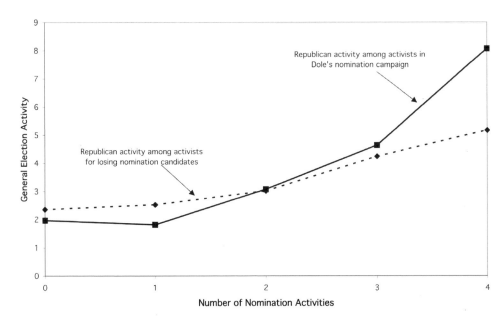

Fig. 2.3. Republican activists' general election activity by nomination involvement, 1996

candidates in the fall.[7] Activity breeds activity, even when the initial mobilization is in support of a losing cause. This evidence led us to challenge the view that nomination campaigns irreparably damage the party. We concluded instead that the candidate-centered nomination process recruits individuals into party activity. Candidates who mobilize new constituencies different from the prevailing interests of the party may be important avenues for party change and responsiveness (Pastor, Stone, and Rapoport 1999; Rapoport and Stone 1994; Stone and Rapoport 1997).[8]

The fact that these effects exist from the nomination to general election stages in the Democratic and Republican parties does not necessarily mean they occur between an independent campaign and major-party campaigns in ensuing elections. After all, nomination participants are strongly committed to their political party, even when they vigorously

7. Figure 2.3 does not break the data down, but positive relationships exist between activity for a losing nomination candidate and the Dole-Kemp campaign and activism in the fall GOP House races.

8. These mobilization effects hold up when we control for previous campaign involvement, predispositions toward activism, and the mobilizing effects associated with the general election.

disagree about who should be its nominee. Therefore, disaffected activist supporters of losing candidates, though they may have to accept a bitter defeat, are nonetheless likely to prefer almost any nominee from their own party to any opposition candidate.[9] An independent campaign, such as Perot's, may attract individuals who are fundamentally disaffected from the parties, much as the "push" side of our model of support contends. Thus, a crucial difference between Perot's candidacy and that of a nomination contender is that supporters of vanquished nomination candidates have their partisanship in common with supporters of the winner. This common partisanship may enable spillover effects to work. In the case of Perot backers, not only might they have been disappointed at the outcome of the 1992 election, but they did not necessarily share a partisan bond with either major-party candidate. Although he was not a candidate for a major-party nomination, Ross Perot's campaign represents the culmination of candidate-centered politics in American elections. Not only was he a candidate who relied heavily on his own resources to attract a following; he mounted an independent antiparty campaign that mobilized hundreds of thousands of activists to place his name on the ballot in all fifty states. Perot took the personalized, candidate-driven politics of presidential nominations one step further by making a populist appeal for the White House, bypassing the nomination process altogether.

The Perot case provides a very severe test of the positive spillover hypothesis because of the antiparty character of his campaign, but the mere fact that it was candidate-centered does not deter our expectations. Perot's attacks on the major parties were not fundamentally different from the assaults nomination contenders regularly visit upon each other. Participation in Perot's campaign may have elevated the stakes his activists felt in the electoral process and sensitized them to their ability to make a difference through their participation. Verba, Schlozman, and Brady (1995) show that participation in one arena—for example, in a work or church setting—builds the skills and efficacy that encourage

---

9. Note that this general preference of one's party over the opposition does not explain spillover effects. The mobilization effects from the nomination campaign persist even with controls for party identification and the strength of preference between the general election candidates.

participation in the political arena. These sorts of effects have been noticed in other studies and are doubtless part of the mechanism that produces spillover effects (Greenberg, Grunberg, and Daniel 1996). In addition, individuals who have been active in one campaign may be more easily identified and mobilized by subsequent campaigns, either through social networks and interest groups that engage them or through more overtly political sources that identify them as potential campaign activists (Rosenstone and Hansen 1993).

Although a shared partisan commitment cannot account for spillover effects between participation in a third-party movement and subsequent major-party campaigns, when either the Democratic or Republican party bids for the third party's constituency, a potential bond is created. Therefore, spillover is possible because activism in the third party's campaign sensitizes participants to the stake they have in politics and enhances the potential for involvement elsewhere, including in a major party actively bidding for their support. Thus, we expect the major-party bid to be a condition for spillover from activism in a third-party movement to later major-party campaigns.

The occurrence of spillover effects from a third-party movement is consistent with the dynamic of third parties, which claims that such a movement could stimulate change in the major parties. Not only might the third party encourage a major party to adopt part of its program to attract its followers, but it may also "train" and stimulate its adherents to become more involved in major-party campaigns. Such effects can produce change if the individuals mobilized into party activity differ substantially from ongoing party cohorts and if they are mobilized in sufficient numbers to change the complexion of the party (Pastor, Stone, and Rapoport 1999).

CONCLUSION

Our theory explicitly connects support for third-party candidates, such as Ross Perot, to larger processes of major-party change. The support model suggests that third-party candidates are most likely to emerge when there is "room" for them because the major parties ignore significant interests or because the major parties' records and candidates leave substantial portions of the electorate dissatisfied (Rosenstone, Behr, and Lazarus 1996). This underrepresentation by the two parties amounts to the "push" factor in our model: the less satisfactory the better major candidate or party is to potential supporters, the more they turn to the third-party or independent candidate. When choice between the two parties is reduced, the stake individuals have in major-party conflict goes down, making support for a third-party candidate more likely. The theory recognizes that a third-party candidate attracts support on his own merits as well. The push-pull model brings into relief the first condition of the dynamic of third parties: support of successful third parties, such as Perot's 1992 campaign, depends on significant issue concerns.

If "push" and "pull" factors are grounded in the issues, the major parties have both the means and the incentive to respond to a third-party's success by trying to woo its constituency. Successful co-optation of the third party's constituency can produce major-party change if it is based on an explicit commitment or bid from the major party and if the third party's supporters respond positively. The major party can bid successfully by shifting its positions so that they are attractive to supporters of the third party. The shift may be in the form of coordinated policy commitments in national party platforms or other visible arenas, or it may result from the uncoordinated actions of individual candidates and officeholders seeking to maximize their chances for election in their prospective constituencies. This reduces the push away from the major-party system and should produce declining support for the insurgent candidate.

In addition to the push-pull model of third-party support, we expect to find spillover effects from activism for Perot to subsequent major-party campaigns. These mobilization effects are contingent on the parties' behavior, especially on a strong and attractive bid for third-party backers' support. Evidence of these spillover effects among Perot activists would provide a microbehavioral foundation for broader patterns of electoral change. Thus, we do not rest with our tests of the spillover hypothesis on our potential activist sample. Taken by itself, such evidence is of limited interest, in part because activists make up such a small proportion of the overall electorate. So what if a relative handful of citizens active in a third-party movement is mobilized into a major party? But if activists' behavior is associated with broader patterns in the electorate as a whole, it provides a plausible mechanism for such change, as well as illustrating the processes of change in individuals' behavior.

Our view of third-party support and change in the two-party system embeds insurgent movements, such as Perot's, in the ongoing development of the American party system. It emphasizes the open and permeable character of the major parties, and it stresses the importance of candidates, including third-party and independent candidates, in mobilizing support and motivating change. It is also optimistic in suggesting that third parties stimulate responsiveness in the major parties as they jockey for support and attempt to balance the interests in their diverse coalitions. Of course, much depends on what motivates third-party supporters to become actively involved for their candidate in the first place, the question to which we now turn.

III

The Rise & Fall of Ross Perot & the Reform Party, 1992–2000

⌁

Ross Perot's 1992 popular-vote share represented a major success in the annals of American third parties. Furthermore, it set in motion a series of events that eventually changed the political landscape in far-reaching and long-lasting ways. Although the ingredients for third-party success and the dynamics of major-party response reflect in this case the broad theory outlined in chapter 2, it is important that we situate our analysis in the specifics of the Perot movement. In this chapter, we outline the conditions for success that existed in 1992 and the major ways the Perot movement took advantage of these opportunities. We also provide a brief account of the movement through its decline in 1996 and its ultimate demise in 2000.

Observers of elections in the United States and abroad saw 1992 as a remarkable presidential election year. President George H. W. Bush experienced an unprecedented decline in popularity, and Bill Clinton, a Southern governor from a small state, embroiled in charges about his personal behavior, emerged as the Democratic nominee and eventual winner. But the most unusual aspect of 1992 was the meteoric rise of Ross Perot—a Texas billionaire running as an independent candidate— who ultimately received a larger vote share than any third-party presidential candidate since Theodore Roosevelt in 1912.

BACKGROUND TO THE 1992
PEROT CANDIDACY

Successful third parties are rare in American political history, perhaps because their fate is almost never in their own hands. As the push-pull
model suggests, third parties need the push of major-party failure before
there can be an opening for them. In their comprehensive survey of
American third parties, Rosenstone, Behr, and Lazarus (1996, 126–27)
conclude, "because the cost of exit [from the major parties] is high and
the likelihood of achieving desired goals through third party activity is
low, severe deterioration of the major parties must take place before significant third party activity occurs."

Almost since the beginning of the Republic, third parties have
emerged under similar conditions: economic dislocation, unpopular
major-party candidates, and significant issues that both major parties
ignore or on which they take unpopular stands (Rosenstone, Behr, and
Lazarus 1996). The most successful third parties have exploited combinations of these conditions. A confluence of conditions strong
enough to motivate significant numbers of Americans to reject both
major parties is rare, but 1992 exhibited all three of the enabling conditions. In 1992, the decline in the economy led to the undoing of
President George Bush's reelection prospects, which had seemed virtually certain as late as a year before the election. The economic decline contributed directly to popular dissatisfaction with Bush, but it
also implicated the Democratic Party and its nominee sufficiently to
promote widespread dissatisfaction with "politics as usual." This disaffection, situated against a backdrop of economic decline, also affected
the sorts of issues that an insurgent candidate—Perot—could tap. Indeed, Clinton's weaknesses as a candidate in 1992 meant that the
major-party system failed to serve up an opposition candidate on
whom the hopes of those disillusioned by the incumbent could comfortably rest. Ross Perot, as an outsider with no political experience or
liabilities, became the conduit for much of the discontent in the
American electorate, especially in the months leading up to the summer nominating conventions.

ECONOMIC DECLINE &
POLITICAL FALLOUT

By February 1992, unemployment had reached a nine-year high. In response, Bush's job approval had plunged from a record high of 89 percent almost a year before to 40 percent in early 1992.[1] During the Bush years, significant concerns were ignored by both parties—concerns that were politically charged in the election campaign because of the faltering economy. The federal government's deficit had almost doubled from $152.5 billion in Bush's first year in office to $290.4 billion by 1992 (Stanley and Niemi 2001). Furthermore, neither party seemed willing to provide a credible solution. The 1990 budget summit was supposed to provide a bipartisan compromise, but it became best known for Bush's retreat from his pledge "Read my lips: no new taxes!" Although the summit promised a five-year deficit of $92 billion, the national debt grew between 1990 and 1992 by more than eight times that projection, to $750 billion. By the end of Bush's term, the deficit had grown by 50 percent, reaching $3 trillion, which amounted to one-half of the U.S. gross national product (Stanley and Niemi 2001, fig. 8.2). During those four years, neither Bush nor the Democratically controlled Congress proposed—let alone produced—a balanced federal budget (Ornstein, Mann, and Malbin 2002, 158–60, table 7-3).

The 1992 Clinton campaign famously emphasized, "It's the economy, stupid!"—in a drive to convince the American public that it could solve the nation's economic woes. However, the Democrats, too, had ignored the deficit, resolutely opposing reform proposals to limit expenditures, such as the balanced-budget amendment and the line-item veto. Other reform proposals—such as term limits, which commanded large majorities in the public and would be adopted by eleven states in 1992 alone—were opposed by Democrats and received little more than token support from Republicans. Leaders of both parties supported U.S. participation in the global economy through such measures as the North American Free Trade Agreement (NAFTA) and the General Agreement on Tariffs

---

1. The polling data are from the Gallup Brain, http://www.brain.gallup.com (site accessible only to subscribers).

and Trade (GATT), which represented more threat than opportunity to many workers.

Nineteen months before the election, in the spring of 1991, things had looked much more positive for George Bush's reelection prospects. Republican Pierre Dupont and Democrats Mario Cuomo, Jesse Jackson, Al Gore, Bill Bradley, and Richard Gephardt—all savvy politicians—gave up possible bids for the presidency because of Bush's perceived strength (Germond and Witcover 1993, 83). The incumbent Republican president's popularity was at record levels, and pundits had all but given him the election. At that point, a prediction that a third-party movement would achieve historic success in the 1992 election would have seemed preposterous.

The perception of Bush's invincibility came to a great degree from his success in the Gulf War against Iraq. Yet in October 1990, just prior to the war, Bush's job approval rating had dropped from its postinaugural high of 80 percent to 52 percent. As the economy declined in 1990 and Bush recanted his "no new taxes" pledge, his domestic job approval rating dropped even lower, to 34 percent (Frankovic 1993). With the Gulf War, Bush experienced a surge in popular approval to 89 percent in March 1991 (ibid., 112). However, while his overall approval was climbing by thirty-seven points, his domestic approval increased by only eight points and, despite this improvement, remained below 50 percent. Whereas his overall approval was twenty-four points above that which he received right after he took office (Gallup survey, March 1, 1989), his handling of the economy was rated fifteen points lower than when he began his presidency. The gap between his overall approval and his economic approval ratings, which was always substantial, ballooned from twenty-two points in July 1990 to fifty points in March 1991.[2]

As the Gulf War ended, the economic news did not improve. Unemployment continued to climb (as fig. 3.1 shows), reaching 6.9 percent by June 1991 and 7.8 percent in the summer of 1992. In the two years leading up to the election, unemployment increased by 50 percent. Samuel Popkin (1994, 242) reflects that the "momentary upsurge in consumer confidence" brought on by the Gulf War success "once again dropped far below the predicted level of consumer confidence [based on objective

---

2. http://www.brain.gallup.com.

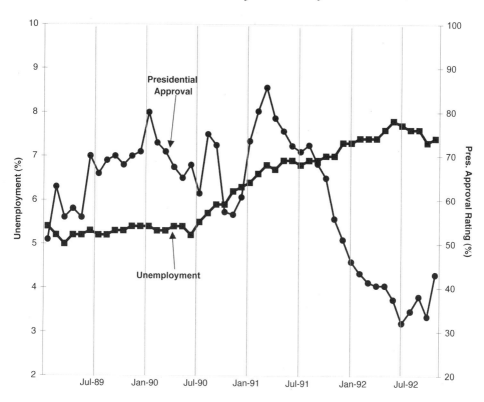

Fig. 3.1.   Percentage unemployment and presidential approval rating (January 1989–November 1992). (Data from Gallup Poll [approval] and Bureau of Labor Statistics [unemployment].)

measures of inflation, production, and unemployment] and stayed there for the rest of the Bush presidency."

President Bush's reactions to the faltering economy exacerbated his problems. After the 1990 election, Bush claimed to be "not sure there is a recession" (Goldman et al. 1994, 311), even though unemployment had steadily increased for six months. In fact, it was not until almost a year later, at the end of 1991, that Bush admitted, through his press secretary Marlin Fitzwater, that there really was a recession (ibid., 316). By this point, Bush's overall approval rating had dropped below where it had been prior to the Gulf War, and on the domestic front, his approval rating stood at 25 percent. The precipitous and unexpected nature of Bush's drop in popularity came too late for the potential Democratic and Republican nomination candidates who had already ruled out a presidential run.

Unfortunately for Bush, he did have one nomination opponent. Conservative commentator Pat Buchanan seemed to offer only token opposition. However, after the New Hampshire primary, any remaining illusions about Bush's invincibility had been shattered. That Buchanan, who had never held elective office, attracted 37 percent of the primary vote in New Hampshire testified more to Bush's weaknesses than to Buchanan's strengths. Buchanan emphasized the president's violation of his "no new taxes" pledge and "King George's" inability to relate to ordinary people affected by the recession, coupling conservative rhetoric with a populist message tapping economic discontent, alienation from politicians, and concern about America's status in the world. As a result, his electoral support plumbed a reservoir of anti-Bush feeling and drew almost equal percentages of moderate, conservative, and liberal Republicans (Ceaser and Busch 1993, 41). Buchanan's challenge to an incumbent president who had recently enjoyed astronomical popularity exposed Bush's weakness and presaged the success of Perot's insurgent candidacy.

Nevertheless, Bush was not the only major-party candidate with significant weaknesses. As figure 3.2 shows, throughout the nomination process and even after he was the presumptive Democratic nominee, Bill Clinton was viewed more negatively than positively by the American electorate. It was not until the eve of the Democratic National Convention that Clinton's positive evaluations nudged past his negatives. Even within his own party, Clinton lacked strong support. After he won enough delegates to clinch the nomination at the end of March, a *New York Times* poll found that 67 percent of registered Democrats would have liked another candidate to enter the race (Popkin 1994, 289). In early June, with the convention only a month off and no other candidate on the horizon, 30 percent of Democrats thought the Democratic convention should dump Clinton and find another candidate.[3]

THE RISE OF H. ROSS PEROT

As a result of President Bush's poor handling of the economy and continuing doubts in the public's mind about the Democratic nominee, Bill

---

3. *Newsweek* survey, June 4–5, 1992, accession 0177336, question 024.

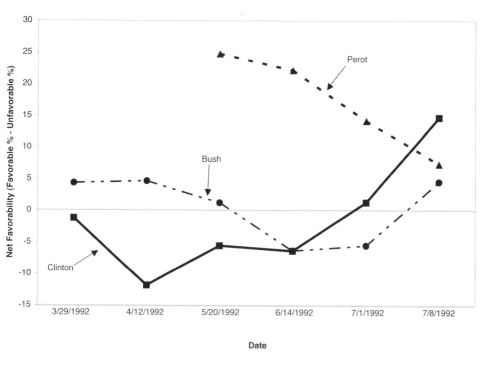

Fig. 3.2. Comparative candidate favorability ratings before Perot dropped out, 1992. (Data from Gallup Poll.)

Clinton, there was a significant push away from both the Democratic and Republican parties in the months leading up to the major-party national conventions. Stepping into the breach, Ross Perot, a plainspoken and independent-minded self-made Texas billionaire, who called on the American people to "take their country back," was seen by some as the right man to challenge the political establishment in 1992. The triumph of his maverick approach was epitomized in his orchestration of a 1979 rescue of his Electronic Data Systems employees from Iran, which stood in marked contrast to the U.S. government's failure to secure the release of American hostages held in its embassy in Tehran.

Perot's entrance into the 1992 presidential race can be traced to the tenacity of the first two Perot "volunteers": John Jay Hooker, publisher of the *Nashville Tennessean* and former Democratic congressional candidate, and Jack Gargan, retired Florida businessman and political gadfly. Hooker phoned Perot out of the blue in November 1991 to ask him to run for president. In spite of Perot's refusal, Hooker continued to call persistently and by December was speaking with Perot as frequently as three or four times a week (Goldman et al. 1994, 415). The timing of the first call was fortuitous, since Perot had just spoken to a rally of anti-Congress activists assembled by Jack Gargan. Unbeknownst to Hooker, Gargan had already been pushing the idea of a Perot candidacy for six months. Gargan was a retired businessman who, in June 1990, had spent forty-five thousand dollars of his personal savings on a series of newspaper ads calling for the defeat of all incumbent members of Congress. Gargan's ads for his group THRO (Throw the Hypocritical Rascals Out) exhorted readers to replace incumbents in response to congressional scandals, their failure to deal with the federal deficit, and their willingness to give themselves pay raises. The ad struck a chord, as readers sent in not only enough money to cover Gargan's original expenditure but enough—nearly one million dollars—for him to buy many more ads.[4] One individual impressed by these ads was Perot himself, who, according to Gargan, "called him that November and 'asked if he could help.'"[5] Although the goal of Gargan's group was to recruit new people to run for Congress, he felt that the country needed a reform president along with a movement to reform Congress and that Perot was the man for the job.[6]

On May 29, 1991, Gargan met with Perot in Dallas to convince him to run. He told Perot that he was going to start a "draft Perot" movement, and Perot's reaction did not assuage his enthusiasm.[7] Even before his trip to Dallas, Gargan had secured Perot's agreement to speak to a rally of members of various "good government" groups that had joined together in a national coalition for political reform. Perot spoke to the overflow rally of three thousand in Tampa on November 2 after being introduced by John Anderson, at that time the most recent successful third-party candidate. Perot outlined the themes that would shape his 1992 presidential campaign: eliminate the budget deficit; reform the sys-

---

4. Jonathan Moore, "Political Activist Calls for Perot, but Texan Doesn't Want to Hold Office," *Houston Chronicle*, September 22, 1991, A20.

5. Michael Isikoff, "Unlikely Suitors Pushed Perot Bid; Efforts to Get Texan to Run Began Nearly a Year Ago," *Washington Post*, May 31, 1992, 1.

6. Authors' interview with Jack Gargan, September 29, 2003.

7. Gargan interview, 2003.

tem that produced deficits by reining in political action committees (PACs) and lobbyists; limit congressional pay raises; give the president the line-item veto; and provide candidates for office with free television time (Barta 1993, 15).

Meanwhile, continuing to act independently of Gargan, Hooker pursued Perot, talking to him periodically and emphasizing his duty to run. Hooker worked to compile information on ballot access and arranged for Perot to meet with political pollster Pat Caddell in January 1992 to discuss a possible third-party campaign.

PEROT'S COMMITMENT TO RUN

In February 1992, Perot flew to Nashville for a radio interview on WLAC. After the show, the station sponsored a reception where, responding to a question from a local businesswoman and activist about a possible run for president, Perot said: "If you feel so strongly about it, register me in fifty states. If it's forty-nine, forget it. If you want to do fifty states, you care that much, fine, then I don't belong to anybody but you." He also asserted, "I would not want to run in any of the existing parties because you'd have to sell out." (Germond and Witcover 1993, 216–17).

Hooker then called Larry King to request that he invite Perot to be on the *Larry King Live* show. Hooker's call piqued King's interest in a possible Perot bid for the presidency (ibid., 217). On the show, King, displaying his usual tenacity, asked Perot five times if he would run. In response to King's final repetition, Perot repeated his promise from two weeks earlier that he would run if volunteers got his name on the ballot in all fifty states, and his campaign was launched. However, like the earlier challenge in response to the question following the Nashville radio interview, this declaration received virtually no media coverage. The *Los Angeles Times* buried it in a three-paragraph story on page 18,[8] and the *New York Times* did not mention Perot's declaration for another three weeks (until March 7).

Despite Perot's expectation that nothing would come of his *Larry King Live* challenge, so many calls came in to Perot's offices that the

8. "If Drafted, Perot Says He'd Run," *Los Angeles Times,* February 22, 1992, 18.

phone system was soon overwhelmed.[9] On March 13, Perot set up a toll-free number with thirty lines; by March 16, there were a hundred lines, with voice mail for overflow. Eventually Perot hired the Home Shopping Network, which set up twelve hundred lines. He also recruited his lawyer and friend Tom Luce to take charge of the ballot-access effort (Germond and Witcover 1993, 224)

Less than a month after Perot's appearance on *Larry King Live,* he gave his "We Own This Country" speech to the National Press Club. It reemphasized the issues he had mentioned in Tampa and added others: the budget deficit and the need for reform to deal with the lack of accountability in government were centerpiece issues, with concerns about trade (including NAFTA), jobs, and economic recovery also prominent. Response to the speech, which was televised on C-SPAN, was unprecedented. It drew seventy thousand mail and two thousand phone requests for transcripts, compared with a usual response of twenty such requests.[10] During the next week, Perot followed up with appearances on *This Week with David Brinkley,* the *Donahue Show, 60 Minutes,* and a return appearance on *Larry King Live.* After his appearance on *Donahue,* during which his toll-free number continuously flashed, phone company officials reported that Perot's headquarters received 257,139 calls.[11]

Without being a declared candidate or spending money on media advertising, Perot's ratings in a three-way face-off with Bush and Clinton skyrocketed (see fig. 3.3), allowing him to get significant media coverage. In a mid-March *Newsweek* poll, less than a month after his initial *Larry King Live* appearance, Perot was the choice of 9 percent of the American public;[12] in a Gallup Poll conducted at about the same time, only 45 percent of Americans had heard of Perot.[13] However, in a survey conducted a week later, Perot's support reached 21 percent, and by the end of April, he had vaulted to a 27 percent share of the three-way vote (Barnes 1992). In mid-May, Perot took the lead in the presidential race for the first time,[14] and by later that month, Perot was the choice of

---

9. Authors' interview with Clay Mulford, November 22, 1999.

10. "Perot: 'Flame in the Political Gas Tank'?" *The Political Hotline,* March 27, 1992.

11. Peter Applebome, "Perot, the 'Simple' Billionaire, Says Voters Can Force His Presidential Bid," *New York Times,* March 27, 1992, 14.

12. Lexis–Nexis, March 19-20, 1992, ascension 0180103, question 007.

13. Lexis–Nexis, March 20–22, 1992, ascension 0172349, question 017.

14. http://www.brain.gallup.com.

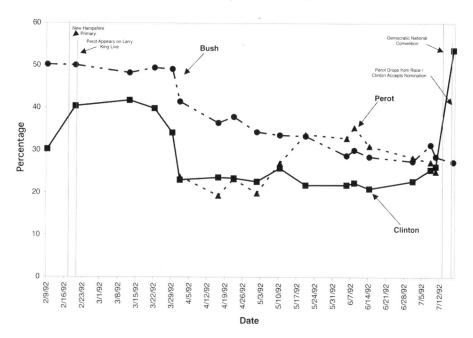

Fig. 3.3.   Candidate voting intention: First phase of presidential campaign, 1992. (Data from Gallup Poll.)

33 percent of the electorate, compared with 28 percent for Bush and 24 percent for Clinton.[15] By early June, Perot had his largest lead of the campaign, with 37 percent of respondents preferring him—at least 13 percent more than either Bush or Clinton.[16] Even partisans were attracted to Perot, as both Democratic and Republican primary voters in such states as Oregon and California liked Perot as well or better than their own party's nominee (Barta 1993, 155). By the end of June, the *Political Hotline* showed Perot leading the three-way race in states, with 284 electoral votes to 158 for Bush and 16 for Clinton (ibid., 208).

PEROT'S VOLUNTEERS & THE PETITION DRIVE

How was Perot able to catapult from a blip on the political radar screen to lead the presidential race in barely three months, and how was his

---

15.   Lexis-Nexis, May 27–30, 1992, accession 0177109, question 004.
16.   *Time*/CNN, June 3–4, 1992, accession 0177395, question 003.

campaign able to fulfill his demand to get him on the ballot in all fifty states? As discussed in chapter 1, some observers claim that Perot's electoral success depended almost entirely on his willingness to expend a huge share of his personal fortune on his campaign (Rosenstone, Behr, and Lazarus 1996). While we do not deny the importance of money in politics for candidates to get their message out, Perot's personal wealth and campaign expenditures fall far short of explaining his late-spring surge in the polls.

Figure 3.4 shows cumulative expenditures by month for Perot and for Bush, Clinton, and two other major-party nomination contenders. At the point when Perot had his largest lead over Clinton and Bush in trial-heat polls, he had spent less than any of the other four candidates, including nomination losers Paul Tsongas and Pat Buchanan. Moreover, he had spent less than a third of what either Clinton or Bush had spent. The claim that Perot's wealth was responsible for the early success of his campaign cannot be reconciled with the results in figure 3.4.

In spite of Perot's appeal to average voters, his ability to attract activist volunteers comprised one of the most remarkable achievements of his 1992 campaign, reinforcing our claim that money was not the key to the success of his movement. Perot's volunteer cadre constituted the largest set of activists of any third-party campaign for which we have relevant data.[17] Activists were critical in spreading the word and legitimizing the movement early in the campaign, and they were absolutely essential to the success of the ballot petition drives. As Clay Mulford—Perot's son-in-law, advisor, and, ultimately, campaign chair—put it, "By mid-March, without us intervening, there were organizations all around the country."[18] Volunteers mobilized "from Maine to California, . . . opening petition offices and manning petition tables in shopping malls at their own expense to advance the cause" (Germond and Witcover 1993, 306). As a result, "Perot-for-president petition campaigns were springing up all

---

17. According to American National Election Studies data from the relevant years, 55.1 percent of Perot voters reported engaging in at least some political activity in 1992, versus 53.7 percent of Anderson supporters in 1980 and 53.2 percent of Wallace voters in 1968. Because Perot's vote greatly surpassed either of these independent candidacies, the numbers of volunteers mobilized was much greater.

18. Mulford interview, 1999.

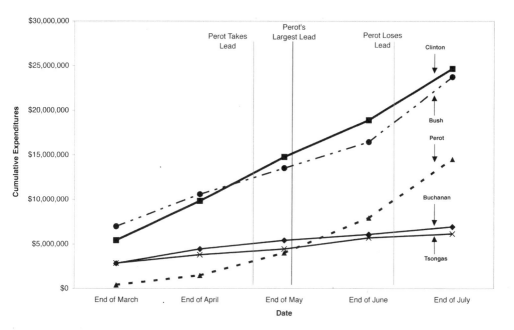

Fig. 3.4.   Cumulative expenditures of selected presidential candidates (January 1992–July 1992). (Data from Federal Election Commission.)

over the country in a self-starting political operation unprecedented in its scope" (ibid., 229).

The spontaneity of the volunteer effort was remarkable. By shortly before California's primary, volunteer activists "had self-selected their own leadership, opened up 20 offices statewide, and recruited 38,000 volunteers who collected 500,000 signatures" (Royer 1994, 162). Eventually Perot's California activists accumulated 1.4 million signatures, with only one paid staffer visiting the state. In our 1992 national survey of over thirteen hundred callers to the Perot toll-free number, more than one thousand had been active in Perot's spring campaign—collecting ballot petitions, canvassing, organizing, and contributing money—but only one held a paid position in the campaign.

In May, with the major-party conventions more than two months off, petition drives provided an opportunity to involve the volunteers and to establish an organization. These drives also demonstrated the level of support that Perot attracted and generated more free publicity, drawing still more supporters.

Historically, ballot access has presented serious problems for third-party candidates. To qualify for the ballot in all states, John Anderson expended almost all of his money over the summer months preceding the 1980 election, leaving him with little to build a media-based campaign in the fall (Germond and Witcover 1981). Richard Winger of Ballot Access News estimated that Perot would need 767,033 names in order to get on the ballot in all fifty states.[19] The *Los Angeles Times* predicted that "given the wide variety of deadlines and requirements to gain access to general election ballots in 50 states . . . [the] standard for becoming a candidate [in 1992] would be virtually impossible to meet."[20]

In state after state, the petition requirements became not only a hurdle but an opportunity to generate a show of support and mobilize volunteers. As a result, the occasions for presenting ballot petitions to Perot (often as down payments toward the promised numbers) served as opportunities both to reenergize the volunteers and to get significant publicity for the campaign. Fortunately for Perot, the first and most challenging state was his home state of Texas. Texas required Perot to accumulate 54,275 petition signers who had not voted in the March 10 primaries. Since primary voters constituted about 40 percent of those who would eventually vote in November, the challenge was formidable. On May 11, after a parade through downtown Austin and a rally at the state capitol, Perot's campaign presented the attorney general with 231,000 petitions—more than four times the number needed.[21] From mid-May until he dropped out in July, Perot repeatedly used successful petition efforts as opportunities for rallies to emphasize the groundswell of support. In fact, petition turn-ins were Perot's only public appearances until he reentered the race on October 1.[22] The numbers of petitions submitted were often overwhelming. In Colorado, which required only 5,000 signatures, the campaign submitted 135,000. In California, which required 139,000 signatures, the campaign collected 500,000 by early June, on its way to a total of 1,400,000 signatures (Royer 1994, 162). Ultimately, Perot submitted a total of 5.3 million signatures across the fifty states and the District of Columbia (Barta 1993, 480).

19. "Perot's Hope: More than 767,000 signatures," *St. Petersburg Times,* April 5, 1992, 6.
20. "If Drafted, Perot Says He'd Run," *Los Angeles Times,* February 22, 1992, 18.
21. "Hannah: Verification Will Move Quickly," *Associated Press,* May 12, 1992.
22. Mulford interview, 1999.

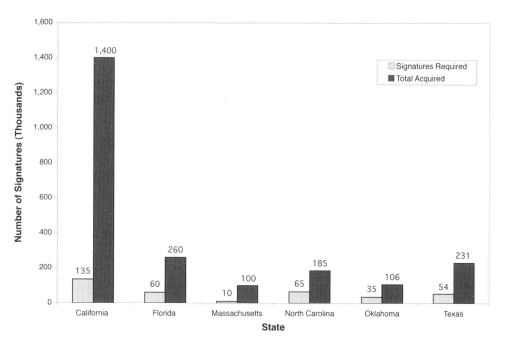

Fig. 3.5.   Signatures required for third-party ballot access; signatures presented by 1992 Perot campaign. (Data from Barta 1993.)

Figure 3.5 shows the success of the campaign in the six states that re-quired ten thousand or more petitions and had deadlines before Perot's July 16 withdrawal. In every one of these states, Perot surpassed the re-quired numbers, submitting at least ten times the required numbers in California and Massachusetts and more than four times the required numbers in Texas and Florida. In other states with more modest require-ments, the story was much the same.

To be sure, Perot's reliance on volunteers had its cost. The coordina-tion of volunteers and the creation of a campaign presented the problem of how to maintain spontaneity among volunteers while creating a co-ordinated national campaign. Since the early petition drives were organ-ized from the bottom up, there was nothing to stop multiple people from declaring themselves the campaign director for a given state, and conflict between groups often resulted (Germond and Witcover 1993, 219). Many of those running the petition drives were unfamiliar with the legal nuances associated with achieving ballot access. In Illinois, which puts electors' names on the ballot, different Perot petition drives had the names of different electors.[23] The campaign was particularly concerned about violating Federal Election Commission (FEC) rules, since campaign finance reform was a high priority for Perot.

In response to these problems, the campaign created an operational field staff out of Perot's Dallas business operation—"Young Turks" as they called themselves, or "White Shirts" as many of the volunteers derisively called them. Their job was to supervise the state organizations, making sure that petitions were consistent with one another and that no laws were broken. Volunteers who were putting in enormous hours for no pay frequently resented them. The campaign was forced to bring order out of the chaos without losing the spirit and spontaneity of the early campaign. Clay Mulford, one of the "brain trust" running the campaign, ultimately came to feel that the campaign's decision to send in a field staff to organize the states was a mistake: "If we had it to do all over again, we should have ignored some of the problems in the tidal wave of activity."[24]

Well into May, aside from Perot's close personal advisors and a small number of field representatives, no sufficient organizational structure existed, especially for a national campaign that would be, as Perot promised, "world-class." Luce, Mulford, and Mort Meyerson, Perot's most trusted lieutenant and head of Perot Systems, decided that more professionalism was needed to turn the petition-gathering effort into a presidential campaign. They persuaded Republican consultant Ed Rollins and Hamilton Jordan, former chief of staff to President Jimmy Carter, to join the official campaign as cochairs beginning on June 3. Although attracting such skilled professionals was something of a coup, it was also a risky strategy that ultimately backfired.

If the "White Shirts" handpicked by Perot elicited anger from volunteers in the field, the entry of "political professionals" provoked far more unhappiness, a response increasingly shared by Perot himself. Ed Rollins elicited particular animosity from Perot. Rollins's relationship with Perot soured almost immediately when he leaked his own appointment to the

---

23. Mulford interview, 1999.
24. Mulford interview, 1999.

media. Perot never trusted him again, and the relationship lasted barely a month. In early July, Rollins resigned under pressure, with Perot dropping out of the race a week later, on the eve of Clinton's acceptance speech at the Democratic National Convention.

Perot's withdrawal precipitated an avalanche of protest from his supporters. Volunteer leaders descended on Dallas to dissuade Perot from his decision, and emotions ran high. "At one point," reports Carolyn Barta (1993, 273), "Nancy Bush of California wrapped her arms around Perot's ankles, begging him to stay in the race." Although Perot refused to reconsider, he encouraged the volunteers to return home, get a feel in their state for the direction the movement should take, and reconvene later in the month in Dallas. When state leaders in the movement met at the end of July, they again failed to get Perot back into the race. They did, however, emerge with an organization, United We Stand America (UWSA), signed onto by leaders from forty-seven states and headed by one of the few people Perot knew well among the volunteers assembled—former Vietnam POW Orson Swindle.[25]

The organization that emerged out of Dallas was far different from the campaign that preceded it. The "more contentious sorts" were eliminated, and "new chairpersons were installed by the corporate white shirts in Dallas" (Goldman et al. 1994, 541); the staff shrank to less than three dozen, all personally loyal to Perot. As a consequence, UWSA was a far more hierarchical organization under Perot as its leader.

Meanwhile, there were still twenty-four states where petition drives had not been completed, although substantial progress had been made in most. Some states, such as New York, presented a particularly difficult challenge. Although volunteers were still available, there were many fewer than there had been before Perot dropped out, and the campaign found itself relying on paid temporary workers to collect petition signatures. As a result, campaign expenditures actually increased after Perot ended his candidacy. Perot spent about four million dollars in August alone—almost as much as he spent in March through May combined.[26]

---

25. Authors' interview with Orson Swindle, July 11, 2000.
26. Federal Elections Commission Web site, http://www.fec.gov.

PEROT'S ISSUE PLATFORM

Perot's popularity in the spring and summer notwithstanding, people knew few specifics about him and the policies he favored. Despite the lack of specifics on the issues, there was an aura of can-do success about the self-made billionaire, and it generated a strong pull toward the Texas independent. In a May poll, with only 5 percent of respondents saying that they knew a lot about Ross Perot, three-quarters of the American electorate nonetheless thought that he showed "strong leadership qualities."[27] Similar percentages felt that the phrase "can get things done" strongly applied to Perot. Tom Luce emphasized this side of Perot's appeal as he reflected on his experience working as a close advisor to Perot.

> In the entire time I worked in phase one of the Perot campaign, I never had a single volunteer ask me if Perot was conservative, liberal, or moderate. As far as they were concerned, those [concerns] were . . . a part of the dialogue of the system which they have rejected. Their basic attitude is, fix the damn problem. (Royer 1994, 163)

Phase one of Perot's campaign, from the spring and early summer until he dropped out, was long on identifying problems that needed to be fixed—the deficit, the need for election reform, the need for general reform of government, the problem of jobs lost to America—but short on specific solutions. As Perot put it, "It's time somebody cleaned out the barn."[28] In an early June poll, when Perot was leading in trial heats against Bush and Clinton, only 25 percent of registered voters said that they understood his issue stands "pretty well," compared with 70 percent who felt that he had "to say a lot more about his positions and policies than he already has."[29] Even among political independents, only one in four said that Ross Perot was telling them "enough about where he stands on the issues . . . to judge what he might do if he won the presi-

---

27. May Campaign Benchmark Poll, Gallup Brain, May 18, 1992–May 20, 1992, question 14b, http://www.brain.gallup.com..

28. "National Briefs," *Washington Times,* November 3, 1991, 2.

29. June benchmark poll, Gallup Brain, 6/41992–6/51992, question qn9, http://www.brain.gallup.com.

dential election."[30] In one of the last polls taken before he dropped out of the race, just 7 percent selected Perot when asked which of the three candidates had "offered the most specific plans for solving the nation's problems."[31] Nonetheless, Perot's spring issue agenda, even without detailed specific policy proposals, attracted a relatively united issue-based constituency, as we show in chapters 4–5.

Perot himself acknowledged his lack of specific positions on many issues. In a speech before the American Newspaper Publishers Association, he announced that he would limit his public appearances and interviews to "spend all my time building an organization, finalizing a strategy and developing carefully thought out positions on each of the major issues." When he was asked about his plan to control entitlement spending and balance the budget, he answered, "See me in 60 days."[32]

It was not until after he had dropped out of the race that Perot released his economic plan and brought out his election manifesto, *United We Stand America,* which laid out specific measures to balance the budget and "take back our country." For the first time, Perot offered a platform that made clear his differences from the major parties, both in the issues that he cared most about and in his proposed solutions. One of his most detailed and distinctive proposals was in response to the federal budget deficit, an issue with substantial potential for Perot because he thought neither major party took it seriously. Perot's "boot-camp approach to fiscal policy: no pain, no gain"[33] contrasted starkly with the "no pain required" approaches of both Bush and Clinton. Clinton was content to blame Bush for the bad economy, claiming that deficit reduction would result from "growing the economy," rather than from cuts in programs or increases in taxes. Bush, in contrast, was hemmed in on taxes by his 1988 "no new taxes" pledge and his violation of it only two years later. The president's approach was to support a balanced budget amendment together with tax cuts, which he contended would stimulate the economy.

---

30. CBS/*New York Times,* June 13–20, 1992, accession 0182727, question 024.

31. Ronald Brownstein, "Spotlight Finds Clinton Locked in a 3-Way Tie," *Los Angeles Times,* July 12, 1992, A1.

32. Robin Toner, "1992 Campaign: Perot to Curtail His Appearances to Study Issues," *New York Times,* May 26, 1992, A26.

33. Susan Dentzer and Jerry Buckley, "Ross Perot's Bitter Tonic," *U.S. News and World Report,* August 3, 1992, 28–31.

But he said little about the debt that had grown radically during the Reagan-Bush years or the fact that he had never submitted a balanced budget to Congress (Ornstein, Mann, and Malbin 2002).

Perot proposed increasing the marginal tax rate on the wealthy from 31 to 33 percent, taxing employee health insurance benefits, eliminating the cap on Medicare taxes, taxing Social Security benefits, increasing the gas tax by fifty cents over five years, and increasing tobacco taxes by eighteen billion dollars over five years. With these proposals, Perot positioned himself to claim that he was the only candidate serious about eliminating the federal budget deficit.

Although deficit reduction was important to Perot, he emphasized a variety of other issues in his campaign manifesto and during his abbreviated fall campaign. In the month between his October 1 reentry and the election, he spent significant effort distinguishing himself from his opponents on political reform, trade, and foreign involvement. His reform proposals included term limits, campaign finance reform, lobbying reform for both foreign governments and former U.S. officials and officeholders, serious cutbacks on staffing of the Congress and presidency, and a panoply of other proposals that played a limited role in the major parties' 1992 platforms. He stated in the second presidential debate: "We have to reform government. If you put term limits in and don't reform government, you won't get the benefits you thought. It takes both. So we need to do the reforms and the term limits. And after we reform it, it won't be a lifetime career opportunity."[34]

He also made clear his commitment to safeguarding the U.S. economy from threats from other countries, both from damaging trade agreements and from U.S. foreign involvement. He stated his reservations about NAFTA by declaring in *United We Stand America,* "I do not want a trade agreement that trades away jobs" (Perot 1992, 105–6). In the second presidential debate, he declared, "We've shipped millions of jobs overseas," bemoaning "these one-way trade agreements that we've negotiated over the years." He promised, "If the people send me to Washington, the first thing I'll do is study that 2000-page agreement [NAFTA] and make sure it's a 2-way street."[35]

---

34. http://www.debates.org/pages/trans92b1.html.
35. http://www.debates.org/pages/trans92b1.html.

Perot's views about putting America's economic interests first were also reflected in the lead heading in his manifesto chapter on foreign policy, "Start at Home" (Perot 1992, 99). He reiterated this view in the second presidential debate: "[F]or 45 years we were preoccupied with the Red Army. I suggest now that our number one preoccupation is red ink and our country and we've got to put our people back to work."[36]

In sum, between dropping out of the race and the November election, Perot clarified his positions on the federal deficit, governmental reform, and economic nationalism, positions that put him at odds with both major parties and provided an increased issue basis for his third-party challenge. He emphasized these three issue clusters and avoided, for the most part, the issues that traditionally defined the liberal-conservative dimension in American politics. In this, Perot's strategy fit the push-pull model by defining his campaign around issues on which he could charge that the parties did not materially differ from one another while he offered distinctive and potentially popular solutions.

PEROT'S REENTRY AS A CANDIDATE

By September, Perot was making regular statements about reentering the race if the major-party candidates did not deal with the deficit.[37] To reenter, Perot had to show both that the major parties were not serious about his issues and that his volunteer supporters demanded his reentry. To accomplish both goals, Perot invited the Bush and Clinton campaigns to Dallas in late September to present their cases to his volunteers, who would then make the "decision" about Perot's reentry. With the outcome a foregone conclusion, the fear of alienating the sizable Perot constituency nonetheless drew senior Democratic and Republican advisors to present their case to the assembled Perot volunteers. Three days later, on October 1, 1992, Perot reentered the race, fittingly with yet another appearance on *Larry King Live*.

Despite the prominence of his volunteers in "making the decision" for him to reenter the race, the basis of the Perot campaign had already

---

36. http://www.debates.org/pages/trans92b2.html.

37. Jack Nelson, "Perot Says Deal with the Deficit or I'll Reenter," *Los Angeles Times,* September 16, 1992, A1.

shifted from a grassroots movement to a far more hierarchical one, which remained firmly in place through election day. Moreover, outside of the debates—which were crucial to his success—Perot eschewed public rallies and other campaign appearances in favor of direct appeals through the debates and his infomercials, which meant he spent a great deal more money on his campaign after he reentered the race than he had in any comparable time period before he dropped out. In fact, in the first two weeks after his reentry, Perot spent more (twenty-five million dollars) than he had in the previous seven months; from that point until the end of the campaign, he spent another fifteen million dollars.[38] It is this second phase of the campaign that led many analysts to conclude that Perot's success in attracting such a large share of the popular vote was due to his personal campaign expenditures.

There is no question that Perot's media campaign had an impact. His first infomercial drew more than sixteen million viewers, a larger audience than was attracted by a National League baseball playoff game shown concurrently (Germond and Witcover 1993, 462). Perot ultimately produced fifteen sixty-second and five thirty-second commercials (Barta 1993, 329). Although it is certainly true that Perot's heavy expenditures in the fall contributed substantially to the visibility of his 1992 presidential campaign, it is also true that, as Clay Mulford put it, "The debates made us" (Goldman et al. 1994, 578). Perot's unprecedented inclusion in the debates alongside the two major-party candidates was the crucial factor that boosted his campaign's visibility and credibility.

If we allocate a fair share of his popularity and vote to his success in the debates, the question becomes, why was he allowed to participate? The answer was not his popularity in predebate polls. In fact, he had only 9 percent of the popular vote in the last poll before the first debate (Goldman et al. 1994, 734). At the point he announced he would participate in the full set of debates, the Commission on Presidential Debates had invited him only to the first debate, with his poll standings to determine his participation in later debates. However, an agreement reached by the major-party candidates stipulated that Perot was to be invited (Barta 1993,

---

38. Perot Petition Committee, "Report of Receipts and Disbursements by an Authorized Committee of a Candidate for the Office of President," March–December 1992, Federal Elections Commission.

342). The reason for this agreement on Perot's full participation was his as-
tounding popularity in May and June. It was the Perot constituency of the
spring and early summer that neither party could afford to offend. After
all, Perot was the first third-party presidential candidate in the history of
public opinion polling to lead both major-party candidates in trial-heat
polls. And, as we have shown, the success of Perot's campaign in the spring
and early summer cannot be explained by his expenditures, which were
modest compared with his major-party rivals.

The televised debates were crucial to Perot's success in building on his
relatively modest support in the polls after he reentered the race. Perot
was the first third-party candidate to appear with both major-party candidates in televised presidential debates.[39] With an average audience of
66.4 million, the debates gave Perot unprecedented free exposure (Stanley and Niemi 2004, 193). Perot acquitted himself well in the debates,
drawing substantial praise for his performances. An *ABC News* poll conducted the day after the first debate found that 37 percent thought Perot
had won, 24 percent gave the debate to Clinton, and only 11 percent saw
Bush as the winner.[40] Cookie Roberts of *ABC News* said: "Let's call a
spade a spade here. Ross Perot won this debate" (Barta 1993, 345).

Unlike past third-party candidates, Perot's support actually grew during the last month leading up to election day, as he reengaged spring-
summer supporters. His ultimate vote share surpassed his support in the
last preelection polls, something neither George Wallace in 1968 nor
John Anderson in 1980 came close to reaching.

THE PEROT MOVEMENT AFTER 1992

After the election, Perot and his supporters proceeded to institutionalize
the movement by converting the campaign organization United We Stand
America into a legally incorporated, dues-collecting, nonpartisan organization. The organization was committed to influencing lawmakers on the
agenda items that Perot had championed: deficit reduction, opposition to

39. In 1980, Anderson only appeared in one early debate and then only opposite the
Republican challenger to President Carter, Ronald Reagan. Due to Carter's absence, the
debate was carried on only one network and attracted a small audience.

40. *ABC News* poll, October 12, 1992, USABC.101292, R1.

NAFTA, political reform, and a host of other issues (Barta 1993, 425). At its height, the group had a membership of upwards of a million (Posner 1996, 323), indicating the continued appeal of Perot and his agenda. Although this is a remarkable number in itself, what attracted major-party attention after 1992 was the Perot constituency—consisting of almost twenty million people who had voted for him—and the even larger number of voters who found him appealing during the course of the 1992 campaign.

As the 1996 election approached, the Perot movement and United We Stand America refused to fold into either of the two major parties. Instead, it sought to transform itself once again, this time from an interest group into a political party. Fittingly enough, Perot made the announcement that he would launch a new political party on the *Larry King Live* show, on September 25, 1995. The timing of the announcement was related to the hurdles that third parties face. For example, to get on the California ballot as a political party, almost ninety thousand individuals had to change their registration to the new party by October 24, 1995.[41] Perot succeeded, spending about five hundred thousand dollars in the California effort.[42] In the end, the Reform Party succeeded in qualifying for all fifty state ballots, although without the dramatic mobilization effort of 1992.

However, the political world of 1996 was quite different from that of 1992. Most important, the Republican Party did not seem as alien to Perot and the movement as it had in 1992. In 1994, the party had successfully made direct appeals to Perot and his supporters for their congressional votes by emphasizing issues central to the 1992 Perot campaign (as we describe in chap. 7). The most tangible example of this appeal was the Republican Contract with America, which tapped into significant Perot issues and bore fruit in Perot's endorsement of the Republicans in 1994.

41. The task was made even more difficult by the decisions of the California attorney general. He at first allowed that the party could turn in around 890,000 names on petitions (not requiring signers to change party registration), but a week after this effort had begun, the attorney general said that he had made a mistake and that the deadline for submitting the petitions had effectively passed.

42. "The H. Ross Perot Party New Organization is Fueled by Texan's Billions," *San Diego Union-Tribune,* October 24, 1995, B6.

Many of the issues that had been crucial to Perot's support in 1992 had receded in salience by 1996. The deficit was blunted with the decline in federal red ink of more than two-thirds from when Clinton took office.[43] Concerns about issues of reform and trade also declined. After 1995, the drive for congressional term limits stalled, both because the Supreme Court had ruled limits on congressional terms unconstitutional and because the Republicans' success in taking over both houses of Congress without the help of term limits indicated that serious change could occur without that reform (Jacobson 2004). Furthermore, seventeen of the nineteen states that would eventually limit the terms of their own state legislators had done so by 1996. On the issue of trade and NAFTA, the fact that the treaty had been in place for three years indicated that the most draconian predictions had not come to pass. As a result, in spite of the strong opposition to the treaty in 1992 and 1993, only a small minority of voters in 1996 supported withdrawing from the treaty.[44]

In addition to diminished pull toward Perot and the Reform Party on the issues, there was also reduced pull based on Perot's personal appeal. In 1992, he had been an extremely popular figure (as shown in fig. 3.2), but at no point during 1996 did the percentage of Americans rating him favorably equal or surpass those giving him an unfavorable rating (Koch 2001). It is perhaps for these reasons that in the run up to the 1996 election, Perot failed to receive the media coverage that he had enjoyed in 1992. For the month of June 1992 alone, more than twenty-four hundred newspaper mentions of Perot appeared. In the same month, President Bush and the Democratic nominee-in-waiting Bill Clinton each received approximately sixteen hundred mentions, giving Perot 50 percent more stories than either the sitting president or his Democratic challenger. Even after the election, Perot's press coverage remained heavy, but his visibility had decreased drastically by 1994. Over the first six months of 1994, the number of stories about Perot dropped to a third of what it had been in the previous year, and it was only a quarter as great by 1995. During the first six months of 1996, with Perot running as a presidential candidate and working to get the Reform Party on the

---

43. http://www.cbo.gov/showdoc.cfm?index=1821&sequence=0#table11.

44. *Time*/CNN, March 6–7, 1996, accession 0258356, question 037.

ballot, his press coverage was a third less than it had been in the first half of 1993, a nonelection year. In fact, over the first eight months of 1996, Perot received fewer mentions than he had in the single month of June 1992, and he lagged badly behind his major-party rivals.[45]

In contrast, both Dole and Clinton were popular candidates in 1996. Of the forty-four different ratings Gallup reported about Dole or Clinton throughout 1996, there was only one with more unfavorable than favorable ratings of either candidate. Favorable responses significantly outpaced the negative responses by a margin of 23 percent for Clinton and 13 percent for Dole. As figure 3.6 shows, both major-party candidates consistently were favorably evaluated throughout most of the year leading up to the election.[46] In addition, the national economy was far better than it had been in 1992. Unemployment, which was at 7.2 percent when Clinton became president, had declined to 5.2 percent by October 1996; the gross domestic product grew at an average rate of 3.3 percent during the Clinton presidency, as opposed to only 1.8 percent during George Bush's term (Stanley and Niemi 2004, 389–90, table 11.1).

The reduced push from the major-party candidates was mirrored in the noticeably weaker pull toward Perot. Even at the height of his popularity in 1996, Perot was drawing more unfavorable than favorable evaluations. In fact, figure 3.6 is the mirror image of figure 3.2 from 1992, when the major-party candidates were evaluated negatively while Perot's evaluations were strongly positive.

These changes in the political environment meant that Perot's constituency was considerably smaller in 1996 than in 1992. In any other year, the majority-party bid for the third party's constituency might have resulted in the complete disappearance of the third party. The most important reason Perot broke with this pattern and did not disappear altogether after 1992 was a unique combination of incentives and resources, which produced a second Perot candidacy. Perot had the financial resources to support a second run, and although his personal and issue appeals were in decline, these did not seriously threaten his ability to get on the ballot. In fact, he spent more than eight million dollars getting on

---

45. The counts of press reports over the specified time period were taken from Lexis-Nexis searches.

46. http://www.brain.gallup.com.

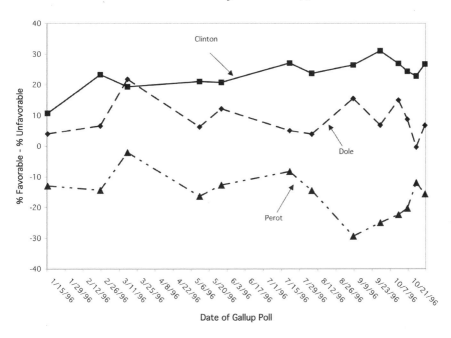

Fig. 3.6. Favorability ratings of Clinton, Dole, and Perot, 1996 campaign. (Data from Gallup Poll.)

the ballot and getting the Reform Party started.[47] The prospect of more than thirty million dollars in federal funds for a second Perot campaign also promoted a run by Perot in 1996.

Perot did his best to raise suspense about who the Reform Party candidate was going to be, claiming, "This is not about me running for president."[48] Based on the expectation that Perot was not going to run, former Colorado governor Richard Lamm entered the race in mid-July. Approximately thirty-six hours after Lamm declared, Perot announced his own candidacy, again on *Larry King Live.* Not surprisingly, Perot became the party's nominee.

Without the presence of favorable issues, the heightened concern about the economy that helped him in 1992, or unpopular major-party candidates, Reform Party prospects were poor. With Perot's early sup-

47. http://www.fec.gov/pres96/presmstr.htm.

48. "Perot Backing a New Party, But Shrugs Off Talk that He'll Run in '96," *St. Louis Post-Dispatch,* September, 26, 1995, 1.

port so much lower than in 1992, he was excluded from the debates by the Commission on Presidential Debates, and this time the major parties had no incentive to come to his aid. With Perot's appeal and support dwindling, there appeared to be a significant chance that he might fall below 5 percent in the popular vote, putting an unmistakable end to his insurgent electoral movement.

At the last minute, however, Bob Dole inadvertently came to Perot's aid by dispatching his campaign manager, Scott Reed, to Dallas to ask Perot to withdraw. The move perplexed Dole's supporters. One of them said: "It's like we gave him an extra debate near the tail end of the campaign. I don't understand it. . . . It may be worth a few points for him."[49] Perot's well-publicized refusal to drop out gave him a platform from which to attack Clinton on campaign finance reform to the National Press Club the next day and produced badly needed press coverage. Perot's final vote was almost two points higher than the last tracking poll before the Dole mission,[50] and with 8.4 percent of the vote, significant FEC funding was guaranteed for a 2000 Reform Party run.

The Reform Party of 2000, a spent force kept on life support by twelve million dollars in federal funds, was mostly an exercise in political theater, playing to a vastly depleted audience. The characters in the drama of 2000 included a former professional wrestler, Jesse Ventura, who had been elected as Reform governor of Minnesota in 1998; multi-billionaire entrepreneur Donald Trump, who briefly flirted with the idea of running; and John Hagelin, the candidate of the Natural Law Party. There were reprise appearances by Jack Gargan, the man who initiated the Perot candidacy in 1992, and Pat Buchanan, the man who had tried to capture the Perot constituency's support for his 1996 Republican nomination run. The final result—a Buchanan hostile takeover of the party and the FEC funding, over Perot's strong objection—had little to do with the movement inspired by Perot in 1992. Buchanan's campaign received just one half of 1 percent of the vote, confirming the demise of the party.

---

49. Richard Berke, "Perot Turns Down Dole Plea to Quit, Calling it 'Weird,'" *New York Times,* October 25, 1996, 1.

50. Gallup tracking poll, week 7 , qn2, http://www.brain.gallup.com.

CONCLUSION

The 1992 campaign was shaped by an unprecedented confluence of events, beginning with an incumbent president's historically high popularity in the wake of a brief and successful war in the Middle East, followed quickly by an economic recession and equally stunning decline in presidential approval. President Bush's plummeting popularity presented the usual opportunity to the challenger party, although it was sufficiently delayed to go unrecognized by many leading Democratic potential contenders in 1992. Partly because of the perceived weakness of the Democratic field of nomination candidates and partly because of long-standing grievances against the two major parties, Ross Perot's maverick challenge on *Larry King Live* struck a chord, energizing hundreds of thousands of potential volunteers, many of whom jumped at the chance to participate in his independent effort to get on the ballot and mount a serious national campaign for the presidency.

By the time Perot's name began appearing on national public opinion polls in the spring, he was far better liked than he was known. While President Bush and the Democratic nominee-in-waiting Bill Clinton languished in the polls, weighed down by as many negative as positive evaluations, Perot benefited from the fact that he had been far more specific about the problems he wanted to solve than he was about the ways he proposed to solve them. Perot's ability to appeal through his television appearances, his rallies of volunteers working to collect petitions in support of his ballot-access drives, and the grassroots nature of his campaign vaulted him in the polls to trial-heat leads over his major-party rivals from mid-May through the end of June 1992.

Ultimately, of course, Perot was able to capture 18.9 percent of the popular vote. It is true that he poured unprecedented amounts of his own money into his fall campaign and that the campaign after he redeclared candidacy on October 1 looked less like a popular grassroots movement and more like a corporate media public relations blitz. However, these characteristics do not ultimately describe what is most important about the 1992 Perot phenomenon, nor do they adequately account for the near-record popular vote he received. But for many keen observers of American politics, these characteristics have disguised the underlying significance of the Perot campaign, causing most to miss the fact that Perot fit a general pattern defined by other successful third-party electoral movements in American history.

Perot's initial surge in popularity was not based on campaign expenditures from his personal fortune, which were modest compared to the major-party candidates, including those of two failed nomination contestants who languished far behind in the polls. His popularity in the spring and early summer legitimized his bid to be the only third-party candidate in history to join the Republican and Democratic nominees in the nationally televised debates. His success in those debates, combined with his record expenditures on his media campaign, increased his popularity between the time he redeclared his candidacy and election day.

If Perot's late-campaign expenditures misled many observers into seeing his movement as unique, his personal style—emphasizing action over substance, problem over solution—also contributed to this misperception. Perot may have oversimplified the problems in Washington and ignored the fundamental realities of the world economy and resulting political forces. But even if that is a fair characterization, it is not correct to conclude that his movement had no programmatic or issue basis. Perot was late in defining his precise positions on many issues, but his concern with issues of reform, the budget deficit, and the economy were clear from the beginning. It remains for us to show how much his volunteer base responded to him because of the issue stands he took. That, indeed, is the question for the next two chapters. However, it is certainly fair to conclude from our analysis of the 1992 campaign that by the time Perot reentered the race in October, he had identified issues and potential solutions at a level of precision roughly consistent with most major-party challengers in American politics.

Ironically, then, those who dismiss the long-term importance of the Perot movement do so by focusing on his extraordinarily high expenditures late in his campaign and his failure to define clear positions on the issues early in his campaign. Our analysis reverses the focus on both counts: he spent little early in the campaign, when his popularity and legitimacy were at their peak; and he defined himself on the issues late in the campaign, as people approached their decisions about how they were going to vote in November. Perot's early popularity is critical to our analysis because it meant the major parties could not afford to risk alienating his constituency by denying him access to the debates in the fall. Perot's appearances and successes in the debates were at least as important to his popular-vote share as was his advertising campaign. He won a spot on the debates because of his preconvention standing in the polls and because of the legions of volunteers he had attracted to the process.

Despite superficial qualities and events that make Perot appear to be a unique flash-in-the-pan insurgent candidate, the dynamic of third parties applies in full to the 1992 Perot movement and its aftermath. From what we know about his campaign, it is clear that his constituency was pushed and pulled toward him not simply because he "bought" their support. An issues basis to his constituency, as we will show, provided the leverage for subsequent change in the two-party system, just as the dynamic of third parties predicts. Applying the dynamic of third parties as our analytic template will lead us to fill in the qualities of the Perot movement itself that are usually missed, as well as its effects on the two-party system, which have also been overlooked as observers have sought to explain the shape of our politics at the close of the twentieth century.

IV

Was There an Issue Constituency for Perot?

U NDER THE LOGIC OF THE DYNAMIC of third parties, the emergence of a successful third party carries the possibility of change primarily because it presents a target to one or both major parties, enabling
them to bid for the third party's constituency in subsequent elections.
The issues that define the third party's constituency provide the basis for
the major-party bid. In the absence of an identifiable issue constituency,
the third party, no matter how successful it is in the short term, would
be unlikely to generate long-term change in the two-party system. A
large vote for a third party might indicate discontent about the performance of the major parties—for instance, a major scandal or the choice
of a candidate whom significant numbers of voters do not trust. In such
a case, the signal to the parties may be clear—avoid scandal and the
temptation to nominate untrustworthy candidates—but the potential for
the third party to bring about enduring change would be limited.

In contrast, when the third party mobilizes a distinctive issue constituency, the signal is clear, as are the major parties' incentives to respond. Their response, of course, is the key to the third-party dynamic.
The question of the third party's issue constituency is important because
it sets up the "pull" side of our model of support, and it posits that successful third-party movements, such as Perot's, are not merely negative
reactions to major-party failures.

How do we decide whether there was an issue constituency supporting Perot? We think of an issue constituency as defined by both issue
preferences and issue priority. Preferences are the positions that support-

78

ers and potential supporters have on the issues; the priority of an issue is the importance individuals attach to the issue concern. Individuals who indicate one issue is more important than another express a priority for one public concern over another. An issue constituency is distinctive in the preferences of the candidate's supporters and in the importance they assign to various issues. One way of assessing the distinctiveness of a third-party movement on the issues is to compare its supporters' preferences with those of the two major parties.

POLICY DIFFERENTIATION

When we say that the Democratic Party's constituency has a preference for imposing stricter controls on gun owners, we do not mean that every Democrat is in perfect agreement on the amount and degree of gun control that is necessary or on the priority that should be given to that issue compared with others. With respect to gun control, some Democrats oppose the dominant view in their party. In matters of national politics, there is never perfect agreement, and describing aggregate preferences and priorities is always a matter of general tendencies, rather than perfect agreement. A constituency's distinctiveness is evident when we compare one constituency with another. Thus, a typical set of Democratic supporters would be more supportive of gun control than a comparable set of Republicans, even if we also find some individual Democrats more opposed to gun control than some Republicans. Moreover, we might find that Democrats were more distinct from Republicans on some issues (e.g., gun control) than on others (e.g., how best to handle federal budget deficits).

A third party's constituency is distinctive to the degree that it differs from the major parties, and this in turn is affected by the degree of choice offered by the two major parties. Consider two alternative ideal scenarios. In the "convergence" scenario, the two major parties take similar positions on the foremost issues; as a result, they do not offer a clear choice. When the parties converge on the issues, activists see relatively little difference between the major parties and their candidates, and divisions between the major-party activists themselves should be muted. This is a scenario ripe for a third party to exploit if there are sizable numbers of activists and voters with preferences that diverge significantly from the consensus represented by the Democratic and Republican parties. There would be a significant opportunity to outflank the major parties, and their similar issue positions would encourage indifference between them among potential third-party supporters. Indifference between the major parties, of course, is one of the conditions in our model that pushes potential supporters toward third-party participation.

Major-party issue convergence provides an opportunity for the dynamic of third parties to work. A third party could emerge to articulate a position on the issue or issues of concern, point out the absence of choice between the parties, and attract significant support. Its success would signal the existence of many supporters of the third party's issue positions, which could set up a bid by one or both major parties. The bid would create change because it would involve a shift in positions or priorities by one or both major parties, and the third party movement would disappear as its constituency was absorbed by one of the major parties.

A second scenario occurs when the two established parties offer a clear choice on the issues, which is reflected in the positions the parties and their candidates take and in the preferences of their activist constituencies. Under this "polarization" scenario, the conditions for third-party success are less propitious because the positions of the parties and candidates are clearly differentiated in potential third-party supporters' minds. The push–pull model indicates that when major-party differences are apparent, a third party has less of an opportunity because of the high stakes voters and activists have in the conflict between the major parties. When the parties are sharply differentiated from one another, there is also less opportunity for a third party to define a unique issue position that can attract significant support. Thus, when a third party does emerge, its candidate typically emphasizes the issues that do not sharply differentiate the major parties (issues that fit the convergence scenario), avoiding or de-emphasizing issues on which the parties are polarized (Sundquist 1983).

These scenarios provide guidance as we search for evidence of a Perot issue constituency in the 1992 and 1996 elections. There is no reason to expect one scenario to apply to all issues: as we just suggested, the issues that formed the core of Perot's campaign should most closely fit the convergence scenario, whereas evidence of a Perot constituency should be less compelling on issues that sharply divide the Democratic and Republican parties. On all of the issues for which we have data, we examine the preferences of potential Perot supporters and assess the distinctiveness of Perot supporters compared with comparable sets of major-party backers. A complete answer to the question posed by the title of this chapter is not possible until we have linked issue preferences to actual support behavior, a task that the push-pull model is designed to do and that we address in chapter 5. However, if we find evidence consistent with these scenarios in the preferences of Perot supporters and major-party activists, we can begin to link the scenarios to the choices presented in the two elections, by mapping the perceived positions of the candidates and parties on the issues. In this way, we can assess the structure of preference and choice across the issue landscape in these two elections.

ISSUE PREFERENCES

Figures 4.1 and 4.2 present mean issue positions of potential Perot volunteers on many of the issues debated in the 1992 presidential election. Figure 4.1 depicts issues that relate directly to the partisan debate in American politics that has divided the Democratic and Republican parties for decades; it therefore most closely approximates the party-polarization scenario. Figure 4.2 describes issues emphasized by Ross Perot in his campaigns for the presidency.[1] Figure 4.1 shows that the Perot sample was not firmly in either the liberal or the conservative camp in 1992, but neither were potential Perot activists consistently moderate in their responses. On the general ideology item, the mean position was just right of center, but on the other six items, Perot supporters were to the liberal side on three and to the conservative side on three—and by sub-

---

1. Some of the Perot issues, notably the balanced budget amendment, also have divided the major parties. Perot's issue items are measured on a seven-point scale ranging from "strongly oppose" (coded as -3) to "strongly support" (coded as $+3$). For liberal-conservative issues, the seven-point scale ranges from "extremely liberal" to "extremely conservative"; a positive score indicates support for the conservative position, and a negative score represents support for the liberal position.

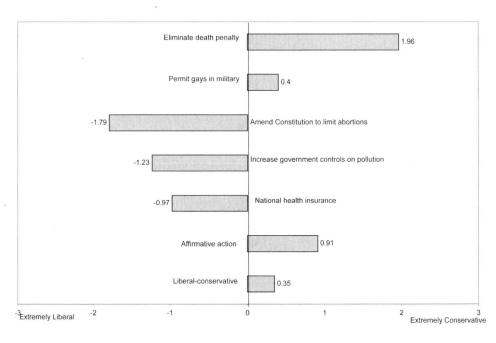

Fig. 4.1.   Mean positions of 1992 Perot sample on liberal-conservative issues

stantial margins on all but one. They took a strongly liberal position against a constitutional amendment limiting abortions, and they expressed strong support for a national health insurance program and increased governmental regulations to control pollution. At the same time, they voiced strong opposition to eliminating the death penalty and opposed affirmative action programs and allowing homosexuals to serve in the military.

Notwithstanding their inconsistency on traditional partisan issues, Perot respondents were unified and consistent on issues associated with Perot's program in 1992, as figure 4.2 shows. Term limits and balancing the budget were two issues that elicited the strongest support, but potential activists in Perot's campaign also favored increased taxes on social security benefits for the wealthy and increased federal taxes on gasoline, both positions in keeping with their commitment to balance the national government's budget.

The 1996 surveys allow us to compare a sample of potential Perot activists with potential major-party campaign activists to examine party differences directly. Several of the items are identical to those asked of the

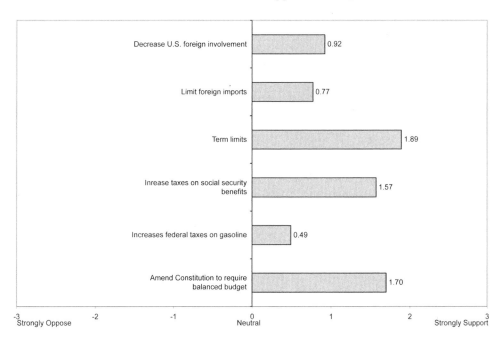

Fig. 4.2. Mean positions of 1992 Perot sample on issues emphasized by Perot

1992 Perot sample, but there are also several different questions. Even where the questions are identical, we cannot directly compare responses to assess change in the Perot movement between 1992 and 1996, because the samples are different.[2] But the comparison does help assess how distinctive the Perot issue constituency was compared with the Democratic and Republican parties four years after Perot's initial foray into the political arena. It is important to remember that Perot's performance in 1996 was successful for third parties in the United States. Indeed, had he received his 1996 popular vote share in 1992, his movement would still have rated among the most successful American third-party movements. Although fewer in number than in 1992, 1996 Perot supporters should be expected to hold many of the issue positions that we find among 1992 supporters.

As in our 1992 results, Reform contributors identified themselves as moderately conservative in their overall political philosophy. On the traditional partisan issues, however, there was less flip-flopping across the

---

2. We investigate the question of change in the Perot constituency in chapter 6 using our panel survey of callers to Perot's toll-free number; the 1992 postelection wave of these callers is the basis of figure 4.1.

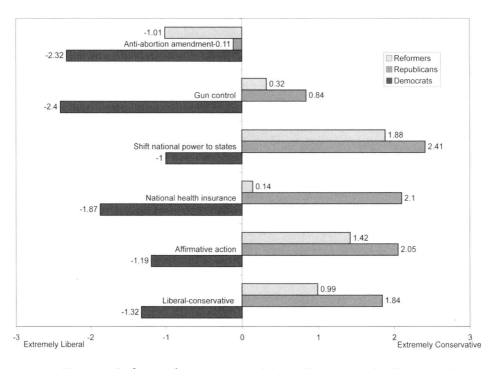

Fig. 4.3.   Reform and major-party activist positions on partisan issues, 1996

ideological divide in 1996 than in 1992, with only the abortion question eliciting a response that nets in the liberal direction.

On liberal-conservative issues, the Democratic and Republican parties differ from one another sharply. On every item, Republican contributors took the conservative position, and Democrats took the liberal position; and on most of the issues, the differences between the parties were large. On every item in figure 4.3, Reform contributors located themselves between the two major parties, although, with the exception of abortion, Reform opinion was in the conservative direction.

Once again the story is different when we look at the Perot issues (see fig. 4.4). As we found in 1992, Reform contributors in 1996 supported Perot issue positions without exception, and on most of the items, their support exceeds the support of contributors to either major party. However, Reformers were more clearly differentiated from the Democrats on Perot issues. Democrats opposed the Perot platform on every issue except increasing taxes to cut the deficit, and Democratic opposition was

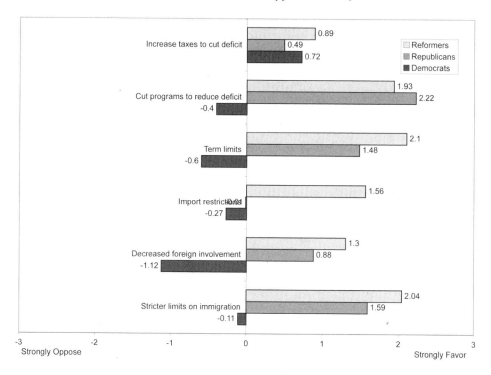

Fig. 4.4.   Reform and major-party activist positions on Perot issues, 1996

pronounced on several items. Thus, distinguishing itself from the Democrats did not present a substantial problem for the Reform Party. In contrast, however, the distinctiveness of Reform contributors compared to the Republicans in 1996 was much less sharp.[3] On one issue—cutting federal programs across the board to reduce the deficit—Republican contributors outran Reformers in their support. However, on all other items, Reform contributors were more supportive than Republicans.

Figure 4.5 summarizes our findings about issue preferences in 1992 and 1996 by presenting potential Perot and major-party activists' preferences on a liberal-conservative index that combines the traditionally partisan issues, alongside a Perot issue index. Note, first, that the Perot constituency was relatively moderate or centrist on the liberal-conservative

---

3. Placements are mean perceptions of the entire sample from the year in question. In 1996, we combine the three party samples, weighted by the proportion each party received of the presidential vote, because the perceptions across the three samples are highly consistent (the mean between-sample correlation of all placement items excluding self-placements is .98).

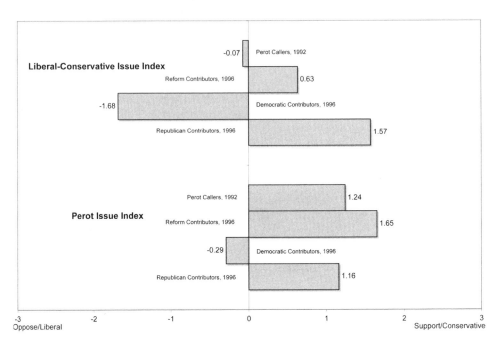

Fig. 4.5. Democratic, Republican, and Reform positions on liberal-conservative and Perot issue indexes, 1992 and 1996

index in both years, while the two major parties were sharply polarized. On these issues, as we have seen, the Democratic and Republican parties were distinct from one another, with the Perot constituency in between. Second, the Perot constituency was relatively distinct on the reform, economic nationalism, and budget-deficit issues that formed the core of both Perot campaigns. In turn, the difference between the major parties was less on these issues than on the liberal-conservative issues that have defined the axis of conflict between them for decades.

At this point, it seems fair to conclude that the evidence for a Perot issue constituency is less than compelling on the liberal-conservative issue dimension, where Perot activists were moderately liberal on some issues and moderately conservative on others. They looked centrist on all issues combined, while distinctively liberal and conservative positions were held by Democratic and Republican activists, respectively. Thus, the major parties distinguished themselves from one another clearly, which should have reduced the incentives to support a third party on these issues. At the same time, the Perot movement's claim to being a centrist alternative was compromised by its liberal positions on some of these issues and its conservative positions on others.

The Perot constituency consistently supported the issues their candidate stressed in his two presidential campaigns—reforming the political process, economic nationalism, and deficit reduction—a pattern more indicative of the presence of a coherent issue constituency than was true of partisan issues. Perot activists were more committed on these issues than either Democratic activists, who generally opposed the Perot agenda, or the Republicans, whose support was less strong and less consistent than among Perot backers. While they did not converge on the Perot issues in 1996, major party activists were also less different from one another on these issues than on partisan issues, although the Perot constituency did not have the separation from either party that the two parties had on liberal-conservative issues.

CANDIDATE & PARTY ISSUE POSITIONS

The idea of an issue constituency implies not only consensus and distinctiveness among supporters of a candidate or party. Issue constituencies are based on a relationship between the positions of leaders and followers. Thus, patterns of differences and distinctiveness evident among activist followers should also be apparent among candidates and parties. We expect leaders' and activists' positions to correspond because leaders take issue stands in response to constituency preferences and because campaign activists support candidates partially based on whether they agree with them on policy issues. We can also gain a more complete picture of how the Perot movement fit with the major parties in 1992, a year when we lack comparative data on major-party activists.

In addition to asking respondents to give their own opinions on the issues in figures 4.1–4, we asked them to indicate where they placed each of the presidential candidates and parties on selected issues. Figure 4.6 maps the issue space for the liberal-conservative political philosophy item in both 1992 and 1996. In both years, potential Perot activists saw the Democratic Party as clearly on the left and the Republican Party as slightly more extreme in its conservatism. They perceived the two major-party nominees as slightly less extreme than their parties, but both

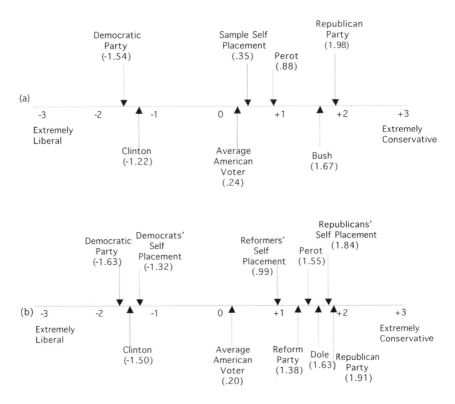

Fig. 4.6. Placements on the liberal-conservative political philosophy, 1992 and 1996: (a) 1992 potential Perot activists; (b) 1996 contributors. (Data from authors' 1992 potential Perot activist and 1996 party contributors surveys.)

were distinctly off-center. For example, less than 1 percent of our 1996 sample thought that Bill Clinton was more conservative than Bob Dole or that the Republican Party was more liberal than the Democratic Party. In short, Democratic activists, party, and candidate placements formed a liberal cluster, while the comparable Republican placements were equally coherent on the right.[4]

Our findings about the self-placement of Perot activists between the two major parties are confirmed by the placement of Perot in 1992 and the Reform Party in 1996. In 1992, Perot was seen as right of center but

---

4. Placements are mean perceptions of the entire sample from the year in question. In 1996, we combine the three party samples, weighted by the proportion each party received of the presidential vote, because the perceptions across the three samples are highly consistent (the mean between-sample correlation of all placement items excluding self-placements is .98).

still to the left of the Republican Party and its nominee.[5] In 1996, both Perot and the Reform Party were seen as approaching the Republican Party and its nominee, Bob Dole, in their conservatism. Thus, although it is true that Perot and the Reform Party were generally consistent with the stands of their activists on these left-right issues, Perot was located between the two enduring parties in 1992 but he was precariously close to the Republicans in 1996. As a result, our expectation is that these issues would not provide as much traction for his 1996 campaign, especially to the extent that it depended on "push" factors to attract support. Large differences between the major parties create an incentive to avoid having the least-favored candidate winning. At least on these issues, the argument for not "wasting" one's support on a third-party movement may have been strong for many potential backers.

Figure 4.7 maps the candidates and parties on measures of the Perot issues in the two elections.[6] In contrast to the liberal-conservative map, the difference between the two major parties on the Perot issues was muted, especially in 1992. In that year, both major parties were seen as opposing the Perot agenda, while Perot was distinctive in his support. Potential Perot activists placed themselves clearly in support of the Perot agenda, although not as strongly as their candidate.

The 1996 Perot issue map shows that Perot was about equally committed on his issues, with the Reform Party and Reform contributors in similarly supportive positions. However, our 1996 reading of the Perot issues is that the Republican Party and its activist base were also in favor of the Perot agenda and sharply differentiated from the Democratic Party and its activist base. The difference between the two major parties on the Perot issues was greater in 1996 (2.27 units on the seven-point scale) than it had been in 1992 (1.09 units), although not as great as the 1996 difference on the liberal-conservative scale (about 3.50 units). Thus,

---

5. There is some variation in where activists placed Perot, depending on which specific liberal-conservative issue we examine: on affirmative action, activists in both years saw Perot as taking the conservative view; on national health insurance and abortion, activists placed Perot to the left of center. On all of these placements, Perot was seen as more moderate than either party.

6. The issues used to construct the 1992 measure were federal tax increases on gasoline, term limits, and limitations on foreign imports. In 1996, the issues were federal deficit reduction (by cutting government programs) and decreased U.S. involvement abroad.

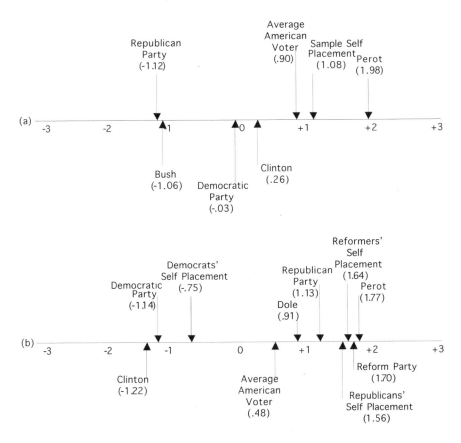

Fig. 4.7.   Placements on Perot issue indexes, 1992 (a) and 1996 (b). (Data from authors' 1992 potential Perot activist and 1996 party contributors surveys.)

our 1996 data continue to show the major parties as less divided on the Perot issues than on the liberal-conservative dimension, although Perot and the Reform Party were significantly more crowded by the Republicans in that year's mapping of the issue space.

We have said that we cannot draw confident conclusions about change by comparing the 1992 and 1996 surveys, because of differences in the samples and the survey items employed. We cannot resist pointing out, however, that the 1992 and 1996 maps of the Perot issue space are consistent with what we would expect from the dynamic of third parties. There was little difference between the major parties in the 1992 election on the issues animating the third-party movement, but by 1996, the Republican Party appears to have made a bid for the Perot constituency by moving sharply toward the Perot positions on these issues, while the Democrats were firmly in opposition. The difference between the major parties should have made supporting Perot more difficult, even among activists concerned about these issues. The fact that Perot was less distinct from the closer major party should also have depressed his support among his constituency. Thus, looking only at figure 4.7, we could conclude that Perot's support between the two elections dramatically declined because the Republican Party successfully preempted the insurgent's constituency by shifting the Republican position on key issues and attracting a significant share of the Reform constituency.

As it happens, that is exactly what we will argue (in chap. 7), although we will not rely on figure 4.7 as our most compelling evidence. Despite the inconclusive nature of the results in figure 4.7, the figure foreshadows the story we tell based on more complete and convincing evidence from the post-1992 period.

Figure 4.8 further clarifies the advantageous position Perot's candidacy had versus the two major parties in that year, by mapping both the liberal-conservative and the Perot issues in 1992 in a two-dimensional plot based on perceptions of potential Perot activists. The liberal-conservative dimension ranges from left to right on the horizontal scale, while the Perot issues are on the vertical scale, from support at the top to opposition at the bottom. Each point represents a position of a candidate or party in a space defined by the two issue dimensions. As other scholars have noted (e.g., Sundquist 1983), a third party can generate significant support by introducing an alternative issue dimension. If the new issue is sufficiently important to enough voters and if the third party is well positioned on it relative to the two parties, the third party can enjoy success.

Perot was well positioned to take advantage of the issues that motivated his campaign in 1992. Democrats and Republicans were sharply different on the liberal-conservative dimension but were close to indifferent or in opposition on Perot issues. Meanwhile, Perot's relative centrism on the left–right scale gave way to a distinctly supportive position on budget, reform, and economic nationalism issues. Potential Perot activists saw themselves and the average voter as relatively supportive of Perot's agenda as well.

This seems about as close to an ideal situation as a third party can

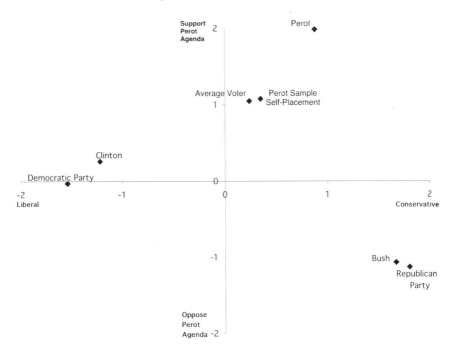

Fig. 4.8.   Two-dimensional map of candidates and parties, 1992 (Data from authors' 1992 survey of potential Perot activists.)

hope for in American politics and helps account for the historic levels of electoral support Perot received in the 1992 election. The key to enduring success, of course, would be in the continuing relevance and importance of the Perot issues. To the degree that Perot could excite interest in his agenda and persuade significant numbers of voters and activists that his issues (rather than the traditional conflict over liberal-conservative issues) should dominate political discourse, the movement might persist (Schattschneider 1975). In addition, of course, the issue map in 1992 provides a clear indication of the signal sent by the Perot movement, a signal unlikely to be missed by entrepreneurial party leaders seeking to add to their base in a competitive electoral environment. Thus, as we have already suggested, the response of the major parties to the Perot challenge would also prove critical to the movement's future, as well as to the shape of major-party politics. Perot's positions on the two issue dimensions in figure 4.8, therefore, not only illustrate the Perot movement's favorable strategic position in that election. It also provides a road map for major-party response and change in the elections that followed.

ISSUE PRIORITY

In addition to taking positions on issues, parties also establish legislative agendas and prioritize policies. Similarly, voters and activists attach a higher importance to some policies over others. Thus, issue priority, or issue salience, is a second way a constituency can distinguish itself from competing parties' followers. For example, even if both Republican and Reform contributors preferred to handle deficit reduction by cutting governmental commitments, Reform backers may have differed from Republicans by giving greater importance to the problem. Especially in his 1992 campaign, Perot emphasized that the Republicans had repeatedly failed to give the budget deficit the priority it deserved, so that their preference for deficit reduction did not reflect a genuine commitment to solving the problem. Although it seems unlikely that a third party could build its success on issue priority alone, differences in issue importance could increase the attractiveness of third-party appeals. As a consequence, such differences help define the issue constituency of third parties.

Unfortunately, we do not have data on 1992 for the major parties, so we cannot compare the importance assigned to issues by Perot activists and by major-party activists. Nonetheless, based on our analysis of each party's platform, the Perot issues took a backseat to traditional liberal-conservative issues in both major parties' 1992 campaigns. Using data for 1996, when we can compare Reform activists with major-party contributors, figure 4.9 reports the percentages that identified a Perot issue or a liberal-conservative issue as most important among all the issues we presented for opinion.

In the 1996 Reform contributor sample, issue priorities lined up behind Perot's agenda, with over three-quarters of Reformers saying a Perot issue was most important to them.[7] Note that almost two-thirds of Democratic contributors indicated that a liberal-conservative issue was

---

7. In 1992, potential Perot activists rated Perot issues as more important than liberal-conservative issues, but by a narrower margin (47 percent) than was true of Reform contributors in 1996 (53 percent).

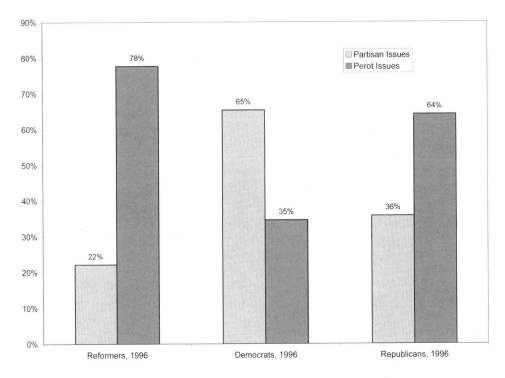

Fig. 4.9. Perot and partisan issues rated "most important" among 1996 contributors

their most important, a result not only consistent with expectations but further demonstrating the separation between the Reform Party and the Democrats in the 1996 election. Republican contributors, in contrast, named a Perot issue as most important much more frequently than they named a partisan issue—more evidence showing that the Republicans crowded the Reform Party and that although the Perot constituency distinguished itself from the Democratic Party, it was much less distinct from the Republicans.

CONCLUSION

The evidence for a Perot issue constituency is suggestive but perhaps not definitive. It is most compelling in 1992, which is appropriate since 1992 is the year the movement emerged and enjoyed historic electoral success. We have seen that the conditions for a Perot constituency are least satisfied in the case of liberal-conservative issues and are maximized in the case of the Perot issues. If we define a third party's constituency by its distinctiveness from the two major parties, the Perot movement failed to distinguish itself on liberal-conservative issues, in part because the major parties were consistently polarized on them. This means, according to the push-pull model, that voters and other potential supporters of a third-party movement have a stake in major-party conflict, even if only to avoid the negative consequences of their least-favored option winning. At the same time, when the major parties are polarized on an issue dimension, it is more difficult for the third party to offer a distinctive alternative. While it is possible to provide a centrist alternative, potential activists in the Perot movement were not consistently centrist in their preferences. When we examined individual issues related to the liberal-conservative dimension, we found that Perot activists were reliably found somewhere between activist supporters of the two major parties, but they alternated back and forth (especially in 1992) between liberal and conservative positions.

Even as the Perot movement failed to distinguish itself as a constituency on traditionally partisan issues, it was distinctive on the three issue concerns we have characterized as central to Perot's campaign, and the two major parties in 1992 cooperated by opposing much of the Perot agenda. These conditions suggest the potential for a third party to tap into an issue constituency and mobilize it as the basis of its electoral support. The Perot candidacy was in a position to do this on the budget, economic nationalism, and reform issues, because these issues did not sharply divide the major parties and because Perot distinguished himself by taking a strong stand. Thus, Perot offered a clear alternative that could attract activists and voters who were in agreement and who were pushed away from the major parties because they did not offer a clear choice or an attractive alternative.

These conditions of a third-party issue constituency are important because they meet the requirements of the push-pull model, which we explore in the next chapter. Linking these issues explicitly to support for Perot is important to establish what we mean by an issue constituency. Note as well that the distinctiveness of Perot coupled with the relative lack of choice between the major parties set up the potential for the third-party dynamic to play out after the 1992 election. Perot was not only attracting followers who supported his stands on reform, economic nationalism, and the budget; he was also signaling to the two major parties the potential these issues had for them. Issues are only one aspect of the push-pull model, so in order for the expectations of the third-party dynamic to hold, it will be important to demonstrate that these issues motivated support for Perot.

V

Explaining Support for Perot

WHILE MAJOR PARTIES HAVE THE advantages of continuous sources of support from interest groups, long-term identifiers, and party institutions, an independent electoral movement, such as Ross Perot's in 1992, must start de novo. It must recruit a cadre of activists, raise money, get on the ballot, and mobilize voters—all in a very short period of time. The Perot movement in 1992 had a particularly short timetable since he did not enter the race until February, when he challenged volunteers to organize and get him on the ballot in all fifty states. Without a large and active army of supporters, the Perot campaign would have been stillborn in 1992. In chapter 2, we developed the push-pull theory of third-party support; in this chapter, we test the theory by evaluating candidate and issue bases of support, before including a broader array of factors that relate more loosely to the push-pull formulation.

WHAT DID THEY DO? ACTIVIST SUPPORTERS FOR PEROT IN 1992 AND 1996

No one can deny that Ross Perot's legions of volunteer activists were directly instrumental to his success in 1992.[1] State ballot-access law for an

1. Our primary focus is on explaining activism in 1992 because that was Perot's first campaign, whereas the 1996 campaign occurred after the major parties had the opportunity to respond to Perot's success in 1992 by bidding for the Perot constituency's support. Nonetheless, because our 1996 surveys enable us to compare Perot/Reform activists with major-party activists, we report some analysis of data from that year.

TABLE 5.1.   Participation by Perot Callers and NES Respondents in the 1992 Campaign (in percentages)

	Preconvention Perot	General Election Campaign For				
		Perot/ Stockdale	Clinton/ Gore	Bush/ Quayle	House Democrat	House Republican
Tried to convince others to support candidate	64.3	49.9	17.7	10.2	7.4	7.2
Attended public meeting or rally	28.8	21.5	5.7	2.7	2.6	2.3
Telephone or door-to-door canvassing	11.7	11.6	2.3	0.5	0.9	1.1
Collected signatures for ballot petition	32.2	—	—	—	—	—
Organized meetings/coffees	4.0	—	—	—	—	—
Held official position in campaign	6.3	—	—	—	—	—
Contributed $100 or less	—	11.4	3.4	1.6	2.0	1.2
Contributed more than $100	—	4.1	1.6	0.4	0.3	0.5
Engaged in fund-raising activities	—	3.8	1.4	0.4	0.6	1.0
Active beyond voting in any way	72.9	57.0	21.6	12.3	11.2	9.1

Source: Authors' September and postelection surveys of potential Perot volunteers.
Note: September wave, N = 1,313; postelection wave, N = 937.

independent candidate varies widely, but in every state, it is a labor-intensive task requiring the circulation of citizen petitions. In addition to performing this task, Perot's volunteers brought his movement visibility and legitimacy that would not have been possible had Perot simply tried to "buy" his way into the election. Table 5.1 provides a summary of the ways in which potential Perot volunteers participated in the 1992 campaign.[2]

We can see from table 5.1 that respondents were quite active in the spring and early summer, before Perot dropped out of the race. During the first phase of the campaign, almost two-thirds of the sample tried to persuade others to support Perot. Although talking with others is an activity that requires only modest effort, almost one-third of the respondents were petition collectors in the ballot drive, an activity that requires a more substantial investment. A similar percentage attended meetings or rallies in the

---

2. Total percentages of activity in a particular way cannot be added together, because some respondents were involved in more than one campaign. The entries for "Active beyond voting in any way" likewise cannot be computed by adding the cell entries for each campaign, because individuals who were active in more than one way for a campaign were counted only once.

spring. About 12 percent canvassed face-to-face or by telephone, and smaller percentages held positions in the campaign or acted as organizers. As already mentioned, all but one of our respondents who participated in the campaign for Perot did so as volunteers, rather than as paid staff.

All told, over 70 percent of respondents were actively involved in some way during the spring-summer phase of the campaign. By surveying callers to Perot's toll-free number, we identified a national sample of potential Perot activists who contributed to the success of the campaign through active involvement in petition-gathering, canvassing, and the like. However, callers to the Perot headquarters were not necessarily active in the campaign. Since over a quarter of the sample was not active for Perot in the first phase of the campaign, we can compare those who were more or less active with those who did not actively support Perot at all.

In the fall campaign, after the major-party nominations were settled and after Perot reentered the race, there was a drop-off in support for the Texan. Across the different activities, the proportion of the sample active for Perot-Stockdale in at least one way other than voting dropped from about 73 percent in the spring to just over half (57 percent) in the general election. On two of three exactly comparable questions posed in the spring and postelection surveys (concerning "convincing others" and "attending a meeting or rally"), there was a decline in activity.[3] This may indicate declining support due to the visible presence of the Democratic and Republican campaigns directly competing with Perot (McCann, Rapoport, and Stone 1999).

Major-party competition with Perot was also reflected in campaign activity for Clinton and Bush in the fall campaign. Over one-fifth of the sample was active in some way for Clinton-Gore, and about 12 percent were involved for Bush-Quayle. There were also detectable amounts of participation in partisan campaigns for the U.S. House of Representatives.[4] Therefore, even though ours is a sample of potential Perot volunteers, some of our respondents were active in major-party campaigns.

3. For the three activities that were common to both waves, 68.1 percent of respondents were active before Perot's withdrawal, versus 55.1 percent after his reentry.

4. We also asked about levels of active involvement in "other state or local campaigns" run by the two major parties. Activity levels were similar to the House campaign activity shown in table 5.1, with 12.7 percent active in some way in Democratic campaigns and 10.5 percent involved in Republican races.

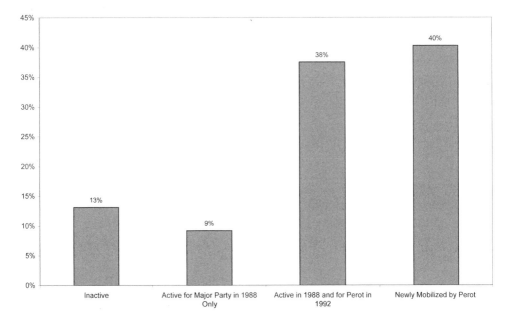

Fig. 5.1.   Campaign activism history of Perot sample, 1988–92

One way of classifying Perot activists is by whether they had been involved in previous major-party campaigns. Figure 5.1 shows that about
13 percent of the sample was inactive in any campaign, partisan or independent, in either the 1988 or the 1992 elections. Another 9 percent
were active in a major-party campaign at the presidential, congressional,
or state and local levels in 1988 but were inactive in 1992. Among those
mobilized into the campaign by Perot, just under half (37.5 percent of
the entire sample) had histories of prior activism in a 1988 major-party
campaign. The remainder (40 percent of the total sample) was newly
mobilized to campaign activism by Perot and had no history of prior
campaign involvement.[5] These newly mobilized Perot activists had a
unique potential to change a major party if they remained active after
the 1992 election.

5. A small percentage of activists newly mobilized by Perot in 1992 were also active
in major-party campaigns in that year. The handful of respondents active in a 1992
major-party campaign who had been inactive in 1988 are excluded from figure 5.1.

TABLE 5.2.   Activity Levels among Reform and Major-Party Contributors, 1996

Percentage Active For	Reform Contributors	Democratic Contributors	Republican Contributors
Perot-Choate	76.2	.8	1.0
Clinton-Gore	2.9	66.2	1.5
Dole-Kemp	3.5	3.2	75.3
Democratic House candidate	2.9	25.2	1.0
Republican House candidate	6.3	1.2	37.0
Reform House candidate	5.6	0.0	0.0
Any Reform campaign	80.3	1.2	1.6
Any Democratic campaign	5.6	73.3	2.5
Any Republican campaign	9.9	3.8	87.7
(N)	1,470	666	789

Source: Authors' 1996 party contributors surveys.

Although we cannot directly compare the 1996 contributor sample to the 1992 caller sample, one of the benefits of the 1996 surveys is that they provide equivalent samples of potential activists in all three parties in that year. In table 5.2, we report the levels of campaign involvement in each of the three 1996 contributor samples.[6]

All three party samples were actively involved in the presidential campaigns in their own party, with relatively little activity in one of the other parties. Substantial majorities—about three-quarters of Reformers and Republicans and about two-thirds of Democrats—were involved in their presidential campaigns beyond voting. Even though the 1992 and 1996 samples are not directly comparable, the most common activity is still "attempting to persuade friends," with 60 percent of Reform contributors, 50 percent of Republicans, and 43 percent of Democrats active in this way, while relatively small minorities of between 5 and 10 percent canvassed for their party's presidential ticket.

Another way of getting a fix on our activist samples is by comparing them to the national electorate. Comparisons are limited because studies of the public do not typically ask detailed questions about active participation. We use the American National Election Studies (ANES) sur-

---

6. The following activities are represented by the data in table 5.2: convincing friends, clerical work, canvassing, contributing one hundred dollars or less, contributing more than one hundred dollars, writing a letter of support to a magazine or newspaper, and other kinds of activity in the campaign.

veys conducted after the 1992 and 1996 elections, which included several activity items comparable to those we asked about in our surveys.[7]

It is no surprise that our potential activist samples were substantially more likely to vote and to engage in activity beyond voting than was the national electorate. For example, in the 1992 Perot sample, about 30 percent attended a meeting or rally for a candidate, and 25 percent contributed money to a party or candidate. In the public, less than 10 percent engaged in either of these two activities during the 1992 campaign. Similarly, in 1996, party contributors were more than twice as likely as voters to engage in activities beyond voting. If we look at attending a meeting or rally, contributors were more than three times as likely to get involved.

Our analysis suggests that we have reasonable, though somewhat different, samples of potential Perot activists from both the 1992 and 1996 campaigns and that these samples captured volunteer activists who were crucial to the success of the Perot movement. The 1992 sample gives us the ability to examine potential activists in the campaign in which Perot first appeared. Calling the Perot campaign headquarters in the spring of 1992 indicated an interest in the movement but was well short of a firm commitment to become involved. Variation in how much callers did for Perot allows us to test our push-pull model of third-party activism.

PUSH-PULL I: CANDIDATE EVALUATIONS

The basic idea behind the push-pull model is that active support for Ross Perot or any third-party candidate results from a combination of negative factors pushing potential supporters away from the Democratic and Republican parties and their nominees, on the one hand, and, on the other, positive attraction to the candidate, pulling backers toward the in-

7. The ANES surveys did not ask respondents to identify the campaign in which respondents participated, so we have aggregated the items in our survey across all of the possible campaigns included on our questionnaire. For example, the ANES surveys asked respondents, "Did you go to any political meetings, rallies, speeches, dinners, or things like that in support of a particular candidate?" A respondent who answered "yes" may have attended a Clinton rally, a meeting in support of her party's U.S. House candidate, or any of a number of other possibilities. To make the two samples as comparable as possible for our analysis, we aggregate across the three campaigns we asked about: presidential, U.S. House, and "other state or local campaigns."

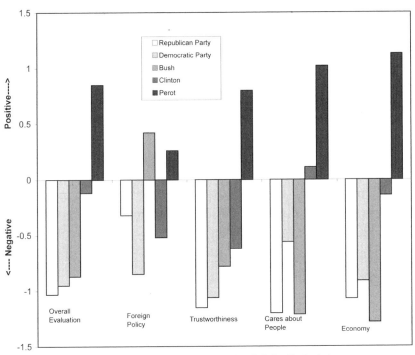

Fig. 5.2.   Ratings of major parties and candidate by 1992 Perot caller sample

surgent campaign. In this section, we provide the simplest possible test of this idea, using candidate evaluations.

We asked respondents to evaluate the abilities of the candidates and parties to provide the basic elements of political leadership. The 1992 survey assessed the candidates' and parties' abilities to solve the nation's economic and foreign policy problems and the degree to which each candidate/party "really cares about people like you" and is trustworthy, along with an overall evaluation of each candidate and party. These items are scored ranging from negative ratings of "poor" (-2) to positive ratings of "outstanding" ($+2$) (see fig. 5.2).

With but two exceptions, all of the major-party candidate and party ratings have negative average scores, while all of the Perot ratings are positive. The major exception to the negativity shown toward the Democrats and the Republicans is the positive score given to George Bush for his ability to solve foreign policy problems (the other is a barely positive rating of

Clinton on the "cares" question). Despite this positive rating for the incumbent, Bush's overall evaluation was even more negative than Clinton's.

These results support the idea that potential Perot volunteers in 1992 rejected both the Democratic and Republican parties and their nominees, while they were at the same time positively attracted to Ross Perot. In Bush and Clinton, potential Perot volunteers saw candidates who lacked the ability to solve the nation's policy problems. Their assessments of the two parties as institutions were no more positive. Likewise, they did not "connect" with the major parties or their candidates in seeing them as trustworthy or caring about ordinary people. In contrast, they rated Perot positively on all five of the items, although they differentiated between his abilities to handle the economy (where he was rated most positively) and his skill in foreign affairs (where his positive rating was relatively low).

In 1996, we did not ask detailed evaluation questions on particular traits or performance items, but we did repeat the "overall evaluation" question used in 1992.[8] Figure 5.3 indicates that 1996 Reform contributors, like 1992 Perot callers, were negative toward both of the major-party candidates and their parties. They tended to be a bit more negative toward Clinton and the Democratic Party than they were toward Dole and the GOP, but all four ratings push the sample as a whole away from the two major parties. In contrast, Reform contributors were very positive toward both Perot and the newly created Reform Party.

Democratic and Republican contributors rated Perot and the Reform Party negatively. With the exception of Democrats' weakly positive evaluation of Robert Dole, they rated the opposition party negatively as well. Major-party respondents rated their own party and its candidate as strongly positive, although their enthusiasm fell short of that displayed for Perot by Reform respondents.

In both years, therefore, potential Perot activists saw their standard-bearer as a positive alternative to the dismal choices the two parties were offering. Their perception of "major-party failure" is plain, but there is also confirmation that the Perot samples saw the Texas independent as a genuine alternative, to whom they were positively attracted. While the results in figures 5.2–3 are consistent with the push-pull conception of

8. We asked for candidate evaluations on seven-point scales in 1996 (-3 to $+3$) as opposed to the five-point scales we used in 1992.

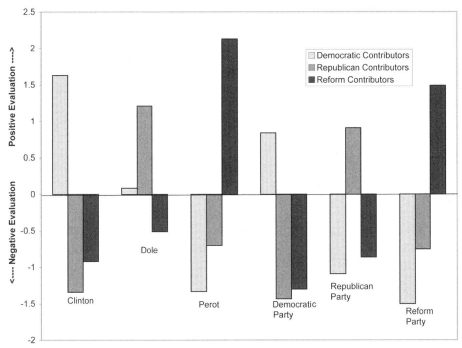

Fig. 5.3. Overall evaluations of parties and candidates by party contributors, 1996

what motivated support for Perot, they do not provide a full test. They demonstrate antipathy toward the Republican and Democratic parties and candidates and positive evaluations of Perot and the Reform Party, but they do not link these feelings to activism for Perot.

In figure 5.4, we show how the ingredients of the push-pull model of candidate evaluations related to campaign activism in the 1992 election. The figure plots the mean levels of campaign activity measured on relative scales that compare Perot campaign participation with activism in a major-party campaign. Positive activity scores reflect a preponderance of activity for Perot, whereas individuals with negative scores were more active for a major party than they were for Perot.[9]

9. This measure is a difference in a count of each individual's campaign activities for Perot minus the activities in major-party presidential campaigns. Thus, a volunteer who engaged in five activities was more involved than respondents who did only one or two of those things or none at all. This is admittedly a rough measure, in part because it treats all forms of active involvement as equal. But we have found, through extensive analysis,

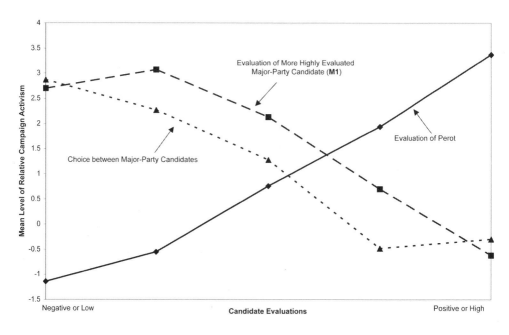

Fig. 5.4.   Push–pull candidate evaluations and campaign activism, 1992

Evaluations of Perot constitute the pull toward the third-party candidate—as evaluations of Perot increase, so should activism in his campaign, an expectation strongly supported in figure 5.4.[10] Among those in the caller sample whose evaluations of Perot were negative, participation in his campaign was practically nonexistent. Indeed, most respondents who gave Perot low evaluations tended to be more active in major-party campaigns than they were for Perot.[11] However, as the evaluation of Perot became more positive, the level of activity in Perot's campaign increased regularly and sharply. Those giving Perot the most positive evaluation on our scale performed better than three activities more for Perot than for the major-party candidates.

---

that it gives us a simple and accurate picture of active engagement in Perot's campaigns and that the simplicity it offers does not distort our ability to understand how and why people became involved.

10. For each respondent, a mean across the five items rating Perot in figure 5.1 was computed. We constructed analogous multi-item indexes to measure the two "push" components in figure 5.3.

11. Mean levels of relative activity for the two lowest ratings of Perot in figure 5.4 were −1.1 and −0.55.

The "push" side of the model includes evaluation of the preferred major-party candidate (**M1**) and the difference between evaluations of the two major-party candidates. The more positive the evaluation of the preferred major-party candidate was, the less active potential volunteers were for Perot, as the negatively sloped line and correlation in figure 5.4 demonstrates. Thus, as Clinton or Bush were evaluated more positively, activism in Perot's insurgent campaign declined because the push away from the two-party system correspondingly declined. Likewise, as the choice between the two candidates increased, activism for Perot also dropped off.

Figure 5.4 shows that both the "pull" and "push" sides of the model are associated with Perot activity and that taken individually, they each have the anticipated effects. However, it is still not certain that both the positive evaluations of Perot and the negative feelings about the major-party candidates stimulated involvement in the Perot movement. In other words, positive attitudes toward Perot might amount to essentially the same thing as negative attitudes toward Bush and Clinton, if individuals positive toward Perot were correspondingly negative toward his competition. Part of our goal in formulating the push-pull model is to assess the relative importance of positive and negative motivations, and we need to know whether these evaluations motivated activism independent of one another.

Multiple regression analysis is a technique that allows us to assess the independent effects of the "push" and "pull" components on campaign activism. It also measures the importance of each effect relative to the others.[12] Figure 5.5 tests the push-pull explanation by using the same evaluation and activity measures employed in figure 5.4. It represents the effect on activism for each variable, independent of the other two.[13]

The results strongly support the push-pull model. Evaluation of Perot is positively associated with campaign activity in 1992. A unit increase in

---

12. Excellent introductions to multiple regression analysis are provided by Lewis-Beck (1980) and Berry and Sanders (2000). Throughout this book, we present regression results in graphical form to make them as accessible as possible to those unfamiliar with multivariate statistical analysis. Appendix B presents the full results, for those interested in the technical details.

13. The analysis also includes dummy variables indicating whether respondents identified with a major party, Republican or Democratic, in 1992.

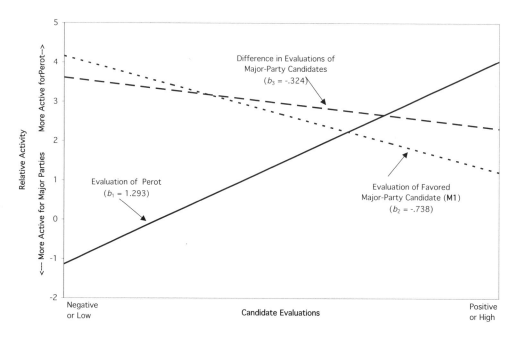

Fig. 5.5.   Push-pull effects of candidate evaluations on relative activity, 1992, controlling for other factors

positive evaluation of Perot produces an average increase of about 1.3 activities to Perot's advantage relative to the major parties, even after we take into account the "push" evaluations of major parties. Likewise, the effect of dissatisfaction with the favored major candidate produced almost the same amount of support for Perot. For each unit decrease in positive evaluation of the better major-party candidate, activity for Perot increased by almost three-quarters of a full activity. This means that activity for Perot was motivated by low evaluation of the major candidates and that these effects were not simply manifestations of positive evaluations of Perot. In addition, the choice between the major candidates had a significant negative effect on Perot involvement. As choice narrowed (represented by reduced difference in evaluation of the two candidates), involvement for Perot increased by about one-third of an activity. The slope for Perot evaluation, which is a "pull" factor, is clearly the steepest, indicating the strongest effect of the three variables involving candidate evaluation. However, if we combine the effects of the two "push" factors—**M1** evaluation and the difference between the two major parties—the total "push" effect is almost as strong as the positive attraction for Perot. Thus, activism in Perot's first campaign was about equally motivated by attraction to the candidate and rejection of the Democratic and Republican nominees.[14]

PUSH-PULL II: ISSUES

In the last chapter, we examined the issue constituency for Ross Perot; in this section, we link support of the Perot issue agenda directly to activism in his campaigns. The push-pull model continues to guide us. The "pull" side, of course, is motivated by positive attraction to the issue positions of the third-party candidate. The "push" side on issues results from dissatisfaction with major-party issue stands, both because the parties and their candidates stand for issue positions remote from the concerns of the third party's backers and because the parties fail to offer a compelling choice on the issues.

To test for the effect of issues, we exploit the fact that Ross Perot was relatively "extreme" on the budget, economic nationalism, and reform issues, while the Democratic and Republican candidates and parties were on the extremes on liberal-conservative issues. Put differently, Perot strongly supported the issues on his agenda, whereas Clinton and Bush took strong positions in support of their positions on issues related to the traditional conflict between liberals and conservatives. Because the candidates took distinctive stands on "their" issues, the more commitment potential Perot activists exhibited on the issues central to his campaign, the stronger their pull to him was. Likewise, the more committed they were on issues related to major-party conflict on the liberal-conservative scale, the closer they were to one of the major-party candidates. Of course, proximity to a major candidate on issues reduces the push toward the third-party option. Our analysis also includes perceptions of the choice between the two major-party candidates on liberal-conservative and on Perot issues. As with candidate evaluation, we expect that the less choice activists saw between the major-party candidates, the more active they were for Perot.

---

14. A similar test using the 1996 contributor data supports identical substantive conclusions.

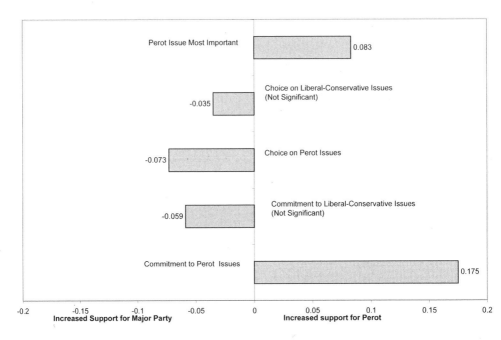

Fig. 5.6.   Effects of issues on relative campaign activity, 1992, controlling for other factors

Figure 5.6 summarizes the "push" and "pull" effects of liberal–conservative and Perot issue clusters on campaign activism, while controlling for the other issue effects and the party identification of the respondent. The magnitude of the slopes is represented by the length of the bars on the chart (rather than by lines as in fig. 5.5): the longer the bar is, the stronger the effect of the variable was on campaign activism.[15] A positive value indicates that as the variable increased, activism for Perot went up on average; a negative value means that as the variable got larger, relative activism for Perot went down.

Notice that the only statistically significant effects are associated with the issues Perot emphasized in his campaign. The impact of the liberal-conservative cluster of issues fails to be strong enough to conclude that it is not due to chance. In contrast, there was a strong enough pull toward Perot that respondents committed to reform, balancing the budget,

15.   Figure 5.6 is based on standardized (beta) coefficients rather than on the unstandardized coefficients used in figure 5.5, because not all of the variables have the same metric.

and economic nationalism were significantly more active for Perot than were those whose commitment to these issues was weaker or absent. Likewise, respondents who said one of the Perot issues was most important to them were more active for Perot than those who did not rate a Perot issue as most important.

Finally, choice between the parties on the Perot issues was negatively related to activism for Perot. We expect this negative relationship because as the perceived choice between the major parties increased, the stakes in their conflict increased, and the push from the two-party system declined. The degree of difference between the major parties on liberal-conservative issues (where the parties differentiate themselves most sharply) did not have a significant impact on campaign activism in 1992, but those who saw the greatest differences between the Democratic and Republican candidates on the Perot issues were less engaged in his campaign, less likely to be pushed away from the major candidates, and more likely to be active in their campaigns as opposed to Perot's.

In short, issues mattered. As with candidate evaluations, both the "push" and the "pull" sides of issues had independent effects. Active engagement for Perot in 1992 reflected attraction to his positions on the issues, in addition to the independent effects of a push away from the two major parties. Moreover, both the issue preferences and the issue priorities of potential activists affected participation. These issue effects are apparent on precisely the issues that Perot emphasized most in his campaign and on which the major parties were most vulnerable to an insurgent candidacy.

BEYOND PUSH-PULL

The push-pull formulation organizes the candidate and issue forces that motivate support for a third-party candidate. We have seen that disaffection from the major-party candidates is not merely the flip side of attraction to Perot, either as a candidate or as an advocate for a set of issue concerns. The pull of Perot's qualities as a candidate and of his issue stands were approximately matched by the disaffection many Perot activists felt toward the Democratic and Republican candidates and the issues they advocated. While the push-pull model captures the core logic of support for Perot, we do not think it necessarily completes the story.

In fleshing out our explanation of participation for Perot, we consider the effects of the economy, alienation from politics as usual, Perot's prospects for victory, contact by the Perot campaign, and prior campaign and group activism.

Evaluations of the Economy

Rosenstone, Behr, and Lazarus (1996) have established that a poor economy promotes the emergence of a third-party candidate. Certainly, the economy was not doing well in 1992, famously prompting the Clinton campaign mantra "It's the economy, stupid!"—to keep the Democratic challenge to George Bush on course. The poor performance of the economy provided grist for Perot's campaign as well, not only because it was another foothold against Bush, but because the Democrats, who held majorities in both the House and Senate, could also be blamed. High unemployment and other indicators of economic failure supported Perot's concern with balancing the budget, reforming the government to limit the influence of entrenched interests, and staunching the flow of jobs out of the country to foreign competitors. Seen in this light, a negative state of the economy is the first cousin of "push" factors in our model, since it triggers a negative response to one or both major parties.

We do not explicitly include evaluations of the state of the economy in the push-pull model, in order to set them apart from issue preferences and priorities. Economic evaluations may influence issue preferences and priorities, but we do not give them the same theoretical standing. As we have argued, issue preferences and priorities are central to the dynamic of third parties because the existence of an issue constituency provides both a foothold for a third-party movement and a target for the major parties. Economic evaluations do not have the same effect, except indirectly—through their effects on candidate evaluations and issue preferences and priorities. When the economy suffers, predisposing many voters and activists to support the major-party challenger or a third-party movement, a constituency of discontent is created, but it does not uniquely adhere to the third party. The challenger party is usually in a better position to exploit it, because it is more likely than the third party to win the election.[16] This puts the third party at a distinct disadvantage relative to the out-of-power major party, unless it can offer more plausible programmatic options. Of course, more plausible programmatic options amount to issue appeals, which is why they are prime movers in our model and why we expect economic evaluations to work indirectly through issues and candidates. Thus, a poor economy may yield rich potential to a third-party movement seeking to build a constituency, but it does not automatically create the constituency that differentiates the movement from the major party out of power. To achieve that differentiation, the movement must appeal based on its candidate and its issue positions and priorities, in the manner described by the push-pull model.

Alienation from Politics as Usual

A general sense of political alienation is also a factor closely related to the push-pull model, because it can push activists and voters away from the two-party system and from politics as usual in the United States. We think of this as distinct from dissatisfaction with the current performance of the two major parties and their candidates, though alienation may predispose individuals to be dissatisfied with the parties and candidates in any given election. Rather than dissatisfaction tied to the specifics of a particular campaign (as in the "push" factors in our model), this sort of alienation is general and presumably continues from election to election. It is also a factor that has been widely cited as important in third-party success (see Koch 1998 and Gold 1995 for contrasting views of the relevance of alienation to third parties).

Perot activists were more likely to express broader discontent with politics as usual in the United States than was the electorate as a whole. For instance, as high as the level of distrust in the government was in the electorate as a whole in 1992, with fully 71 percent saying they could trust the government to do what is right only "sometimes" or "never," the percentage adopting this skeptical view in our sample of potential

---

16. As we already noted, under divided government, both major parties may share culpability. Nonetheless, a poor economy hurts the party in control of the presidency much more than it does the party that controls Congress.

Perot activists was practically unanimous, at 95 percent. In 1996, similar differences prevailed. When we compare Reform contributors with contributors to one of the major parties, we find that Reformers were more likely to express distrust of all levels of government, less likely to feel that the political system represented their concerns, and more likely to assert that the country was in need of radical change. These sorts of differences characterize comparisons of third-party activists with the electorate as a whole (McCann, Rapoport, and Stone 1999).

Strategic Participation

Third-party candidates may have difficulty adequately distinguishing themselves from major candidates on the issues, since they lack an established tradition and record in national politics and typically do not have the legions of officeholders, activists, and voters available to the major parties. Considering such institutional barriers as ballot-access laws and campaign finance laws, one may wonder how third-party candidacies get off the ground at all.

Once a third-party candidate is on the ballot and visible to voters, however, he faces yet another problem in attracting support. Even if the independent candidate espouses popular positions on the issues and is otherwise more attractive than the major-party alternatives, it may still not make sense for potential activists to support him, if they believe he has little or no chance of winning the election. Supporters who otherwise might back a third candidate out of agreement with that candidate's issue positions may shift their support to a second-choice major-party candidate to avoid "wasting" their efforts on a hopeless cause.

This problem was hotly debated in 2000, when Ralph Nader ran as the Green Party's nominee, but it is a problem in all elections with a third party whose supporters prefer one of the major parties to the other but prefer the third party to both. Not surprisingly, there is evidence that third-party candidates in two-party systems usually lose support by the logic of strategic voting (Black 1978; Cain 1978). For recent presidential elections in which a third-party candidate ran, Abramson, Aldrich, and Rohde (1998, 199) report evidence of strategic voting by showing that 96 percent of citizens who rated a major-party candidate most highly on a question involving a standard "feeling thermometer" voted for that candidate, whereas fewer (about 70 percent) of those who favored third-party candidates—such as George Wallace, John Anderson, and Ross Perot—voted for them. Instead, for strategic reasons, the latter voted for the less objectionable major-party candidate.

If strategic voting occurs, it is reasonable to suppose that a similar phenomenon occurs with respect to activism.[17] In the preelection wave of our 1992 survey, we asked respondents to estimate the percent of the total vote each of the three candidates would receive.[18] Activism for Perot should have been greater among those who saw his prospects as stronger, since they would have faced less tension between their preferences and the likelihood that their efforts would be wasted on a candidate with no chance of winning.

Previous Political Involvement and Campaign Contact

Previous political involvement in campaigns and in other social settings—such as work, church, or politically relevant groups—can facilitate campaign participation in several ways (Verba, Schlozman, and Brady 1995). Our expectation is that the more individuals were involved in social, economic, vocational, and political groups outside of the overtly partisan arena of campaign politics, the greater their campaign activism would be, including activism in a third-party campaign, such as Perot's.

As Rosenstone and Hansen (1993) and Verba, Schlozman, and Brady (1995) have shown, contact by a campaign also increases involvement in electoral activities. Interpersonal mobilization through social networks plays on the ties of work, friendship, and neighborhood to mobilize individuals into campaigns, in part because these social connections help compensate individuals for the costs of participation (Huckfeldt and Sprague 1995). Particularly in the case of a third party, which lacks the

---

17. There is abundant evidence of strategic activism in presidential nomination campaigns, where potential activists must decide which candidate, among several candidates, to support for their party's nomination (Stone, Rapoport, and Atkeson 1995).

18. It is remarkable how close our respondents came in their September estimates of the vote totals each candidate would receive in the general election. Respondents' mean estimates of the popular vote for Clinton, Bush, and Perot, respectively, were 43.9, 38.9, and 17.4 percent. None of the mean candidate estimates is more than 1.5 percent off the actual popular vote received by these candidates.

long-standing social networks in workplace, union, and church communities, direct contact with potential supporters is likely to be especially important.[19]

A Comprehensive Explanation of Activism for Perot

Figure 5.7 provides a comprehensive analysis of campaign activism in the 1992 campaign. A positive effect indicates that the factor stimulated respondents toward greater activism in Perot's campaign; a negative effect indicates that the variable pushed respondents toward activism in one of the major-party campaigns.[20] In the analysis we present (based on a multiple regression model), all effects take account of all the other factors. For example, the effect of the predictions of Perot's vote share that were made by respondents prior to the fall campaign is in the positive direction, which is in keeping with our expectation of a "strategic activism" effect. This means that the greater respondents' estimate of Perot's prospective vote was, the more active they were in his campaign, holding constant the effects of all other factors.[21]

Consider, first, the other variables included in figure 5.7 that do not explicitly fit into the push-pull model as we have conceived it thus far. As we might expect, a history of active campaign participation for major-party candidates in 1988 drew individuals away from Perot activity and toward major-party activity. In contrast to major-party activism, prior involvement in social, economic, and political groups stimulated activism for Perot in 1992. Previous group involvement builds the sorts of skills and social connections that predispose individuals to campaign

19. We limit the notion of "contact by a campaign" to direct, interpersonal contact. It would be fair to say that virtually anyone who supports a political campaign does so as the result of some sort of contact emanating directly or indirectly from the campaign. Such contact might be through interpersonal relations with friends, neighbors, or coworkers or (most commonly) through the mass media. From this perspective, it is surely the case that no one supports a campaign—either by voting or by the sorts of activism we measure in this study—without being mobilized in some way. Our intent here, in keeping with much of the literature on campaign mobilization, is to assess the effects of direct, interpersonal mobilization by representatives of the campaign.

20. The effects reported in the figure are standardized (beta) slope estimates.

21. It is plausible, for instance, that respondents' estimates of Perot's prospective vote share were influenced by their attraction to him as a candidate. In an analysis that failed to include evaluations of Perot, the simple effect of Perot's predicted vote share on activism would overstate the effect of strategic factors on campaign activism for Perot in 1992.

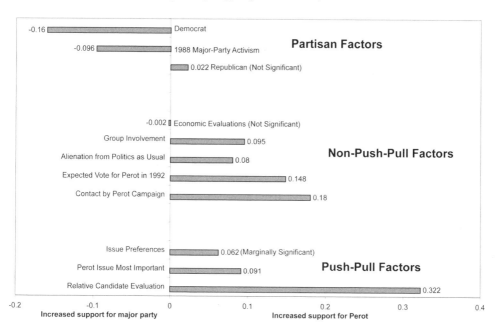

Fig. 5.7.   Impact of push, pull, and other factors on 1992 relative campaign activism. (A negative number indicates that the factor decreases support for Perot.)

activism on behalf of candidates they like, and it identifies them as targets of mobilization. It is important to stress that while an effect based in group involvement should generalize to other samples of potential campaign activism,[22] we do not argue that group membership motivates activism in a third party's campaign in the population at large. Rather, group involvement should stimulate political activism on behalf of any candidate individuals are otherwise predisposed to favor, and since most in the Perot caller sample were positively disposed toward Ross Perot, a history of social and political group involvement affected campaign activism within this sample.

Contact by the Perot campaign also had the expected positive effect. In fact, its independent effect is greater than that of any other factor with the exception of relative candidate evaluation. Alienation from politics as usual also had a significant independent effect on Perot activism in 1992.

---

22. This expectation is borne out in our 1996 major-party and Reform samples (Stone, Rapoport, and Schneider 2004).

As anticipated, these factors play an independent role in explaining active support for Perot and supplement the push-pull model in rounding out our understanding of the sources of third-party support. Evaluations of the state of the economy in 1992 did not have a significant, independent effect on campaign activism, although, as we shall see, economic evaluations did have indirect effects, working through the elements of the push-pull model.

In addition, the analysis presented in figure 5.7 includes several basic indicators of "push" and "pull" factors, the most prominent of which is based on candidate evaluations.[23] Indeed, candidate evaluations have far and away the strongest direct impact on campaign activism.

Issues Revisited

The weak to nonexistent effects of issue salience and preferences in figure 5.7 may suggest that we have overstated the importance of issues in the Perot constituency. The priority of Perot issues stimulated activism in his campaign, but its effect was much weaker than candidate evaluations and noticeably weaker than the effect either of contact by the Perot campaign or the strategic influence of Perot's prospective vote share. The effect of the issue proximity comparison between Perot and the favored major-party candidate was even weaker and reaches only a marginal level of statistical significance.[24] What are we to make of the apparent absence of strong issue effects?

In order to assess the full impact of issues on Perot activism, we must recognize that the impact of issues is heavily mediated by other variables in the analysis. These mediated, or indirect, effects of issues are not represented in figure 5.7. For example, candidate evaluations mediate the relationship between issue preferences and activism, because when potential activists have issue preferences that agree with the third-party

---

23. We combine "push" and "pull" factors related to candidate evaluations and issue preferences into a single indicator in order to simplify the analysis. Doing so does not allow us to see that the "push" and "pull" sides of issues and evaluations independently affect activism (although more detailed analysis indicates that they do in this case), but it does permit us to assess both direct and indirect effects of issues, a key concern that this analysis is designed to address.

24. The significance of issue preferences is less than .10 in the two-tailed test and less than .05 in the one-tailed test.

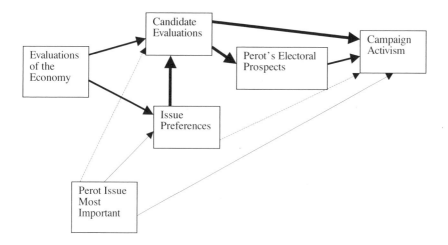

Fig. 5.8. Effects of issues, candidate evaluation, and Perot's electoral prospects on campaign activism for Perot, 1992

candidate's position more than they agree with the positions of the better major-party candidate, they evaluate the third-party candidate more positively. Because issue preferences influence candidate evaluations, which in turn affect activism, we understate the impact of issue preferences if we do not take into account this mediated, or indirect, effect of issue preferences.

Figure 5.8 presents one plausible ordering of the principal variables in our analysis.[25] We assume that issue preferences are causally prior to candidate evaluations, Perot's electoral prospects, and campaign activism. In addition, respondents' perceptions of Perot's prospects may have been influenced by their attraction to him as a candidate, which is also reflected in the causal ordering in figure 5.8.[26] The heaviest lines in the figure indicate the strongest causal effects, medium-weight lines indicate moderate impact, and the lightest solid lines indicate weak but statistically significant effects. The broken lines indicate weak and marginally significant

25. In our analysis behind the diagram in figure 5.8 and the summary results in figure 5.9, we controlled for partisanship, major-party activism, group involvement, alienation, and contact. However, to focus the presentation here, we depict the causal effects only of economic evaluations, issue priority, and issue preferences, along with the variables that intervene between them and campaign activism.

26. We also assume that evaluations of the economy are causally prior to candidate evaluations and issue preferences.

effects, and the absence of a line between two variables indicates that there is no statistically significant effect.[27]

The causal diagram shows modest to weak direct effects of issue preferences and the importance of Perot issues on campaign activism. This merely restates our findings from figure 5.7. However, note that issue preferences have a strong effect on candidate evaluations, which in turn directly and strongly affect campaign activism. Candidate evaluations also strongly influence perceptions of Perot's electoral prospects, which in turn have an impact on how active individuals were in his campaign. It is clear, therefore, that issue preferences have indirect effects on campaign activism, through candidate evaluations.

Figure 5.9 summarizes the effects—both direct and total—that economic evaluations, issues, and candidate evaluations had on activism for Perot in 1992. The total effects of a variable are composed of the direct effect and the indirect effects through mediating variables. By taking into account the indirect effects of issues—preferences as well as priority— we conclude that issues had a greater effect than any other factor in our analysis except candidate evaluations.[28] Likewise, evaluations of the economy have no direct effect on activism but, as expected, do have an indirect effect, through the components of the push–pull model that involve the issues and candidate evaluation. As a result of our analysis of issue effects, we have renewed confidence in our conclusion that Perot's constituency was motivated in a strong and fundamental way by the issue positions and priorities that defined his campaign.

CONCLUSION

Our examination of why potential activists became involved in Ross Perot's third-party campaigns supports several conclusions that we think

---

27. In figure 5.8, heavy lines indicate standardized regression coefficients between .3 and .4, medium lines indicate effects between .1 and .3, and light or broken lines designate effects less than .1. Marginally significant effects are at the .10 level in the two-tailed test or the .05 level in the one-tailed test; all others are at least at the .05 level.

28. The total effect (direct + indirect) of issues in the model is .333; the total effect of candidate evaluation is .381. We also computed the indirect effects of alienation, assuming its influence worked through its effect on candidate summary evaluations, summary issue preferences, and Perot's electoral prospects. The total effect of alienation was .168.

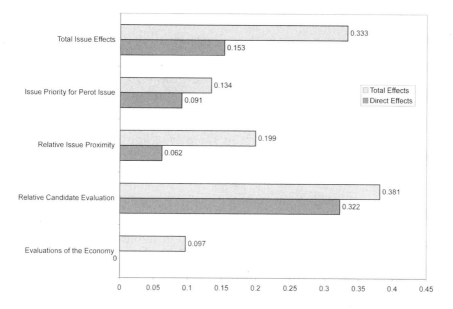

Fig. 5.9. Direct and total effects of economic evaluations, candidate evaluations, and issues on Perot campaign activism, 1992

apply to most successful insurgent electoral movements in U.S. politics. Of course, our close study of activists and potential activists is limited to a single example of such a movement, but it is worth speculating about how general our conclusions are likely to be.

First, we consistently find that activists were motivated both by a push away from the major-party candidates and the issues they stood for and by a positive attraction, or pull, toward Perot. Activism in Perot's 1992 campaign cannot be explained solely because his supporters were repulsed by the candidates nominated by the major parties, nor did their participation result exclusively or primarily from enduring dissatisfaction with the normal conduct of American politics. While negative attitudes toward and perceptions of the major candidates consistently emerged as part of the explanation for Perot's support, we have also found that attraction to Perot because of positive evaluations of his traits as a candidate and because of his stands on the issues was about as strong as the impact of "push" factors in accounting for his support.

We strongly suspect that both attraction to the candidate and rejection of the major-party alternatives would explain successful third-party movements in the past. A third-party candidate must stand for something and be able to convey his message convincingly to attract significant support. At the same time, a significant opening for an insurgent challenge to the two-party order must exist. The particulars of major-party failure have varied substantially in our political history, as Rosenstone, Behr, and Lazarus (1996) convincingly demonstrate. Our model of support and the evidence we have from the Perot example illustrates the importance of both perceptions of a breakdown in the two-party system and positive attraction to an outsider who would challenge the established order in American electoral politics.

Within the context of the push-pull formulation, our second broad conclusion about Perot is that there was a clear and strong issue basis to his support. Perot emphasized issues related to reform of the political process, balancing the federal budget, and economic nationalism, and these issues were especially notable in identifying his constituency and motivating his support. As we expected, the preferences of potential supporters matter in explaining campaign involvement, as do issue priorities independent of preference. There is ample evidence that attraction to Perot on the issues stimulated activism, as did distance from the major-party candidates and the perception that the major candidates failed to offer adequate choice on the issues. In our most complete model of support, issue effects are mediated by candidate evaluations and perceptions of Perot's electoral chances, but the overall impact of issues is nonetheless strong. Perot was attractive because of his personality, and his cause was doubtless furthered by his great wealth, but there is no doubt that substantive issues also drove his campaign.

The strength of issues in defining and motivating Perot's constituency may surprise those who wrote Perot off as a gadfly who sought to "fix what's wrong in Washington" without offering specific programmatic alternatives, as well as those who saw Perot's personal wealth as the primary reason for his remarkable electoral success. Indeed, the strength of issues in explaining his support emphasizes their more general importance in successful third parties. If Perot's following had a strong issue basis, it is not difficult to imagine other recent movements—such as those of George Wallace, John Anderson, and Ralph Nader—also being defined by issue appeals. As much as these candidates tapped voter anger and frustration, they also advanced clear issue agendas.

A third conclusion to our examination of support for Perot looks ahead to our analysis of change and his impact on the two-party system. Understanding the place of third parties in our political system requires us to understand their effects on the party system once they are gone, at least as much as it requires us to understand the sources they tap for their strength. The dynamic of third parties guides us, and our findings thus far are consistent with its broad expectations. Our findings supporting the "push" side of the model mean that Perot exploited openings offered by disaffection from the Democratic and Republican parties. This aspect of the signaling function of third parties, then, is confirmed in the Perot case. The importance of issues further means that the signal the two parties received after the 1992 election gave them a clear direction they could take in response. We should find, therefore, evidence of a major-party bid for Perot supporters following the 1992 election and of a corresponding response in the Perot constituency. That response should be evident both in the movement toward one or both major parties and in the shift away from Perot support between 1992 and 1996. For our explanation to be correct, change of this sort not only must occur but must be rooted in identifiable ways to the dynamic of third parties. Much of the rest of this book is devoted to exposing these patterns of change and tying them explicitly to this general pattern of third-party emergence, major-party bid, and subsequent response. In this way, we place the Perot movement into a broader pattern of behavior in the political system that has characterized insurgent electoral movements in the past and that will doubtless typify them in the future.

VI

The Decline in Support for Perot

⊘↗

B̲ʏ ʀᴜɴɴɪɴɢ ᴀ sᴇᴄᴏɴᴅ ᴛɪᴍᴇ, ɪɴ 1996, and attracting over 8 percent of the popular vote, Ross Perot broke from the pattern of previous successful third parties. According to the dynamic of third parties, third-party movements, such as Perot's, should immediately die after the sting of their success. By attracting so many votes in 1992 and by signaling the issue concerns of his constituency to the major parties, Perot's supporters became ripe for appeals by the Democratic and Republican parties. A successful bid by one of those parties should have swept the legs out from under Perot's movement, denying him any chance of an electoral return in 1996.

In fact, events ultimately unfolded in a manner consistent with the dynamic of third parties, as we demonstrate in chapters 7–10. However, the expectation that Perot would disappear following the 1992 election was obviously mistaken. While his decline in popular support after 1992 was substantial, he was still left with a larger popular-vote showing in his second election than was achieved by any other third party in its second run except the Republican Party in the 1850s.

Despite the failure of his movement to follow the precise trajectory of the third-party dynamic, the large drop in Perot's popular vote only four years after his initial success is consistent with third-party dynamics. In this chapter, we explore the decline in his support among activists, which we expect to have resulted from essentially the same factors that produce the decline in all third-party support. Because Perot ran again and lost a significant amount of his 1992 support, the 1996 election provides an intermediate step between his historic success in 1992 and the implosion of the movement in 2000. In 1996, Perot's 1992 supporters could remain active, drop out, or move to one of the major parties. Thus, 1996 enables us to observe both the process of third-party decline and the movement of third party supporters to the major parties. In this chapter, we focus on understanding this decline in Perot's support; in subsequent chapters, we study his supporters' movement to the major parties.

PARTICIPATION FOR PEROT AFTER 1992

Figure 6.1 shows the drop in activism for Perot among our panel respondents between 1992 and 1996. Whereas over three-quarters of the respondents were involved in some way in the 1992 Perot movement, the proportion involved in 1996 plummeted to only 20 percent.[1] In addition to the comparisons of overall activity (which include different activities from the two campaigns),[2] we compare identical activities between the two campaigns. On each item, the decline is precipitous, indicating an across-the-board and dramatic falloff in involvement for Perot among activist members of his 1992 constituency. Across the three items concerning general election participation, activity drops from 52 percent of respondents engaged in one of the activities in the fall of 1992 to only about 13 percent in 1996. This amounts to a relative decline in activity of 75 percent. In contrast to these more demanding forms of participation, the percentage voting for Perot dropped by only 58 percent between 1992 and 1996 (from 52 to 22 percent), which is almost identical to the falloff in voting support in the electorate as a whole (a relative drop of 56 percent, from 18.9 to 8.4 percent).

How does the decline in activism for Perot compare with what we would find among similar activists in the major parties? Those involved

---

1. The analysis in this chapter is based on the panel survey of the 1992 potential Perot activists, whom we resurveyed in 1996. The panel allowed us to monitor individuals through time and to study changes in behavior and attitudes in the years following the 1992 election.

2. The items for 1992 were contributing money, collecting signatures, organizing meetings, volunteering, canvassing, convincing friends, fund-raising, and attending meetings. In 1996, the items were writing letters of support to newspapers and magazines, clerical work, contributing money, convincing friends, and "other kinds of activity."

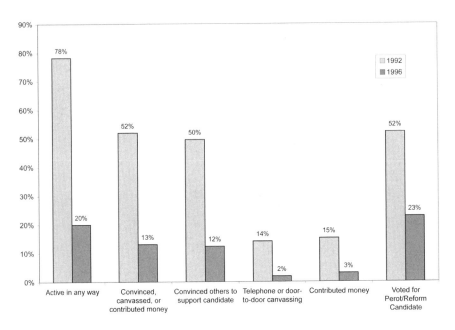

Fig. 6.1.   Percentage involved in selected campaign activities for Perot, 1992 and 1996

with Perot in 1992 had no opportunity to participate in a prior Perot campaign, so for a comparison with major-party activists, we look to 1988, in which large numbers of political newcomers became active in both major parties. One-third of respondents to a survey we conducted of 1988 Republican caucus attendees were newcomers, many of whom supported Pat Robertson's insurgent challenge to more traditional Republican nomination candidates; a little less than a quarter of Democrats were newly mobilized to presidential caucuses in that year (Pastor, Stone, and Rapoport 1999).

Table 6.1 shows that newcomers to major-party activity display a pattern strikingly different from the Perot activists. Whereas three-quarters of those involved for Perot in 1992 dropped out of active campaign involvement in 1996, large majorities of newly mobilized Democrats and Republicans remained engaged the year after their first foray into campaign activism. Remarkably, 70 percent of 1988 Republican newcomers stayed active for the party even though most backed Pat Robertson, who was defeated for the GOP nomination. And while majorities of major-party caucus participants who were inactive in 1988 remained uninvolved in the next presidential campaign, many more became active than was the case for Perot's 1992 potential activists, only 3 percent of whom were newly mobilized for Perot's 1996 campaign. In short, the major parties retained and engaged their newly mobilized activists much more successfully than the Perot movement did between 1992 and 1996.

Several differences between the major parties and the Perot movement probably account for the greater activism among newcomers to the parties than we find in the Perot movement. Most important, the major parties are enduring institutions that potential activists, including newcomers to the active ranks in any given year, have probably identified with for many years. Once mobilized into the ranks of the party, therefore, it is not surprising that major-party activists are easier to hold. Perot activists in 1992, in contrast, were attracted by Perot's appeal or by their dissatisfaction with one of the major parties, but as conditions changed and as they were subject to major-party appeals, their commitment to Perot declined, particularly without a strong national or local organization to keep them involved.

MAJOR-PARTY INVOLVEMENT IN 1996

Another way to assess the decline in active support for Perot is to compare it with the increase in major-party activism among 1992 Perot sup-

TABLE 6.1.   Continuity in Activity for Perot/Reform Newcomers, 1992–96, and for Major-Party Newcomers, 1988–92 (in percentages)

	Perot/ Reform		Newcomer Democrats		Newcomer Republicans	
	Active in 1992 Perot presidential campaign?		Active in 1988 presidential campaign?		Active in 1988 presidential campaign?	
Active in next presidential campaign?	No	Yes	No	Yes	No	Yes
No	97	75	61	36	57	30
Yes	3	25	39	64	43	70
Total	100	100	100	100	100	100
Number of cases	93	334	41	52	35	64

Source: Authors' potential Perot activist panel, 1992 and 1996 postelection waves; and authors' three-state major-party caucus-attender survey, 1988 and 1992 postelection waves.

TABLE 6.2.   Comparisons of Mean Activity Levels in 1992 and 1996

	1992 Perot	1992 Democratic	1992 Republican	1996 Reform	1996 Democratic	1996 Republican
Presidential only	1.06	0.31	0.20	0.36	0.28	0.38
All campaigns	1.06	0.68	0.62	0.44	0.57	0.93

Source: Authors' potential Perot activist panel, 1992 and 1996 postelection waves ($N = 427$).

porters. Table 6.2 shows the mean number of activities performed by our sample for Perot and major-party candidates. Note that 1992 activity for Perot far outstrips involvement for either major-party presidential campaign. Callers to Perot's toll-free number were somewhat more involved in the Clinton/Gore campaign than they were for Bush/Quayle, but the difference between involvement levels in Perot's campaign and those of his major-party competitors strongly favors the insurgent candidate from Texas.[3] In short, the 1992 campaign saw potential Perot activists much more engaged in the Perot-Stockdale campaign than in major-party presidential campaigns. Involvement for Perot in 1992 was also greater than Democratic and Republican activity in campaigns at the national, state, and local levels combined.

By 1996, however, the differences between the Perot and major-party presidential campaigns were all but erased. The average activism for Perot dropped from about one activity per respondent in 1992 to about one-third of an activity in 1996. At the same time, mean activism in Republican presidential campaigns almost doubled, from 0.20 to 0.38 activities, while activities for Clinton/Gore remained about at the same level in 1996 as they had been in 1992. Thus, a dramatic decline in active involvement for Perot between his two presidential campaigns was accompanied by increased Republican campaign activism. Our focus in the remainder of this chapter is on the decline in activism for Perot, before we turn, in the remainder of the book, to explaining movement by Perot supporters into the major parties.

---

3. Since respondents were unlikely to be involved in both major-party campaigns, the results in table 6.2 might artificially deflate support for the major-party candidates. However, if, in calculating the mean activity for the Democratic and Republican campaigns, we exclude respondents who identified with the opposite party, activity for each major-party ticket remains less than half as great as for Perot-Stockdale.

EXPLAINING THE DECLINE IN ACTIVISM
FOR PEROT, 1992–96

Since a combination of "push" and "pull" factors explains why people became actively involved for Perot in 1992, it stands to reason that declining activity can be explained either by declining pull toward Perot in 1996 compared with his first campaign or by declining push away from the major-party candidates. Did the drop in active support for Perot result primarily from a decline in attraction to Perot as a candidate? Was declining involvement for Perot the result of reduced agreement with or commitment to his issue agenda? Perhaps Perot's attraction did not fade as much as factors pushing supporters away from the major-party candidates declined. Answers to the preceding questions can help us understand whether the drop in Perot activism is consistent with the dynamic of third parties and what the implications are for major-party change.

Affect toward the Candidates

Figure 6.2 compares evaluations of Perot and the more attractive major candidate (**M1**) in 1992 with the same evaluations in 1996 for the entire sample. It also makes these comparisons for those who remained active for Perot in both years ("continuing activists") with those who dropped out of active involvement in 1996 ("dropouts"). By comparing activists who remained involved in Perot's campaign with those who dropped out, we may identify factors that help explain the decline.

There was substantial change in the full sample from a positive evaluation of Perot in 1992 to a mean rating of just below average. This change reflects a significant reduction in the overall pull toward Perot. At the same time, there was a significant but less dramatic increase in the rating of **M1**, from 0.19 in 1992 to 0.43 in 1996. Thus, along with severely decreased pull toward Perot, push away from the major parties also declined, as evaluations of the more favored major-party candidate became more positive. Declining positive affect for Perot may be explained by his dismal performance in the NAFTA debate with Vice President Al Gore and by the lower amounts of press coverage he received after the 1992 election (as discussed in chap. 3).

To put the decline in affect for Perot in perspective, 1992 respondents

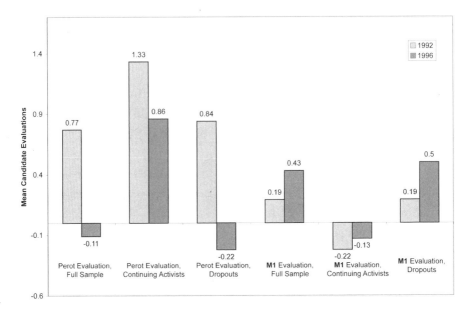

Fig. 6.2.   Comparing candidate evaluations among continuing Perot activists and dropouts, 1992–1996

were seven times more likely to rate Perot above average (71.1 percent) as to rate him below average (10.1 percent), but by 1996, the percentages rating him above and below average were almost equal (45 and 42 percent, respectively). Of those individuals who rated Perot above average in 1992, just over half continued to do so four years later, while one-third rated him below average four years later. All told, fewer than one in every ten respondents in the sample as a whole improved their opinion of Perot between the two elections, while almost half of the respondents lowered their ratings of him.

While evaluations of Perot were in steep decline, much of the push away from the major-party candidates present in 1992 had evaporated by 1996. In 1992, 57 percent of our respondents gave both Clinton and Bush average or negative ratings; by 1996, a majority were positive toward at least one major-party candidate, and only 43 percent rated both Clinton and Dole average or below.[4] By a ratio of two to one, respon-

---

4. Although affect toward Clinton in our sample declined slightly over the four-year period, it was more than made up for by the increase in positive evaluations of the Republican nominee. In 1992, Bush was rated above average by only 14 percent of the sample; by

dents became more positive rather than more negative toward the favored major-party candidate. With the drop in Perot evaluations, it is not surprising that Perot activity declined in 1996.

Figure 6.2 also compares continuing Perot activists with dropouts. The comparisons for evaluations of Perot indicate that two patterns were consistently replicated. First, those who dropped out of activity for Perot between the two elections were less positive in their evaluations of him in 1992 than were those who continued to be involved in Perot's second presidential campaign. Second, dropouts changed their attitudes toward Perot more dramatically than did continuing activists. Dropouts lowered their rating of Perot by more than a full point on the five-point scale, to an average negative rating of 0.22. In contrast, while continuing activists rated Perot lower in 1996 than in 1992, they remained positive in their rating, and their overall decline was lower. This pattern was reversed in the evaluations of major-party candidates, where continuing Perot activists remained negative toward **M1**, although their ratings increased slightly between 1992 and 1996. In contrast, dropouts started out rating their preferred major candidate positively in 1992, and by 1996, their evaluations improved more than evaluations among those who remained active for Perot. As a result, those who dropped out in 1996 rated their preferred major-party candidate almost three-quarters of a point more favorably than they rated Perot.

These results suggest a "predisposition" explanation and a "change" explanation for the decline in Perot activism. The predisposition explanation is rooted in 1992 attitudes and explains dropping out as a result of the lower initial levels of pull toward Perot and push away from the major parties in 1992. In this view, activists dropped out in 1996 because they were never as enthusiastically attracted to Perot or as repulsed by the major candidates as those who remained involved through 1996. They were, in short, predisposed, by their 1992 attitudes, to be less solidly committed to Perot, and they were therefore more likely to disengage over time. This predisposition toward disengagement may have made these activists more susceptible to changing events following the 1992

1996, Dole was rated above average by three times that proportion. Clinton's positive ratings remained fairly constant, at just over a third (39 percent in 1996 and 36 percent in 1992), while the percentages rating him negatively increased from 36 percent to 44 percent.

election, or it may simply have led to eroded enthusiasm for Perot after 1992. Dropouts were always less enthusiastic about Perot and less disaffected from the major parties, so the initial pull away from and push toward Perot in 1992 were both relatively weak. It is therefore no surprise that these supporters did not remain active, even if the "pull" and "push" factors were strong enough in 1992 to nudge them toward active support for Perot in his first campaign.

The change explanation emphasizes that dropouts differed from continuing activists in the amount they changed after 1992. According to this explanation, those who dropped out of Perot activity did so because they changed their opinion of Perot (signifying reduced "pull") and/or came to hold one or both major-party candidates in higher regard (signifying reduced "push"). These changes could have occurred due to stumbles by Perot (as in his debate with Vice President Gore), because of the reduced media attention given to Perot in 1996, or as the result of active bids by one or both of the major parties. The dynamic of third parties leads us to favor the change explanation, because we expect one or both major parties to bid for the third party's backers after the initial election. Such a bid, of course, could result in both reduced pull toward the third-party candidate who runs again and reduced push away from the major party making the bid. Our analysis must take into account both explanations—predisposition and change—for declining support for Perot, especially since the results in figure 6.2 are consistent with either explanation. Indeed, both explanations may be true, since they are not mutually exclusive.

Change in Issue Preferences

Although many observers questioned how much of an issue basis there was to Perot's 1992 campaign, we have shown that issue concerns were critical to Perot's activist supporters. The question is whether part of the decline in support for Perot after 1992 resulted from declining enthusiasm for Perot's issue agenda and/or from increased commitment to traditional partisan issues. If Perot's declining support was due to dramatic issue change in his constituency, the chance that his supporters would promote significant change in the political system would be reduced.

Figure 6.3 shows the average percentage favoring Perot's position

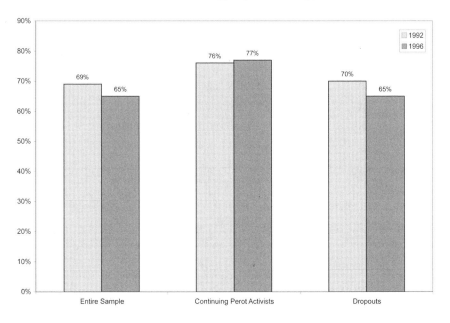

Fig. 6.3. Mean percentage of continuing Perot activists and dropouts favoring Perot issues, 1992–96 panel

across a range of issues in 1992 and 1996.[5] In the full sample, opinion was only slightly more favorable to the Perot agenda in 1992 than in 1996, so there was only a modest drop in support of the Perot issues. However, activists who remained involved in the 1996 Perot campaign were more in agreement with the Perot position in 1992 than those who dropped out, and they experienced no significant drop in their issue support over the four years. Dropouts were also strongly supportive in both years, although they were a bit less favorable to the Perot issue agenda in 1992 than were continuing activists, and they did decline in their support after 1992. Even so, their level of support in both years was high. It is certainly fair to conclude that evaluations of

5. We constructed indexes of three identically worded items related to the Perot agenda: term limits, limits on foreign imports, and limits on U.S. involvement abroad. The indexes are counts of the number of items that the respondents favored. Our survey also included budget-deficit items, but because the wording changed, we did not include these items in figure 6.3; separate analysis of these items indicates a pattern similar to that in figure 6.3.

Perot as a candidate were far more volatile than preferences on the issues behind his campaign.[6]

Figure 6.3 suggests two provisional conclusions. First, there was little loss in enthusiasm for the reform and economic nationalism issues between 1992 and 1996. Large majorities of continuing activists, as well as those who dropped out of the Perot movement, supported these issues. Second, even if the modest decline in commitment to the Perot issues helps explain the drop in his support, there was considerable potential for activists who were committed to these issues to carry their interests with them as they migrated out of the Perot movement and into the major parties.

We saw in chapters 4–5 that reform and economic nationalism issues motivated activist support for Perot, but partisan issues—such as affirmative action, national health insurance, and other matters related to the liberal-conservative debate—were also prominent during the 1992 and 1996 campaigns. To the extent that potential Perot activists increasingly took partisan positions on these issues by strongly supporting the liberal or conservative position, they would have experienced reduced push away from major-party involvement and reduced pull toward Perot's third-party challenge.

Figure 6.4 shows a slight increase in the entire sample in the average level of commitment to liberal-conservative issues among continuing Perot activists and among those who dropped out in 1996.[7] This suggests a modestly reduced push away from the major parties, with no meaningful difference between continuing activists and dropouts. Thus, we can expect to find that liberal-conservative issues had little or no impact on the decline in activism for Perot.[8]

---

6. The panel correlation between respondents' evaluations of Perot in 1992 and 1996 is .37; on the three-issue index, it is .58. Thus, over the four years in the panel, individuals were much more consistent in their issue positions on Perot issues than they were in evaluating the candidate.

7. To measure commitment on liberal-conservative issues, we used five items that were identical in both years: abortion, affirmative action, national health insurance, pollution control, and the overall liberal-conservative item. Entries in figure 6.4 are mean percentages of items (out of five) on which respondents gave a "strongly oppose/favor" or, on the liberal-conservative scale, "extremely liberal/conservative" response.

8. Including analysis of the importance of Perot issues compared with liberal-conservative issues is complicated by the fact that the issues included in the 1992 and 1996 surveys differ—in number and identity—between the two years. There is actually a modest

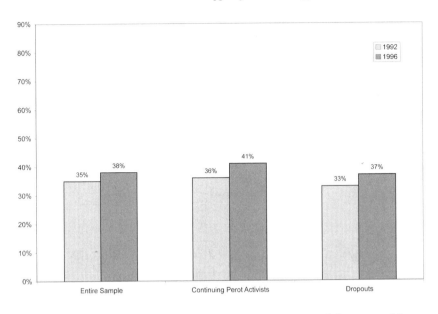

Fig. 6.4. Mean percentage of continuing Perot activists and dropouts taking a strong stand on liberal-conservative issues, 1992–96 panel

Changes in Economic Evaluations

Negative shocks to the political and economic environment contribute substantially to third-party success (Rosenstone, Behr, and Lazarus 1996), and if these shocks subside and the environment becomes more positive, third-party support may decline. The 1992 election took place at a time of severe economic pessimism, which reflected badly on the major parties and stimulated support (through the push-pull model) for Perot's campaign. In 1992, consumer confidence was low, and pessimism about the economy was high. By 1996, the economy looked stronger, the trajectory was positive, and consumer confidence was higher.[9]

increase in the percent who designate one of the Perot issues as most important to them (from 54 to 60 percent in the two years for the entire sample). A similar increase exists for both continuing activists and dropouts, although continuing activists were consistently more likely to indicate that a Perot issue was most important to them.

9. In 1992, *ABC News* and *Money Magazine* reported the lowest level ever recorded for the consumer comfort index (at −44). Using the same measure, *ABC News* and *Money Magazine* showed the index improving every year from 1992 through 1996, and although it still rated in the negative range in 1996 (at −11), the trajectory was positive. The data are available online at http://abcnews.go.com/images/pdf/m1229.pdf.

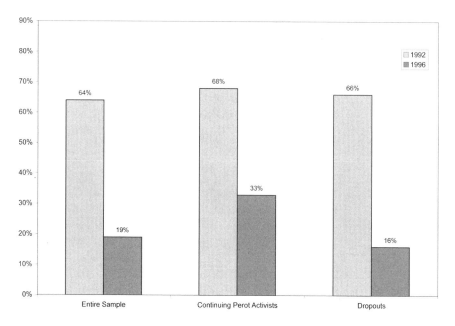

Fig. 6.5. Percentage of continuing Perot activists and dropouts responding that the economy in previous year has gotten worse

Potential Perot activists saw the economy as headed in the wrong direction in 1992 but had substantially changed their views by 1996 (see fig. 6.5). Over 60 percent of the sample judged the economy in 1992 as "worse" or "much worse" than in the previous year, compared with only 19 percent who made the same judgment in 1996. Both continuing activists and those who dropped out became much less pessimistic in 1996 than they had been four years earlier, although continuing activists were far more pessimistic in 1996 than were dropouts. The overall change and the difference between dropouts and continuing activists suggest that changing assessments of the economy are likely to figure prominently in our explanation of the decline in Perot activism.[10]

Multivariate Analysis of Change in Perot Activism

Thus far, we have seen evidence consistent with both the predisposition and change explanations for the decline in Perot activism. For example, we

10. We have also investigated the impact of alienation from politics as usual, but it does not change significantly between 1992 and 1996, nor does it differentiate between continuing activists and dropouts.

found that those who eventually dropped out of active support for Perot in 1996 started out less positive in their evaluations of him in 1992 than did continuing activists. They were less active on average in 1992 than were those more positively inclined toward Perot, which is consistent with our earlier findings that positive affect for Perot produced a significant pull toward his campaign. That they were also more likely to disengage in 1996 raises the question of whether dropping out was due to their relative lack of enthusiasm about the candidate in 1992, their lower levels of activism in 1992, or post-1992 changes in the pull toward his candidacy.

If the predisposition explanation is correct, we should find that differences in the levels of 1992 factors from the push-pull model, between those who eventually dropped out and those who remained active, explain the decline in Perot activism. Of the five 1992 factors of interest—evaluation of **M1**, evaluation of Perot, perceptions about the economy, strength of support for Perot issues, and strength of support for liberal-conservative issues—only support for Perot issues has even a slight impact on the decline in Perot activism. In short, 1992 predispositions offer almost no purchase on explaining the decline in activism for Perot.[11]

When we add measures of change to the analysis, however, we gain considerably more leverage on explaining the decline in Perot campaign activism than when we restrict ourselves to predispositions from 1992.[12] Figure 6.6 shows that all changes but change in support for liberal-conservative issues are statistically significant.[13] Support for Perot issues and evaluations of Perot are both pull factors and therefore should have positive effects on Perot's 1996 support. Activists who became more positive for Perot or more committed to the issue positions he emphasized increased their level of activism for Perot between 1992 and 1996. Likewise, the positive effect resulted in decreased activism among those whose issue preferences became less committed or whose evaluations of

---

11. The statistical model supporting these conclusions is reported in table B.7 in appendix B (see also fig. 6.6).

12. Since the R^2 statistic increases from .11 to .31 when we add the change variables to the analysis, the explanatory power of the statistical model nearly triples over a model based solely on predispositions.

13. The analytic model includes 1992 activity level as one of the independent variables, along with the 1992 level (i.e., the predisposition) for each change factor. As a result, the effects in figure 6.6 reflect the impact of change in each of the variables.

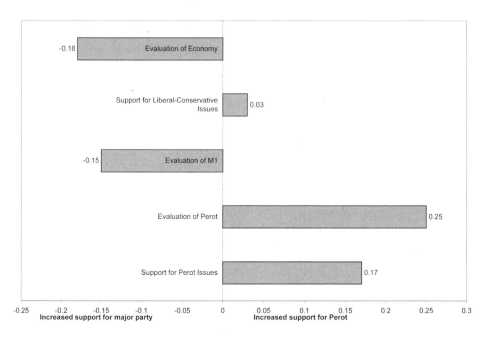

Fig. 6.6. Effect of change factors on 1996 Perot activity, controlling for 1992 predispositions

Perot declined. The negative effects of evaluations of **M1** and of the economy are also consistent with expectations: as activists evaluated the better major-party candidate more positively and/or saw the economy as improving between 1992 and 1996, their activism for Perot declined.

We conclude that 1992 attitudes and preferences did not predispose individuals to reduce their activism for Perot. Rather, it was the changes that occurred after the 1992 election that produced the decline in activism for Perot. Individuals who had been strongly positive toward the Texas independent as a candidate became much less enthralled by 1996. Additionally, the economy improved, and disaffection from the major-party candidates softened. We know, from our analysis earlier in this chapter, that the amount of change on these factors varied considerably, with relatively little aggregate shift in activists' commitment to Perot's issues and with substantial shifts in evaluations of the economy and evaluations of Perot himself.

Figure 6.7 reports the net effect of each change factor on the overall change accounted for by our analysis. Each bar represents the impact of the factor on the net decline in activism, by combining the average ef-

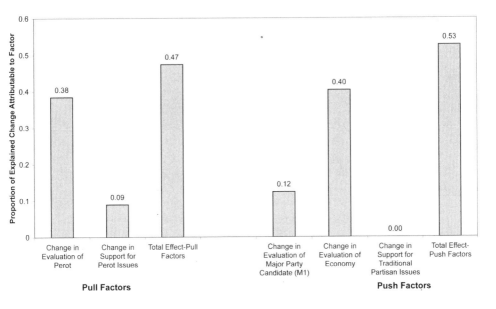

Fig. 6.7.   Impact of change in push and pull factors on Perot activity, 1992–96

fect of the variable with the average change of opinion in the sample.[14] For example, the net effect that change in Perot evaluations had on the change in activism is about 38 percent of the total change attributable to our model.[15] This is because individual activists were affected by the change in their attitudes toward Perot and the average respondent lowered her evaluation of the Texas billionaire substantially (from a positive evaluation of 0.83 in 1992 to a negative evaluation of 0.08 in 1996).[16] If there had been no effect of evaluations of Perot on changed activism between 1992 and 1996 (i.e., if the coefficient in fig. 6.6 were insignificant), there could be no impact on change no matter how large the

---

14. Each bar captures the net impact of the variable by multiplying the magnitude of its effect on changing activism by the amount of aggregate change that occurred on the variable: % Effect $= b_j(\bar{x}_{j96} - \bar{x}_{j92})/(\bar{x}_{96} - \bar{x}_{92})]$, where b_j = regression coefficient for variable j; $\bar{x}_{j96}$ = sample mean of "push" or "pull" factor in 1996; $\bar{x}_{j92}$ = sample mean of "push" or "pull" factor in 1992; $\bar{x}_{96}$ = the predicted mean activism in 1996; and $\bar{x}_{92}$ = the predicted mean activism in 1992. See appendix B for the statistical analysis.

15. Our statistical model accounts for about 25 percent of the net aggregate decline in Perot campaign activism between 1992 and 1996.

16. These scores do not exactly match those reported in figure 6.1 for the entire sample, because of missing data introduced in the multivariate analysis. The differences, however, are not systematic, nor do they affect our substantive conclusions.

change in the evaluation of Perot, because individuals' campaign activism would not be influenced by changes in pull toward Perot. Likewise, if there had been no aggregate change in the factor (i.e., if mean evaluation by activists in 1996 had not changed since 1992), there could be no net impact on our explanation of change, because individual change would have canceled out in the aggregate, producing no overall shift in evaluation. Because there was both an effect of evaluations on activism and an aggregate change in evaluations of Perot, change in the pull toward Perot explains part of the decline.[17]

Changed evaluations of Perot and of the economy had the greatest net impact on the decline in participation in Perot's campaigns: both factors influenced changes in individuals' participation, and both changed markedly over the four-year period in the sample as a whole. The change in the overall state of the economy between 1992 and 1996 reflected a substantial improvement, which was registered in the perceptions of our activist respondents. This supports the view that the state of the economy can be a driving force in accounting for changes between elections (Fiorina 1981; Rosenstone, Behr, and Lazarus 1996). When the economy is doing poorly, challenger candidates have an advantage, and the time may be ripe for an insurgent challenge, such as Perot's. However, when the economy rebounds, the push toward an insurgent candidacy is correspondingly reduced. Under such conditions, insurgent candidates cannot get as much traction sounding the alarm about economic decline, and perceptions of the major parties improve. In our analysis, there was indeed an improvement in evaluations of the favored major-party candidate (**M1**), which also reduced the push away from the major parties. But in 1996, increased optimism about the economy proved to be a more powerful factor than improved evaluations of the Republican and Democratic candidates. At the same time, the decline in evaluations of Perot independently discouraged participation in his second presidential bid. Thus, the diminished pull toward the Texan and the reduced push from the economy were the biggest factors in producing the drop in Perot activism.

17. We do not include contact as a possible "pull" factor toward Perot in figure 6.7, because the measures of campaign contact in the two surveys were not identical. Thus, we have no way of assessing the effect of change in average contact on decline in Perot activity.

With the exception of taking extreme positions on traditional partisan issues, which had no impact whatsoever, changes in Perot issue support had the smallest effect among the change factors. How can the core issues in Perot's campaigns, which had an important impact on why individuals were active for Perot in 1992, count for so little in explaining the net drop in activism? Because Perot activists continued to be committed to Perot issues in 1996, the overall change among activists on this dimension was slight, and the effect on net change is correspondingly small. Had Perot activists reduced their commitment to reform, economic nationalism, and budget-reduction issues, campaign activism would have diminished even further, and the net impact of Perot issues would have been greater (see fig. 6.7). Overall, the reduction in push away from the major parties, including the improved economy, only slightly outweighed the effect of changed pull toward Perot.

CONCLUSION

The decline in campaign activism for Perot's 1996 presidential bid was pronounced and was rooted in many of the same factors that explain activism for his campaign in 1992. Just as we can explain why individuals supported Perot in his campaign, we can use the same factors to account for why they pulled back four years later. However, the mix of these factors in explaining the two phenomena is quite different. Whereas we found that perceptions of the state of the national economy in 1992 were in the background of our explanation of activism in that year, changes in these evaluations leap to the foreground in accounting for the decline in activism by 1996.[18]

---

18. One reason for this shift is embedded in the nature of our design. In our analysis of 1992 activism, the actual state of the national economy does not vary (because we have only one year in the study), although perceptions, experiences of the economy, and evaluations of its health did vary among the potential activists we surveyed. We used these variations to account for the effect of "the economy" in 1992. When we analyzed change, however, we had the actual change in the state of the economy between the two years (which was substantial), along with variation in individuals' perceptions and evaluations. For further discussion of the implications of assessing the impact of the economy from a single year versus multiple years, see Markus 1988. Markus demonstrates that cross-time variation in the economy has a much stronger effect on presidential voting choice than has individual variation in perceptions in the same election.

We have ruled out 1992 predispositions as the explanation for the decline in Perot activism between the two campaigns, in favor of changes in attitudes and perceptions rooted in the push-pull formulation. This conclusion fundamentally supports the dynamic of third parties, because it does not locate the explanation for declining support for Perot in weaker commitments to him (or against the major parties) in his first campaign. It focuses our attention, instead, on what occurred after the 1992 election. To be sure, one important occurrence was improvement in the economy. That aside, however, changes in evaluations of Perot and of the major parties also helped produce the decline in Perot activism. Finding, as we do, that change rather than predispositions best accounts for the decline brings into focus questions posed by the third-party dynamic.

The noneffect of change in the Perot issues is also an important finding from this analysis. Despite our evidence that there was a strong issue base to the Perot movement in 1992 (both in the positions activists took on the issues at the center of Perot's campaign and in the importance his supporters assigned to these issues), Perot issues played only a small part in explaining the decline in his support, because there was no meaningful decline in support for these issues. That suggests that the Perot issue constituency remained essentially intact through the 1996 election, even if many of its members chose not to continue their active support for his candidacy. What happened to these activists? Where did they go and with what consequences? The dynamic of third parties leads us to speculate that their issue commitments provided a basis for major-party bids for their support after 1992. To the extent such a bid occurred and Perot activists responded to it, the absence of change on these issues testifies to the potential these commitments had for producing change in the major party making the bid. By migrating to one of the major parties, Perot activists carried the potential to change that party's stands on core Perot issues, such as reform, economic nationalism, and the federal budget. Activists retaining their issue commitments even as the third-party movement dies is an important condition for the movement's long-term impact on the two-party system, a condition met in the case of the activist followers of Ross Perot.

III. The Major-Party Bid

VII

The Major-Party Bid for the Perot Constituency

⧜

ALTHOUGH THE MAJOR PARTIES ARE generally oblivious to third-party activity, when a third party or independent candidate attracts a large share of the presidential vote, the signal is unmistakable. If the dynamic of third parties is to work, one or both major parties must make a serious attempt to attract supporters of the third-party movement. This chapter examines the bids made by both parties—especially by the Republicans—to attract the Perot constituency after the 1992 election. The sheer size of the Perot vote and the legions of volunteer activists his movement mobilized demonstrated the depth of dissatisfaction with the Democratic and Republican parties that existed before the 1992 election; but it also presented an opportunity for each major party to appeal to a pivotal group of supporters that might expand its coalition. The party that could successfully appeal to Perot supporters in the postelection period stood to gain an enormous advantage not only in the 1994 midterm elections but well into the future.

The success of the Perot movement, in other words, signaled the potential for a sea change in the American two-party system. However, for enduring change to occur, the second stage of the dynamic of third parties, the bid stage, was essential. The blueprint for a bid was spelled out in the issue priorities of the Perot movement—reform, a balanced federal budget, and economic nationalism—and both parties had strong incentives to make an appeal.

Although the 1992 election produced one-party control of both houses of Congress and the presidency for the first time in twelve years, the Democratic hold on government was tenuous. Bill Clinton had won an outright majority of the vote only in Arkansas and the District of Columbia, and despite Clinton's national plurality over President George H.W. Bush, the Democrats lost ten seats in the House and failed to gain any in the Senate. As a result, Democrats were sensitive to the importance of Perot's constituency. Even before the inauguration, Clinton's budget director, Leon Panetta, his secretary of treasury designate, Lloyd Bentsen, and his secretary of labor designate, Robert Reich, each told Congress "that getting the deficit down is priority one."[1] On the day President Clinton gave the 1993 State of the Union Address to Congress, outlining his economic and budget plans, he called Perot and spoke with him for about fifteen minutes.[2] Such appeals seemed to work at first—the day after the speech, Perot said, "Let's give the president an A+ for raising the issue of the deficit."[3] However, Perot's criticisms of Clinton's failure to pursue other reform proposals, including a balanced budget amendment and congressional reform, began to escalate. By April 1, tensions were such that the *New York Times* reported, "President Clinton and Ross Perot abruptly dropped all pretense of diplomacy today in a fit of cross-country name calling that noisily shattered their uneasy peace."[4]

Even so, the importance of Perot's supporters remained obvious. In April 2003, Stanley Greenberg, Clinton's pollster, conducted a survey of twelve hundred Perot voters. The survey, conducted on behalf of the Democratic Leadership Council (DLC), concentrated on how the Democratic Party might attract Perot voters to its fold. In the introduction to the survey report, DLC leaders Al From and Will Marshall called the Perot voters "the pivotal force in American politics."[5] In the report, itself, Greenberg concluded, "The Perot bloc is for real and has consider-

1. J. Dillin, "Post-Election, Clinton Economic Team Paints Stark Budget Picture for Congress," *Christian Science Monitor,* January 15, 1993, 1.

2. Paul Richter, "State of the Union; Pages Used from Perot Playbook," *Houston Chronicle,* February 18, 1993, A12.

3. Adam Pertman, "3 Critics of Deficit Voice Optimism," *Boston Globe,* February 19, 1993, 11.

4. Gwen Ifill, "Clinton and Perot Call Off Truce," *New York Times,* April 2, 1993, A1.

5. Al From and Will Marshall, "The Road to Realignment: Democrats and Perot Voters," Democratic Leadership Council, 1993, I-1.

able staying-power."[6] He argued that it "represents an important indicator of our country's direction."[7]

However, shortly after the DLC report appeared in May, prospects for Democratic success with Perot supporters worsened. Perot decided to focus on opposing the North American Free Trade Act (NAFTA), which was a critical part of the Clinton administration's commitment to the global economy as a mechanism of economic recovery. In September 1993, he published *Save Your Job, Save Our Country: Why NAFTA Must be Stopped—Now!* By November, Perot had taken such a leadership role in fighting the administration on NAFTA that Vice President Al Gore took him on in a nationally televised debate. By all accounts, Gore bested Perot in the debate, and Perot's national appeal declined as a result. Perhaps the most important result from the perspective of a Democratic bid for the Perot constituency was that the debate made future accommodation between Perot and the Democrats all but impossible.

Many Republicans agreed with President Bush's estimation that "[i]n the final analysis, Perot cost me the election" (Bush 1999)—a belief that not only provoked anger toward Perot but also pointed to the necessity of winning this constituency in the post-1992 period. With the advantage (as the party out of power) of having to take only limited responsibility for national policy, the Republicans reached out to Perot and to the Perot constituency. Only a month after President Clinton's inauguration, former Perot pollster Frank Luntz was invited to speak at a three-day Republican retreat in Plainsboro, New Jersey. His presentation, "The Perot Vote and the GOP's Future," won over then–Republican whip Newt Gingrich, who recommended "that every Republican candidate and every Republican official read his presentation."[8]

However, the idea of reaching out to the Perot constituency was not universally embraced in Republican circles. In early May, Haley Barbour, the new chairman of the Republican National Committee (RNC), said, "I've had no contact with [Perot], and I have no plans to."[9] Bob Dole,

---

6. Ibid., II-2.

7. Ibid., II-1.

8. Kevin Merida and Thomas B. Edsall, "Perot's Ex-Pollster in the Limelight at GOP Retreat," *Washington Post,* March 1, 1993, A10.

9. Tom Baxter, "Perot's Ride in Polls Remains Stuck in Rut," *Atlanta Journal and Constitution,* May 13, 1993, D2.

the Republican Party's presidential nominee-in-waiting and Senate minority leader was equally blunt. In a CNN interview, Dole called Perot
a "hit-and-run artist"; and in a speech to Republican lawyers in mid-
May, Dole called Perot "a walking sound bite . . . [who] can give 25
sound bites without ever addressing the issue."[10] Dole also attacked Perot
for his policy proposals, pointing out that "there are more new taxes in
his program than in Clinton's program."[11]

Nonetheless, while Barbour, Dole, and some other party leaders were
displaying little affection for Perot, House Republicans had already begun
meeting and reaching out to the Texas independent and his supporters.
The first meeting occurred on March 31, a month after Luntz's speech to
the postelection Republican retreat, just as Perot's relationship with the
White House was souring. Republicans on the House Budget Committee, under the leadership of ranking minority member John Kasich, qui-
etly invited Perot to Washington to brief him on their proposal to reduce
the deficit through deep spending cuts. In the ensuing three weeks leading up to Perot's April 25 infomercial on the budget and the economy,
Perot and Kasich spoke with each other on the phone five times.[12] In the
infomercial, Perot endorsed Kasich's plan while attacking the Clinton
economic plan, which he said would result in the "American people . . .
[getting] . . . hit with the largest tax increase in the history of this country."[13] A few weeks later, Kasich, Representative Bill Paxon (chair of the
Republican National Campaign Committee), and New York Republican
Representative Jack Quinn went to a gathering of United We Stand
America (UWSA) in Amherst, New York, to speak about the dangers of
Clinton's economic plan.[14] On May 19, Perot held a private meeting with
the freshman class of House Republicans, saying: "The Republican Party

10. Craig Hines, "Perot Puts the GOP on Horns of Dilemma," *Houston Chronicle,*
June 7, 1993, A1.

11. John Aloysius Farrell, "Perot Draws More Fire—from Right This Time," *Boston
Globe,* May 26, 1993, 3.

12. Roland Evans and Robert Novak, "Perot Warms up to GOP Plan on Trimming
Deficit," *Chicago Sun-Times,* May 2, 1993, 46.

13. Dan Balz, "Perot Sharply Attacks Clinton Economic Plan; New Taxes without
Spending Cuts Opposed," *Washington Post,* April 26, 1993, A6.

14. Henry L. Davis, "Lawmakers Tell Perot Supporters of the Need for Citizens to
Change Government," *Buffalo News,* May 16, 1993, 13.

needs a strong, aggressive program. You've got one"; though he specifically declined to endorse the freshmen representatives' nineteen-point plan, Perot urged the Republicans not to let their efforts "deteriorate to whitewash, which is what we're getting a big dose of now"—a reference to his disappointment with Clinton's lack of progress on the deficit and campaign finance reform.[15]

The May meeting with Republican freshmen occurred in defiance of House minority leader Robert Michel but with the encouragement of Minority Whip Newt Gingrich, who had also encouraged the relationship between Kasich and Perot.[16] The struggle over the House Republicans relationship with Perot mirrored the ongoing struggle for control between Gingrich and Michel. On both Perot and the question of power in the House, Newt Gingrich proved ascendant.

The relationship between the Republicans and Perot solidified in early June 1993, as opposition within the Republican Party softened. In an interview with reporters, RNC chair Haley Barbour refused to criticize Perot and spoke approvingly of his work for smaller government.[17] On June 21, Barbour announced the creation of the National Policy Forum, a GOP organization that would hold town-hall meetings aimed in part at winning Perot voters.[18] Barbour even invited two UWSA organizers from Illinois to attend the July RNC meeting in Chicago.[19]

On June 24, when Perot came to Washington to deliver 2.5 million petitions to Congress urging that spending be cut before taxes were increased, several Republicans, including Senators Phil Gramm and Kay Bailey Hutchison of Texas, appeared with Perot at his rally and news conference on the Capitol lawn.[20] Senator Bob Dole retreated from his earlier criticism of Perot by meeting in Kansas City with a dozen regional

---

15. Kenneth Cooper, "Perot Gives Pep Talk to House GOP Freshmen," *Washington Post*, May 20, 1993, A9.

16. Robert Novak, "GOP Freshmen Defy Michel in Meeting Perot," *Chicago Sun Times*, May 23, 1993, 41.

17. Craig Hines, "Perot Puts the GOP on Horns of Dilemma," A1.

18. Richard Benedetto, "GOP Sets Sights on Swaying Perot Faithful," *USA Today*, June 22, 1993, 6A.

19. Fred Barnes, "Like a Moth to a Flame, the GOP Just Can't Resist Wooing Perot," *Louisville Courier Journal*, July 30, 1993, A9.

20. Richard Wolf, "Perot, GOP Keep Attacks Coming Fast," *USA Today*, June 25, 1993, A4.

coordinators for Perot's 1992 presidential campaign.[21] The *New York Times* quoted Dole as saying in early July: "I talk to Ross Perot. . . . I don't want to leave the impression that there's any hostility between myself and Ross Perot."[22]

The GOP effort to seek support from Perot and his constituency extended to formal affiliation with Perot's advocacy group, UWSA. Newt Gingrich, Representatives John Doolittle of California and Joe Barton of Texas, and Senator Kay Bailey Hutchison of Texas all became dues-paying members.[23] These Republican congressional UWSA members were soon joined by several more, including Senator Alfonse D'Amato and Representatives James Inhoff of Oklahoma, Tim Hutchinson of Arkansas, and Peter Hoekstra of Michigan.[24] By the summer of 1993, reaching out to Perot and his supporters had become an important goal of the Republican Party.

THE CONTRACT WITH AMERICA

For the Republican bid to succeed, the party needed to develop a Perot-friendly issue agenda, to communicate this agenda to Perot supporters, and to recruit high-quality candidates to put the strategy into effect. According to conventional wisdom, congressional campaigns have become more candidate-centered over the last fifty years, relying less on party recruitment efforts. Although parties provide some money and modest amounts of other resources to candidates, U.S. House candidates usually must develop their own issue agendas and formulate their own district-based appeals (Mayhew 1974; Fenno 1978; Herrnson 1998; Jacobson 2004).

In 1994, the GOP offered a partial repudiation of that decentralized issue-appeal approach, through the Contract with America, a party platform endorsed by 357 Republican candidates for Congress, including virtually all Republican House challengers. As Barry Jackson, staff director

---

21. Barnes, "Like a Moth to a Flame."

22. Richard L. Berke, "Republicans Forget Clinton, the Big Worry is Perot," *New York Times,* July 11, 1993, A1.

23. Joel P. Engardio, "Officials Join Perot Movement: Congress Members Sign up, Attend Rally," *Boston Globe,* June 28, 1993, 2.

24. Authors' email from Clay Mulford, August 18, 2003.

of the House Republican Conference, pointed out, Perot voters were the target (Gimpel 1996). Joe Gaylord, a close associate of Newt Gingrich and one of the architects of the Contract, said that the title "Contract with America" was aimed at Perot voters who "wanted accountability and reform and for whom, based on Frank Luntz's polls, a 'Contract' was more binding than a platform."[25] Similarly, calling it the "Contract with America" rather than the "Republican Contract with America" signaled a nonpartisan appeal to Perot voters who had not previously supported the Republican Party. Indeed, the idea of a contract with voters reflected language Perot used in his book *United We Stand America,* which he concluded with a "Checklist for All Federal Candidates." According to Clay Mulford, Perot's campaign manager and son-in-law, the idea of "getting a contract of issues that candidates would have to sign in order to get an endorsement . . . was transferred to the Republicans, and of course, Perot was delighted by it" (Posner 1996, 331).

Although "all of the proposals had long been floating in the GOP's primeval policy soup" (Pitney and Connelly 1996, 50), a selective serving was offered up in the Contract with America using Newt Gingrich's recipe. Gone was the 1992 Republican platform emphasis on family values (the first section of the platform that year), along with strong antiabortion and religious rhetoric. This decision was contentious, but Gingrich fought hard for it. He declared categorically, "There will be no social issues"—a decision made with Perot voters explicitly in mind.[26] Gaylord explained: "What Newt made clear to those who objected was that gaining control of Congress mattered more than the specifics of the platform. He said, 'The wagon train is going west, and it doesn't matter what color the wagons are.'"[27] Gingrich's logic carried the day. The Christian Coalition, recognizing the importance of the Perot consistency and knowing that a Republican House would be more supportive of its aims, praised an agenda that left out many of its most important issues.[28]

Figure 7.1 illustrates how the Contract with America mirrored the

---

25. Authors' interview with Joe Gaylord, August 22, 2003.
26. Gaylord interview, 2003.
27. Gaylord interview, 2003.
28. Jeffrey M. Peyton, "GOP Promises Change," *Christian America,* October 1994.

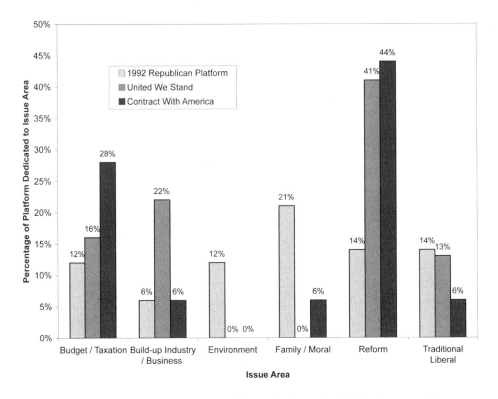

Fig. 7.1.   Emphasis in 1992 Republican platform, *United We Stand,* and Contract with America

checklist at the end of *United We Stand America* and deviated from the Republican platform of only two years before. It is immediately clear how much changed in only two years and how much that change was focused on the issues on the Perot checklist. At the 1992 Republican Convention, Buchanan gave a prime-time speech on the "culture wars," which set the tone for the convention and the party's platform. Family and moral issues comprised more than a fifth of the 1992 platform, half again as much as any other topic; all reform issues together comprised only 14 percent of the platform. Two years later, moral and family issues, which received no mention in the United We Stand checklist for candidates, together comprised only 6 percent of the Republican Party's Contract with America, barely one-eighth as many mentions as reform issues. In fact, reform issues were the dominant topic in the Contract, comprising slightly more of the Contract than they did of the Perot candidate checklist.

The Contract with America began with eight proposals to reform government in general or Congress in particular, including making employment laws and other laws applicable to Congress, limiting the number of years of service for committee chairs, cutting the number of committees, and providing outside auditors for Congress. After these process reforms, the Contract turned to its legislative commitments. The first item dealt with the balanced budget amendment and line-item veto, both widely favored in the Perot constituency. The Contract promised "[a] first-ever vote on term limits to replace career politicians with citizen legislators." As Balz and Brownstein (1996, 332) point out, "Term limits occupied one of the central planks in the Contract because Perot voters, not Republican incumbents, favored them, and Republican leaders enshrined the Balanced Budget Amendment at the top of the Contract to lure the Perotistas."[29] The term *citizen legislators* was selected based on focus groups with Perot supporters.[30] The Contract's foreign policy section promised "[n]o U. S. troops under U.N. command" and increased funding for national defense, while ignoring GATT and NAFTA, which were seen by Perot supporters as international commitments that undermined the ability of the U.S. economy to create and hold high-paying jobs. This strategy was also reflected in "a growing number of Republicans . . . running for Congress with campaign platforms that avoid[ed] any mention of free trade."[31]

The Contract with America was a national document committing the Republican Party to a policy agenda, but it was also a set of talking points for Republican candidates. It gave them a coherent agenda to push in their individual campaigns, an agenda on which large numbers of Republican challengers relied.[32] Although the Contract appeared nationally in only a single ad run by the Republican Party, it was trumpeted by Republican candidates, who stressed its inherent appeal to Perot supporters.

---

29. Not only did Republicans sign the Contract with America, but the vast majority of the 211 candidates signing the pledge of the U.S. Term Limits organization were Republicans—and not coincidentally, challengers (Germond and Witcover 1993).

30. Gaylord interview, 2003.

31. Keith Bradsher, "The Nation: The G.O.P. Looks Homeward on Trade," *New York Times*, October 16, 1994, D3.

32. Gaylord interview, 2003.

TARGETING PEROT SUPPORTERS

Building on the Contract with America, the Republican Congressional Campaign Committee worked to identify Perot voters in congressional districts with a strong 1992 Perot vote and to mobilize them on behalf of Republican candidates. It was clear to Republican pollsters that to win in these districts, "we had to get 70 percent of the Perot vote."[33] The goal was to use direct mail and personal contact to address Perot voters by making issue-based appeals emphasizing taxes and government accountability.[34]

To target Perot supporters, Republicans sought lists controlled by state or local Perot organizations. For example, Newt Gingrich and Georgia Republican Representative John Linder met with the former Georgia state coordinator for UWSA to see if former members of UWSA would share lists or members with Republican congressional candidates.[35] The New Jersey Perot organization shared lists of Perot supporters with Republican candidates in that state.[36] Maria Cino, director of the Republican Congressional Campaign Committee in 1994, pointed out: "Republicans tried to work with Perot people. Anywhere Perot did well [in 1992], the Republicans went to Perot people (local campaign chairs and organizers) to get lists . . . and contact[ed] people off that list."[37]

In many cases, however, either lists were not readily available or the Republicans could not get access to them, so they relied on voter-identification projects. As Dave Sackett, a senior partner with Lance Tarrance Associates, describes this project, the Republican Party selected precincts nationwide in which Perot did well in 1992. They removed from their list registered voters who habitually voted in either major party's primaries, and they used telephone canvassers to contact the remaining households to identify individuals who had voted for Perot in 1992. Significantly, anyone whom they could not identify as a major-party supporter

---

33. Authors' interview with Dave Sackett, July 31, 2003.

34. Sackett interview, 2003.

35. Joan Lowy, "Nervous Lawmakers Court Perot Voters for '94," *Cleveland Plain Dealer,* August 1, 1993, 18.

36. William McClintock, personal correspondence, July 2, 2003.

37. Authors' interview with Maria Cino, December 11, 2003.

they assumed was a potential Perot backer and was targeted for additional contact. All individuals on this list who were identified as actual or potential Perot supporters in 1992 were directly contacted by telephone, direct mail tailored around Perot's issues, and door-to-door canvassing prior to the 1994 elections.[38]

Although some estimated that as many as 25 to 40 percent of voters on the list had not supported Perot in 1992, this was not a concern to Republican strategists, because they felt that the targeted message would work with traditional Republicans as well.[39] It is significant that the process used to identify Perot voters erred on the side of making sure that Perot supporters were included even if others were included as well, rather than excluding nonsupporters of Perot. For the Republicans in 1994, Perot voters were crucial. As Sackett put it, they were "equivalent to the importance of older voters in low-turnout elections—they were the people who would make the difference."[40] Republicans knew they could not win in 1994 without strong support from Perot voters and that the traditional Republican congressional campaign would be insufficient to get this support.

CONTACT FROM
MAJOR-PARTY CAMPAIGNS

It is one thing for Republican leaders to tell us they had a strategy to contact Perot supporters in advance of the 1994 midterm elections; it is quite another to demonstrate that it worked. If the GOP strategy of identifying and contacting Perot supporters was adopted nationwide, we should find that respondents in our sample of Perot activists were more likely to be contacted by Republican campaigns than by Democratic campaigns in 1994. In addition, Republican contact should have been greater for those more active for Perot in 1992, because their activity made them more visible targets for the 1994 election campaign.

Figure 7.2 shows that the level of contact by the two parties among those inactive for Perot was almost identical. As Perot's 1992 campaign

38. Sackett interview, 2003.
39. Sackett interview, 2003.
40. Sackett interview, 2003.

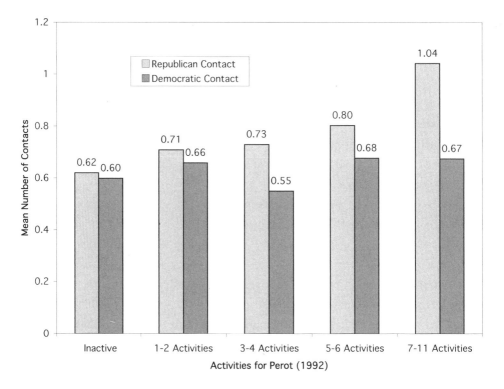

Fig. 7.2.   Contact by 1994 Republican and Democratic House candidates by level of activity in Perot's 1992 campaign

activity went up, however, the level of Republican contact in 1994 increased monotonically.[41] Those at the highest level of Perot activity were contacted by Republican House campaigns almost twice as much as those who were least active. In contrast, Democratic contact did not increase with higher levels of 1992 Perot activism.[42]

The positive relationship in figure 7.2 between Perot activity and Republican contact could result from other factors, such as activism in previous Republican campaigns. Figure 7.3 shows the effect of Perot activity on Republican contact, taking into account the level of past Republican campaign activism, party identification, education, age, and

41. The Pearson correlation (r) between Perot activity in 1992 and Republican contact is .135 ($p < .05$).

42. There is no significant correlation between 1992 Perot activism and 1994 contact by the Democrats.

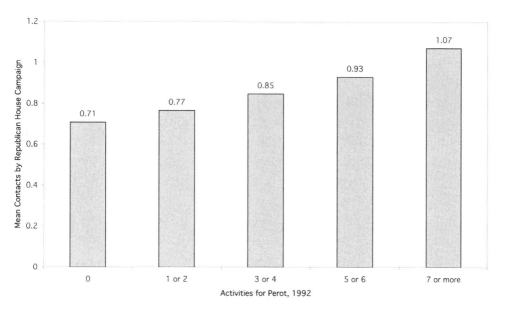

Fig. 7.3.   Effect of 1992 Perot activity on contact by Republican house campaigns in 1994, controlling for other factors

income—all factors that have been shown to influence party contact in midterm elections (Rosenstone and Hansen 1993, 165). The results confirm our expectation that Republican campaigns contacted individuals who were made visible and attractive as targets of mobilization by their activism for Perot two years earlier.[43]

THE QUALITY OF REPUBLICAN CANDIDATES IN 1994

Thus far, we have shown that the Republican bid was coordinated by such national leaders as Representative Newt Gingrich, who, after the 1994 GOP victory, would become the first Republican Speaker of the House in forty years. This sort of bid is reflected in such actions as drafting the Contract with America and Republican Party financial support of candidates running for the House (discussed later in this chapter). The

---

43. The analysis is based on multiple regression results in which respondents are placed at the sample mean for all variables except for Perot vote. The dependent variable is the mean number of contacts.

experience and quality of House candidates, however, does not depend primarily on coordinated action by party leaders in Washington. Potential candidates for the House make their own decisions about whether to run, based on what is best for their political careers, their prospects of winning, and their assessments of the quality and strength of the incumbent (Fowler and McClure 1989; Kazee 1994; Maisel and Stone 1997; Stone, Maisel, and Maestas 2004). When individual potential candidates' strategic decisions reflect national conditions that favor one party over the other, they aggregate to a significant advantage for that party (Jacobson 1989; Jacobson and Kernell 1983).

In the case of the 1994 elections, one factor that helped create an attractive opportunity for strong Republican potential candidates was the existence of large numbers of 1992 Perot voters in many House districts. These former Perot voters, as we have seen, did not escape the attention of party leaders. A leading strategist of the 1994 Republican victory explained:

> Part of the pitch in recruiting candidates . . . was, "Look at the Perot and Bush vote together. Say it represents 60 percent; then you can win." This identified a winning coalition and made the district more appealing.[44]

Of course, the existence of large numbers of Perot voters in a House district sent the same message to local political leaders and potential House candidates. Thus, it is likely that strong Republican potential candidates saw that a large 1992 Perot vote in their district was an opportunity for a Republican candidate to win. If this is correct, we should observe strong Republican House candidates emerging in districts where Perot had done well in 1992. By running in these districts, these candidates participated in the Republican Party's bid for Perot supporters just as surely as Newt Gingrich and other national leaders did, even if their decisions to run were not promoted by any centrally coordinated GOP effort to recruit and support them.[45]

---

44. Gaylord interview, 2003.

45. We cannot assess the impact of the Republican Party's recruitment efforts relative to the importance of individual candidates' decisions based solely on the opportunity 1994 offered them in their district. We know that the national Republican Party engaged in efforts to recruit strong House candidates as part of the Republican strategy of

The quality of a party's House candidates is closely related to the success of the party in congressional elections (Jacobson 2004; Jacobson and Kernell 1983). One of the reasons that the Democrats held their majority in the House for so long was their routine ability to field stronger candidates than the Republicans. Political scientists typically measure the strength or "quality" of congressional candidates by whether they had elective office-holding experience prior to running for the House. Those who have held office have the experience and the ability to mobilize resources—such as activists and campaign contributions—that inexperienced candidates often lack. As a result, experienced candidates routinely win more votes than inexperienced candidates.

Experienced candidates are also strategic actors who are unlikely to get involved unless their prospects for victory are good. Thus, high-quality candidates are more likely to run when national or local conditions are favorable, and less likely to do so when conditions are unfavorable. Congressman Bill Paxon, chair of the Republican Campaign Committee in the House in 1994, observed:

> There were office holders that the Republicans had tried hard to convince to run [previously], who had not. Many of them decided to take a shot in 1994. The level of Perot activity meant they would have a good chance. Dossiers were coming in over the transom [without our doing anything].[46]

The increased experience of Republican candidates in 1994 is undeniable (Jacobson 1996; Krasno 1997), but what matters most for our argument about the Republican Party's bid for Perot supporters' backing in 1994 is that experienced Republicans ran disproportionately in the districts with the greatest numbers of former Perot voters. As expected, there is a significant correlation between the emergence of experienced Republican House candidates in 1994 and the size of Perot's

---

winning control of the House, and we know that national party contacts have a positive effect on potential candidates' chances of running (Maestas, Maisel, and Stone 2005). But we do not have the data on 1994 that we would need to assess the relative importance of individual versus national party factors in the decision-making processes of Republican House candidates prior to the 1994 elections.

46. Authors' interview with Bill Paxon, October 29, 2003.

1992 vote share in the district,[47] but there is no significant effect of Perot vote share on the emergence of experienced Democratic candidates. This suggests that the size of the Perot vote in a district signaled an opportunity only to Republican candidates. Even so, other factors must be taken into account in considering whether the Perot vote was responsible for stimulating more experienced Republican candidates to run: the electoral strength of the incumbent Democratic officeholder, the long-term partisan complexion of the district, whether the incumbent was running for reelection, and the quality of the Republican candidate in 1992 (to capture strategic factors that may be otherwise missed by our analysis).[48]

Figure 7.4 shows the relationship between the size of a district's 1992 Perot vote and the probability that an experienced Republican candidate would run. Because the analysis takes full account of the Republican voting history of the district, this relationship is strong evidence that the Perot vote sent an unmistakable signal about Republican prospects beyond those that could be predicted from its previous tendency to vote Republican. In contrast, the chances that an experienced Democratic candidate would run show a slight (statistically insignificant) tendency for decline as the Perot vote share increases. In districts where Perot received only 5 percent of the vote in 1992, the probability that an experienced Republican candidate would run was only about one in twenty (.06), but where Perot got 25 percent of the vote, it increased to better than one in five (.21), and where Perot received 30 percent, the likelihood reached almost one in three (.31).[49] Thus, experienced potential Republican candidates saw the size of the Perot vote in their districts as an indicator of the opportunity they had to win the seat and were more likely to enter the race in districts with a substantial Perot constituency.

47. The correlation is .266 ($p < .001$).

48. Our measure of candidate quality is whether the candidate has office-holding experience, so we employ logistic regression. The statistical model controls for the vote share of the incumbent Democrat (or, in the case of an open seat, the outgoing incumbent), the three-party percentage for Bush in the district in 1992, the 1988 percentage vote for Dukakis as a measure of long-term partisan predispositions in the district, whether the 1992 Republican candidate was experienced, and whether the seat was open.

49. These probabilities are computed by setting all other independent variables at their means and varying the Perot vote in 1992.

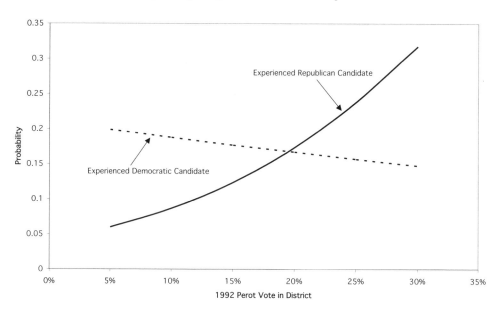

Fig. 7.4. Effect of 1992 Perot vote in district on probability that an experienced Democratic or Republican challenger would run in 1994

REPUBLICAN PARTY CONTRIBUTIONS

We can extend our analysis of the commitment of the national Republican Party to bidding for the Perot constituency by asking whether the party invested resources in districts in response to the percentage of 1992 Perot voters. If, as we have argued, Perot districts were targets of opportunity for Republicans in 1994, we should find that the national party's contributions to candidates increased as the size of Perot's district vote went up.

National party financial allocations reflect strategic decisions about where investment is most likely to produce desirable outcomes (Herrnson 1998). That is why parties invest more in marginal districts and in open seats than in districts held by entrenched incumbents in either party. In the 1994 campaign, the Republican Party was most interested in districts held by Democratic incumbents that might be vulnerable to the Republican candidate, either because the Democratic incumbent had retired or because the Democratic representative running for reelection was vulnerable. As we have said, one important signal about the potential for

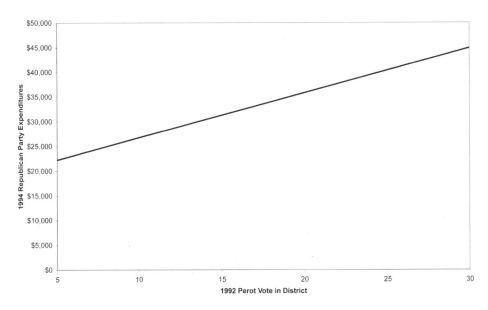

Fig. 7.5.   Effect of 1992 Perot vote on 1994 Republican Party expenditures in districts held by Democrats, controlling for other factors

a Republican takeover was the size of the 1992 Perot vote in the district. Thus, as with the decision of experienced potential candidates to run, the greater the Perot vote in a district was, the greater the GOP expenditure in that district should be, because that investment was more likely to bear fruit.

Our analysis, illustrated in figure 7.5, reveals that Republican contributions and expenditures were twenty-two thousand dollars greater in marginal districts than in nonmarginal districts. Likewise, open seats attracted just over fourteen thousand dollars more in Republican Party expenditures, holding constant the effects of the other factors in the analysis. However, a strong effect of the 1992 Perot vote on the level of the Republican Party's financial support remains even after we take into account other explanations for Republican Party investment in a race. For every percentage point that the 1992 Perot vote share increases, the Republican candidate received over nine hundred dollars from the Republican Party. The difference between the districts where Perot won 5 percent of the presidential vote in 1992 and those where he won 30 percent of the vote was more than twenty-two thousand dollars in Republican Party aid, about the same as the difference in Republican Party contribution levels between safe and marginal districts. Among all districts in which there was no Republican incumbent, party aid averaged just under thirty-five thousand dollars, so the effect of the 1992 Perot vote on the magnitude of Republican Party investment in the race was indeed substantial.

Thus, Republicans made a bid for Perot supporters in 1994 by shaping their issue appeals to Perot and his adherents and by developing strategies to contact Perot activists and voters directly. In addition, the national party's decisions about where to allocate money in House elections were based in part on the size of the 1992 Perot vote in the district. In 1994, the size of the Perot vote two years earlier sent an unmistakable signal to the Republican Party and its candidates about which districts were winnable, and the party and its experienced pool of potential candidates responded by disproportionately investing in races where Perot ran strongly in 1992.

REPUBLICAN PRESIDENTIAL NOMINATION CANDIDATES

So far, we have seen the Republican bid for the Perot constituency in the 1994 congressional elections—a bid that, as we demonstrate in the next chapter, bore substantial fruit. However, our analysis of the Republican bid would not be complete if we failed to consider other arenas. In particular, our theory of third parties suggests that the Perot constituency also provided a target of opportunity for presidential nomination candidates.

As we pointed out in chapter 2, presidential nomination campaigns are personalized contests among candidate factions within the party, each attempting to mobilize a sufficiently large constituency to capture votes in state primaries and caucuses. Recent nomination candidates have demonstrated that identifying and mobilizing new constituencies is an important part of their strategy—consider, for instance, Jesse Jackson's "Rainbow Coalition" in 1984, Pat Robertson's mobilization of the Christian Right in 1988, and Howard Dean's Internet-based mobilization strategy in 2004. This strategy is less likely to be pursued by front-runner candidates who dominate the party's core constituency, but outsider and maverick candidates often must attract newly mobilized supporters. In chapter 5, we found that a plurality of potential Perot activists were newly mobilized by the Texas independent, and the size and distinctiveness of the Perot constituency could not have escaped the notice of Republican nomination candidates in 1996 and 2000.

Pat Buchanan in 1996

In August 1995, Ross Perot offered both Democratic and Republican candidates the opportunity to address the United We Stand convention in Dallas. Bill Clinton declined, while "all ten Republican candidates for the presidency [paid] homage to Mr. Perot and his disaffected United We Stand America followers, [and] an electrifying Buchanan message clearly stole the show."[50] Other candidates may have been more focused on dissuading UWSA from mounting a third-party candidacy in 1996, but Buchanan "made a direct, unabashed appeal for the support of the thousands of voters that gave Perot more than 19 percent [*sic*] of the vote . . . in a 30-minute tirade against illegal immigration, international trade agreements, foreign aid, and affirmative action."[51] By emphasizing economic nationalism issues and portraying a populist style, Buchanan "emerged . . . as a dauphin to the crown of Ross Perot."[52]

Even after Perot announced the formation of the Reform Party, Buchanan continued to see former Perot voters as his natural constituency. A comparison of Buchanan campaign brochures from 1992 and 1996 indicates a shift in emphasis in his attempt to lure Perot voters to his standard in the primaries.[53] Buchanan's 1992 campaign brochure emphasized populist themes, such as economic nationalism, his opposition to affirmative action quotas and abortion, and his support of prayer in school, but there was less emphasis on campaign reform or the balanced budget amendment, and there was only one reference to term limits (toward the end of the issues list). In 1996, reform took more than double the space it did in 1992, and reform proposals were given pri-

---

50. Tom Rhodes, "Voice of Angry White Male Steals the Show at Perot's Conservative Parade," *The Times,* August 14, 1994.

51. Tony Freemantle, "Perot Supporters Courted by GOP; Buchanan Garners Warmest Reception among 10 Hopefuls," *Houston Chronicle,* August 13, 1995, 1.

52. Rhodes, "Voice of Angry White Male."

53. Compare Buchanan's brochure "Putting and Keeping America First" from his 1992 campaign with his "Putting Americans First: Pat Buchanan on the Issues" from 1996.

macy of place in Buchanan's campaign brochure. In fact, the first five proposals in the brochure committed the candidate to political reform; the first two dealt with term limits, and the next three dealt with correcting "[o]ur national politics [that] have been corrupted by Big Money," a topic ignored in 1992.[54]

Buchanan's appeal was apparently successful: on Super Tuesday in 1996, Buchanan received the support of half again as many former Perot supporters as 1992 Bush general election voters. While Buchanan trailed Dole by better than three to one among those voting for Bush in 1992 (61 percent vs. 20 percent), he trailed by only 7 percent among those who had voted for Perot in the general election (36 percent vs. 29 percent).[55]

John McCain in 2000

Going into the 2000 election, the organizational side of the Perot movement was in disarray, although his constituency of voters and activists remained. Much as Pat Buchanan had before him, Senator John McCain of Arizona saw in the Perot constituency a possible foothold, and in appealing to former Perot supporters, he almost succeeded in breaking front-runner George W. Bush's apparent stranglehold on the 2000 Republican nomination.

McCain had a lot in common with Perot, both in his personal political style and in his emphasis on reform. McCain's reputation as a straight-talking political maverick echoed the style Perot used in his 1992 infomercials, and McCain's campaign bus—the "Straight Talk Express"—sounded like one on loan from Perot's 1992 campaign. But the Arizona senator's identification with reform—specifically, with the campaign finance reform bill that bore his name—became his signature issue. When asked to explain why he was running, McCain replied,

> We've got to reform this government. We've got to reform
> education in America. We've got to reform the military. We've got
> to reform the tax code, which is now 44,000 pages long. We have to
> reform our government. . . . But we can't do it, we can't do it unless

---

54. Buchanan, "Reclaiming the American Dream," campaign brochure, 1996, available online at http://www.4president.org/brochures/patbuchanan96.pdf.

55. CNN, "VNS Exit Polls for Elections Occurring 3/12/1996, Republican Primary Voters, 1996," http://www.cnn.com/ALLPOLITICS/1996/polls/exitpolls/SUP.tue .shtml#pres.vote.

we reform the system of financing campaigns, which has caused the public interest to be submerged by the special interests.[56]

In addition, McCain's commitment to end pork-barrel spending and waste in government was, according to McCain advisor Marshall Wittman, "part of a broader reform message that resonates among the American people."[57] The similarities in style and platform between McCain and Perot prompted Orson Swindle, director of Perot's United We Stand America and a close advisor to McCain, to comment on the "affinity between McCain and Perot because of what they stood for."[58]

With the Reform Party self-destructing in 2000, it would have been counterproductive to try to associate McCain with it in any direct way. It was the larger group of former Perot supporters who were the target of McCain's appeal. However, even without a direct appeal, McCain and his top aids realized how crucial Perot supporters were to the senator's success, and the campaign focused on political reform issues to gain their support. Rick Davis, McCain's campaign manager, explained:

> Attaching McCain to any movement would in the long term come back to haunt him. We didn't pay attention to Republicans, Democrats, or Reform—rather we decided to push the reform message, and the success of the Perot movement showed that there was a constituency for that message. . . . We think there legitimately were reform groups—identified more with the *r* in *reform* and not the *R* in *Republican*. They were waiting for someone to enunciate a message that they liked.[59]

Even more than Pat Buchanan's, McCain's appeal succeeded. A national survey in February 2000 found that 24 percent of McCain's supporters said that they had voted for Perot in 1996, versus only 2 percent of Bush voters.[60] Although this support was ultimately insufficient to secure the nomination for McCain, it provided the boost to make McCain

---

56. Jim Lehrer, "Candid Campaigner," *News Hour with Jim Lehrer,* September 1, 1999.

57. Julia Malone, "War on Waste Gets Election Year Lift; After Finance Reform, 'Prof' Becomes Target," *Times-Picayune,* March 5, 2000, A12.

58. Authors' interview with Orson Swindle, July 11, 2000.

59. Authors' interview with Rick Davis, February 6, 2004.

60. Balz, "Perot Sharply Attacks Economic Plan," A6.

a legitimate challenger and to increase his influence in Congress on issues of political reform.

CONCLUSION

As the dynamic of third parties suggests, after Perot identified and mobilized a large constituency, both major parties bid for its support in subsequent elections. The Republicans, as the party out of power in both houses of Congress and the presidency, had the greater opportunity and incentive to appeal aggressively to the Perot constituency. Beginning with the February 1993 Republican postelection retreat, a group of Republican leaders, spearheaded by Newt Gingrich and John Kasich, established close ties with Perot and his UWSA organization. Despite initial reluctance from other party leaders, including Bob Dole and Haley Barbour, Gingrich and his colleagues brought the Republican Party into line behind a Perot-based strategy. Most impressive in this effort was the Contract with America, which reflected both the form of Perot's checklist for candidates at the end of his book *United We Stand America* and many of the same issue priorities of Perot and his supporters, while ignoring issues—such as abortion and free trade—where differences between the GOP base and the Perot movement were sharp.

Republicans organized a 1994 campaign strategy aimed at reaching Perot supporters with targeted mailings, and stronger Republican candidates were more likely to emerge in districts where Perot had done well. The party committed more funds to these districts as well. As we show in the next chapter, the result was that the Republicans succeeded in taking the House of Representatives for the first time in forty years.

The same opportunity individual Republican House candidates saw in the Perot constituency was seized by Pat Buchanan in 1996 and by John McCain in 2000, in their insurgent nomination campaigns. The persistent courtship of Perot and his movement began shortly after the 1992 election and continued unabated through the 1994 midterm elections, testifying to the issue basis of the Perot movement in 1992 and to the opportunity it created in its aftermath to alter the balance of power between the major parties.

IV. The Perot Constituency's Response & the Republican Resurgence

VIII

Perot & the Republican Resurgence, 1994–2000

&/ρ

W<small>E HAVE SHOWN THAT THE</small> Republican Party made an aggressive bid for Perot backers' support in the 1994 election, but can we show that Republicans were successful in attracting Perot voters to their cause? In this chapter, we demonstrate that the Perot vote was responsible for producing historic Republican victories in the 1994 House elections and in the 2000 presidential election. Ross Perot's success as an independent candidate in 1992 opened the door to a Republican resurgence at the close of the twentieth century.

There is no doubt that Republicans enjoyed historic success in the 1994 elections by winning majority control of both houses of Congress, breaking an apparent Democratic stranglehold on the U.S. House of Representatives. Previously, the Democrats held consistent majorities in the House, even when they lost the presidency by landslide margins, as in 1972 and 1984. Between 1952, when the Republicans won the presidency for the first time in twenty years, and 1992, when Bill Clinton captured the presidency with a popular-vote plurality of 43 percent, the Republicans won seven presidential elections to only four by the Democrats. Nonetheless, the Democrats amassed majority after majority in U.S. House elections after 1952.

Figure 8.1 puts the magnitude of the 1994 Republican victory in the context of Republican performance in House elections since 1948. Between 1948 and 1992, the Republican Party managed to win an average of only 40.6 percent of the seats in the House of Representatives. They

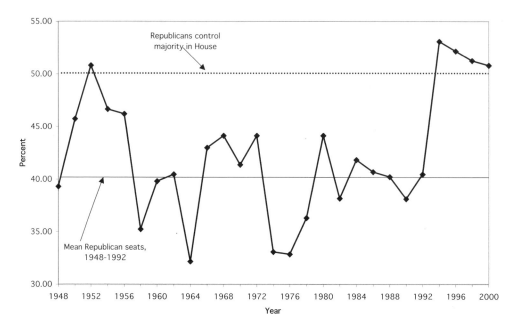

Fig. 8.1. Percentage Republican seats in U.S. House of Representatives, 1948–2000

captured a majority of the House only once, in the 1952 elections, when their presidential nominee, World War II hero Dwight D. Eisenhower, won the presidency. After the 1992 elections, the Republicans held only 40.5 percent of the seats in the House, a hair below their average for the post–World War II period. In the 1994 midterm elections, the Republicans turned the tables, winning 52.4 percent of the popular vote and gaining a 53 percent majority of seats.

It is no coincidence that Republicans won their first congressional majority in the election immediately following Ross Perot's independent candidacy in 1992. The Republicans won in 1994 because they successfully bid for the 1992 Perot constituency in the Contract with America and with strong candidates for the House, especially in districts where Perot had done well in 1992. Not only did the Republicans achieve victory in 1994, but they also enjoyed continued success in House elections and victory in the 2000 presidential election. However, the link between Perot and the Republican resurgence, while a direct consequence of our understanding of the dynamic of third parties, has largely gone unnoticed in the scholarly literature on the 1994 election and its aftermath.

SCHOLARLY EXPLANATIONS OF THE 1994 REPUBLICAN VICTORY

The conventional scholarly understanding of U.S. House elections is that their outcomes can best be explained by a combination of national tides, the partisan makeup of the district, incumbency, and other factors particular to the race in the district. The most important factor is whether the incumbent is running for reelection. Incumbent reelection rates are high, averaging approximately 94 percent since 1966. Incumbents are successful because they usually share the partisanship of the majority of voters in their district and because they make every effort to maintain their personal popularity in their district (Cain, Ferejohn, and Fiorina 1987; Jacobson 2004; Mann and Wolfinger 1980). David Mayhew (1974) offered the classic description of how incumbents maintain their popularity: by advertising their name, by claiming credit for producing policies and benefits that voters in the district want, and by taking positions on issues (in their roll-call voting and in their public pronouncements) in accord with district opinion.

In addition, incumbents have resources—such as their staff and the frank (subsidized mailing privileges)—that challengers lack. Thus, many observers have argued that U.S. House elections are not typically fought on a level playing field, since challengers are outspent and overmatched by incumbents. In many districts, the incumbent is recognized as unbeatable, and no one emerges to mount a challenge. In most other districts, the challenger is neither experienced nor well funded and has little or no chance of unseating the incumbent. One reason challengers are so often underfunded and overwhelmed is because the strongest prospective challengers already hold political office and are reluctant to put their current position at risk, knowing that incumbents are difficult to unseat. They often remain on the sidelines until the incumbent retires and the seat becomes open (Bond, Covington, and Fleisher 1985; Cox and Katz 2002; Gaddie and Bullock 2000). When the seat is open and no incumbent is running for reelection, the campaign is typically far more balanced and competitive, with strong, well-funded candidates running on both sides.

In addition to local factors, congressional elections scholars recognize that national tides in any given election may favor one party or the other. The midterm election of 1974 is an example of an election-year tide against the president's party, owing in large measure to the Watergate scandal and the resignation of Richard Nixon from the presidency. Election tides against a party may also result from the poor performance of the economy or from dissatisfaction with other policy failures that can be pinned on the party in power. When a national tide works against a party, strong potential candidates in the favored party are typically emboldened to run, and incumbents in the party that is out of favor may retire to avoid defeat (Jacobson and Kernell 1983; Jacobson 1989; Cox and Katz 2002).

How does this description of factors, typically used to explain U.S. House election outcomes, account for the Republican victory in 1994? On the Sunday before the election, the *Washington Post* invited fourteen close observers of politics—Republican and Democratic political strategists, media commentators, and academics—to predict the outcome of the 1994 elections. Most forecasters expected a national tide in favor of the Republicans, in part because the party opposite the president's usually picks up seats in the midterm election and in part because of the continued poor performance of the economy, the Clinton budget that raised taxes, and the failure of his national health care reform bill. None of these observers forecast a Republican gain as large as the actual result.[1] One leading academic authority on congressional elections admits that the forecasting models he and others employed, which relied on such factors as incumbency, challenger quality, and national tides, were woefully short of predicting the magnitude of the Republican victory (Abramowitz 1995).

The Republican victory in 1994 produced a virtual GOP sweep into power. Not a single Republican running for reelection was unseated, while thirty-four Democratic incumbents lost their bids for reelection.

---

1. David Broder, "Naked Punditry," *Washington Post,* November 6, 1994, Outlook section, p. 1.

In open seats, twenty-two Democratic-held seats fell to the Republican onslaught, and only four districts flipped from the Republican to the Democratic column. In twelve midterm elections prior to 1994, the president's party lost an average of twenty-six seats in the House, so President Clinton and the Democrats expected to absorb significant losses. But the fifty-two-seat loss came as a surprise to them as much as it did to political scientists. In 1994, the president's party lost more seats than in any midterm election since 1946.

What was different about 1994? The explanations found in scholarly literature usually ignore or dismiss the relevance of the Perot movement. Some have based their explanation primarily on a partisan or ideological realignment in the electorate. In this view, many conservative districts, especially in the South, gradually were dominated by Republican majorities but had continued to elect Democratic incumbents to Congress. The 1994 elections registered this underlying shift in partisanship and ideology toward the Republicans as the national parties polarized and as the ideological differences between the parties became more apparent to voters (Abramowitz 1995; Abramowitz and Saunders 1998).

A second explanation rests on the electorate's rejection of President Clinton's policies and performance, which led to dissatisfaction with Democratic incumbents who had supported Clinton's policies, especially if they were from moderate or conservative districts. This explanation relates to the realignment thesis, because the districts most dissatisfied with Clinton in 1994 had become more conservative and Republican in the years before the 1994 election. David Brady and his colleagues join the realignment and presidential accountability explanations.

> A large number of seats [in the South and West] were represented by Democratic incumbents but were, at best, marginally Democratic. In such areas, it was not just that the Democrats who had won by the smallest margins in 1992 were vulnerable in 1994. It was that the Democratic incumbents who had supported the Clinton program most faithfully were defeated at historically high rates. (Brady et al. 1996, 346)

Gary Jacobson draws on a combination of factors to develop his explanation of the Republican victory. Unlike in previous years, Jacobson points out, the Republicans ran more experienced challengers in 1994 races where a Democratic incumbent was seeking reelection. As mentioned in the previous chapter, Bill Paxon, chair of the House Republican Campaign Committee in 1994, reports that his committee was inundated by resumes from prospective candidates in that year. Jacobson suggests that strong Republican candidates were able to persuade "voters to blame a unified Democratic government for government's failures" (Jacobson 1996, 2) and that local and national factors combined to produce the Republican victory. Jacobson also points out that long-term change toward the Republicans, especially in the South, meant that the GOP was overdue in making significant gains in House elections: in 1994, "the party finally cashed in on favorable changes in party identification that had raised Republicans to near parity with the Democrats ten years earlier" (Jacobson 2000, 11).

Ross Perot receives little or no attention throughout these accounts of the Republican victory in 1994. Jacobson acknowledges the importance of "voter anger" and notes that 1992 Perot voters voted disproportionately for Republicans in 1994, but he does not include district Perot vote in his analyses of the 1994 vote. Brady and his colleagues (1996) include the Perot vote in their analysis but conclude that "Perot's real effect on the election was minimal."

Some observers have noted that Perot endorsed the Republican Party's efforts to win control of Congress in 1994 and that there was an association between the 1992 vote Perot received in House districts and the subsequent Republican victories. Philip Klinkner (1996) reports a correlation between the district Perot vote and the tendency to flip to the Republican Party in 1994, but his analysis does not take adequate account of other explanations that could explain the correlation. Martin Wattenberg (1996) goes so far as to show that the percentage of the congressional district voting for Perot in 1992 is significantly related to the 1994 percent voting Republican outside the South, controlling for several other potential explanations. He concludes that the Republicans owed their victory in significant part to Perot, but he omits any reference to candidate quality in his explanation, and he restricts himself to districts outside the South. Excluding the South may unduly tip the analysis away from the realignment thesis.

In sum, we are left with a confusing situation in the scholarly analysis of the 1994 elections. Some analysts ignore the possibility of a Perot effect altogether. Others take some account of Perot but do not fully accommodate the competing explanations of long-term party change in favor of the Republicans and Republican candidate quality. Of perhaps greatest importance, no one has advanced a coherent theory of why the Perot vote should matter or exactly how it could be expected to influence Republican fortunes. The fact that Perot endorsed the Republican Party in 1994 is often mentioned, but that anecdotal fact about the 1994 campaign fails to differentiate districts from one another. Jacobson's recognition that unified government under the Democrats after 1992 left angry Perot voters with a target for their discontent attaches importance to the disaffected segments of the electorate, rather than emphasizing Perot's impact on major-party change.

THE RESPONSE IN THE ELECTORATE

Our perspective on third parties as stimulants of major-party change leads us to reexamine post-1992 voting patterns, including those of the all-important 1994 election. One simple test is whether 1992 Perot voters changed their voting after 1992 to support Republican candidates. A change of this sort might indicate a response to the Republican Party's bid for their support following the 1992 election. Consistent with these expectations, the Republican percentage of the two-party congressional vote among Perot voters jumped from about half in 1992 to over two-thirds in 1994 (Jacobson 1996; Klinkner 1996; Wattenberg 1996). The difficulty is in determining how much of the post-1992 Republican vote was merely a return to a previously established tendency to vote for the GOP. If 1992 Perot voters had habitually voted Republican in previous elections, their subsequent high levels of support for that party would not be surprising, nor would this sort of coming-home behavior help us tie Republican successes to the Perot movement. If, however, their Perot vote produced a subsequent increase in Republican voting, their behavior would fit our expectation of a response to the GOP bid.

The problem is that the evidence from voter surveys is spotty and somewhat contradictory. In the American National Election Study panel survey, the proportion of 1992 Perot voters voting for Republican House candidates went from 52 percent in that year to 69 percent in 1994 and up to 74 percent in 1996.[2] However, although the ANES panel began in 1992, it did not ask respondents how they voted in previous congressional elections. Respondents in 1992 were asked to recall their presidential vote from four years before, and the response to that question suggest a high level of prior Republican voting among 1992 Perot voters.[3]

The only survey that allows us to ascertain Perot supporters' pre-1992 House voting is a 1990–92 ANES panel survey that was not part of the 1992–96 panel that we have been consulting.[4] This two-year panel has the advantages of beginning in a midterm election year before Ross Perot appeared on the national scene and of continuing through the 1992 election in which he first ran. The results from this survey provide strong evidence of a Republican surge in 1994 compared with both 1990 and 1992. Only 42 percent of these respondents who ended up voting for Ross Perot in 1992 had voted for Republican House candidates in 1990, while 58 percent voted Democratic. Although this particular finding supports our argument that the post-1992 shift among Perot voters to the GOP was not a coming-home phenomenon, we are forced to look elsewhere for more definitive evidence, because the survey record is inconsistent and incomplete.

THE IMPACT OF PEROT ON THE 1994 ELECTIONS

We begin the present analysis by comparing the time series of Republican seats in the South with those in non-Southern states (see fig. 8.2). The realignment in the South throughout this period is evident, as the

2. We use the American National Election Studies panel because, in contrast to 1994 and 1996 exit poll data, it does not rely on recall measures to identify 1992 Perot voters. However, the results are essentially similar, no matter which data source we employ.

3. According to the 1992 ANES recall question, 78 percent of 1992 Perot voters recalled voting for Bush in 1988, a result that supports the coming-home hypothesis, if we assume that Bush voters cast Republican votes for the House and if we accept that a four-year recall question is valid.

4. See ICPSR Study 6230, American National Election Study, 1990–1992: Full Panel Survey, Ann Arbor, MI.

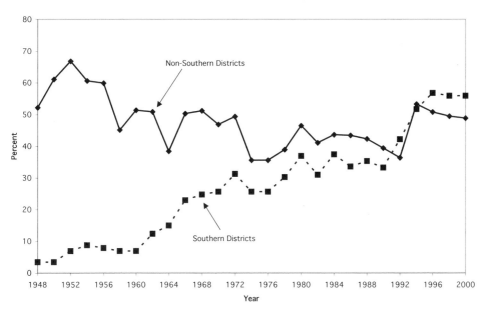

Fig. 8.2.   Percentage Republican seats in U.S. House by region, 1948–2000

percent of Republican seats grew from a paltry 3.5 percent in 1948 to majorities in 1994 and the years following. Prior to 1994, the percentage of Republican seats grew in the South at a rate of 1.8 percent per two-year election cycle.[5] From this perspective, the realignment thesis looks like a strong contender for explaining the 1994 Republican majority in the South. However, a closer analysis reveals that the 1994 election delivered a significant pro-Republican shock to the Southern series. The twenty-three pre-1994 elections in the series contributed a 38.7 percent gain in Republican seats in the South, while the 1994 election alone produced a 9.1 percent increase in seats for the GOP, almost one-quarter of the total from the previous forty-six years.[6] Something happened

---

5. The strength of the trend is indicated by an R^2 of .92. Regressing GOP seat share for all elections through 2000 increases the R^2 to .93 and the rate of increase to 2 percent per election cycle.

6. Regressing Republican seats in the South on year of election and a dummy variable for 1994 yields

$$\% \text{ Republican Seats in South} = -1,719.57 + .88 \text{ (Year)} + 9.10 \text{ (1994)} + \epsilon; R^2 = .958 \text{ (}t\text{-ratios).}$$
$$\quad\quad\quad\quad\quad\quad\quad\quad\quad\quad\quad\quad (-15.7) \quad\quad (15.9) \quad\quad\quad (3.7)$$

between 1992 and 1994 to boost Republican fortunes in the South beyond the long-term trend in the GOP's favor.

In districts outside the South, there is a long-term countervailing
trend against the Republican Party. Republicans lost seats during the
1948–2000 period covered by figure 8.2, but a sharp uptick in Republican fortunes occurred in 1994. When we estimate the trend in districts
outside the South, the decline in Republican seats is not as strong or
consistent as the party's gain in the South, but the impact of the 1994
election is even more pronounced. Each election except for 1994 con-
tributes about a 1 percent decline in Republican seats, whereas the pro-
Republican shock in 1994 amounts to a whopping 16.7 percent increase
in Republican seats.[7]

Again, the implication is that long-term trends do not fully account
for the Republican victory in 1994, nor can the outcome be explained
as a simple consequence of realignment in the South. In fact, the Republican share of seats in that year was slightly smaller in Southern districts than it was outside the South. On the basis of this fact alone, it
would be difficult to attribute the Republican victory to North-South
partisan or ideological differences. However, it is true that Republican
support in the South helped sustain the Republican majority after 1994,
with a distinct regional gap in Republican fortunes emerging in 1996
and persisting through 1998 and 2000. Without their majorities in the
South, the Republicans would have lost control of the House in the
1998 elections.[8]

If we cannot explain 1994 by the North-South differences rooted in
the long-term realignment south of the Mason-Dixon Line, can we link
the 1992 Perot movement to the Republican victory in 1994? Our claim
is that the Republican bid for the Perot constituency after 1992 created
the Republican sweep in 1994 by accelerating the Republican realign-

---

7. The regression equation is

% Republican Seats Outside South = 1,021.9 − .495 (Year) + 16.723 (1994) + ϵ;
 R^2 = .560 (*t*-ratios).   (6.1)   (−5.8)   (4.5)

8. The Republicans captured 53.3 percent of non-Southern seats in 1994 and 50.8
percent in 1996. After 1996, they dropped below 50 percent, winning 49.5 percent in
1998 and 48.9 percent in 2000.

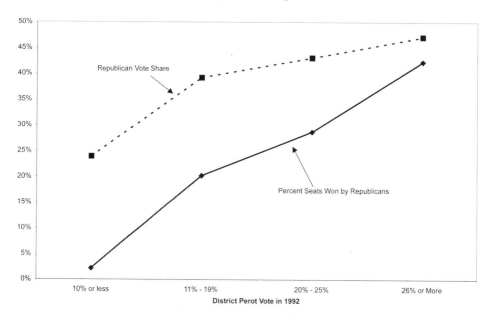

Fig. 8.3. 1994 Republican vote share and seat percentage in districts held by Democrats by 1992 district Perot vote

ment in the South and sharply reversing its eroding fortunes outside the South. The 1994 Republican landslide two years after Ross Perot's remarkable 1992 campaign was no coincidence, nor was it simply the culmination of long-term partisan trends. Rather, the GOP victory was firmly rooted in Perot's electoral success two years before and in the dynamic of third parties.

Figure 8.3 connects the size of the 1992 Perot vote in congressional districts with the Republican vote share and the chances the district flipped from Democratic to Republican control in the 1994 elections. Only 2.2 percent of Democratic districts where Perot received 10 percent or less of the district vote flipped to the Republicans in 1994, while 42 percent of Democratic districts where Perot ran most strongly in 1992 switched to the GOP. The progression of Republican gains in vote share and seats captured is pronounced. The question is whether this relationship between the 1992 Perot vote in districts and Republican success in 1994 holds up in a more fully controlled analysis.

In our analysis of the data for figure 8.4, we take into account each district's major-party voting history (to control for long-term partisan

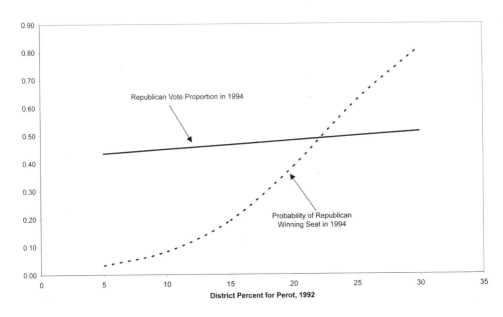

Fig. 8.4.   Effect of 1992 Perot vote on 1994 district vote for Republicans' chances of winning, Democratic-held marginal seats, controlling for other factors

predispositions), the experience and spending of both parties' House candidates, the level of support Democratic incumbents gave to President Clinton (as a control for the possibility that voters were reacting against President Clinton's policies), and whether the district is in the South.[9] Including these controls allows us to take account of the explanations other scholars have offered for the Republican victory in 1994. We restrict the analysis to marginal seats because almost the entire turnover occurred in such races.[10] In marginal Democratic districts where the 1992 Perot vote was only 5 percent, the average Republican vote was well below 50 percent, and the chance that the seat would switch to the Republicans was only 3.3 percent; in districts where the Perot vote was between 25 and 30 percent, the average Republican vote

9. We set all variables in the analysis to their mean values in order to observe the impact of 1992 district vote for Perot on "typical" districts' vote for Republican House candidates and the probability of the Republican winning the seat.

10. We define marginal seats as those in which the Democratic incumbent carried the district in 1992 by 60 percent or less. The effect of the Perot vote in all seats is statistically significant, but its substantive impact on the probability of the Republican winning is muted because most Democratic-held seats did not change party hands.

share was over 50 percent, and the chances that the seat would change to the Republicans were strong—between 62 and 81 percent.[11]

How does this analysis improve on the limitations of the voter survey record previously discussed? Leaving aside for the moment the question of how individual behavior might produce the change toward the Republican Party in 1994 (a question we consider in detail in the next chapter), using district data in this case has several advantages over voter surveys. By including partisan predispositions of the district, we give the coming-home thesis its due. Making full allowance for the Republican predispositions in House districts, a strong independent impact of the 1992 Perot vote on Republican fortunes in 1994 remains.

We do not claim that the coming-home and ideological change explanations are irrelevant. Indeed, it is true that some of the 1992 Perot vote came from the Republican base, and reasonably enough, it returned to vote Republican once Perot was off the scene. Likewise, Abramowitz and others are correct that there was a long-term drift toward the Republican Party in the South. But after taking these explanations into account, our analysis indicates that the Perot candidacy gave Republican electoral fortunes an additional boost.

Based on the same statistical model that we used to isolate the effects of districts' 1992 Perot vote on the 1994 House election results, we can simulate what the 1994 Republican vote in each district would have been with a decline in Perot's vote share in 1992. If we look at all districts, we can assess how the overall election results would have differed had Perot's national vote been lower.[12] Figure 8.5 presents three scenarios in which we set Perot's 1992 popular vote to the level of other successful third-party candidacies in recent decades: the George Wallace vote in 1968, the John Anderson vote in 1980, and Perot's vote in 1996.

---

11. The actual range of the Perot vote in Democratic districts was between 3 and 30 percent. In nine districts, the 1992 Perot vote was 5 percent or less; in thirty-six districts held by Democrats after the 1992 elections, the Perot vote was 25 percent or more. The partial slope value is .309, which indicates that for each percent of gain visible in district votes for Perot in 1992, there was about a 0.31 percent increase in vote for Republicans, other things considered ($p = .014$).

12. The simulation uses the major-party vote share in 1994 as our dependent variable and distinguishes Republican-held from Democrat-held seats and, within each party, whether the district was marginal in the 1992 elections.

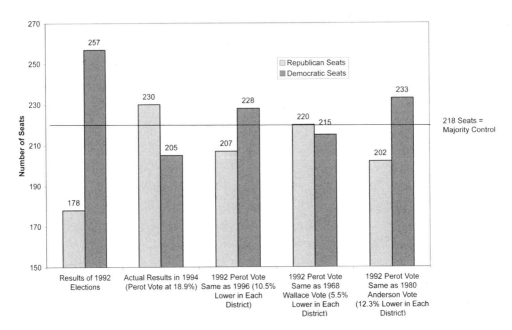

Fig. 8.5.   Simulation of 1994 House results with varying sizes of 1992 national Perot vote

Had Perot won the same popular vote as he captured in 1996 (8.4 percent, less than half of what he actually received in 1992), we estimate that the Republicans would have failed to win control of the House. They would have picked up about twenty-nine seats over what they held in 1992, leaving Democratic control intact. If the Republicans had gained twenty-nine seats, their performance would not have been exceptional for a midterm election—the average number of seats lost by the president's party between 1946 and 1990 was twenty-six. If Perot had received the same popular vote as John Anderson did in 1980, the Republican total in 1994 would have been even lower. Had Perot won the same popular-vote share that George Wallace secured in the 1968 presidential elections (13.5 percent), the Republicans would have won a bare majority of House seats. By our estimate, if the Perot vote in 1992 had been below about 13.2 percent, the Republicans probably would not have won control of the House in 1994.[13]

13.   This analysis begs the question of what might have caused Perot to do better or worse in 1992. We assume only that if Perot had won fewer votes than he actually did in

In sum, we have shown that the Republican victory in the 1994 elections resulted from the party's successful bid for the Perot constituency's support. That bid reflected coordinated actions by national party leaders in the form of the Contract with America, and it came in the form of individual decisions by strong potential House candidates on the GOP side who saw opportunity signaled by the size of the Perot vote in their districts. Districts with the largest concentrations of Perot voters responded, in turn, by producing the change in party control and the GOP House victory.

THE LEGACY OF PEROT AFTER 1994

The Perot movement had a lasting impact on the Republican Party's electoral fortunes in the elections after 1994. The post-1994 equilibrium is obvious in the continuing Republican House majorities in 1996, 1998, and 2000. Table 8.1 compares the Perot effect in Southern and non-Southern districts from 1994 through 2000. The 1994 election was obviously not unique, as there was a lasting effect of the 1992 Perot vote, especially in districts outside the South. The impact of the Perot vote in the 1994 election continued through 2000. Where Perot did not run strongly in 1992, Republicans held only 11.5 percent of non-Southern seats that had been in Democratic hands, compared to one-third of non-Southern constituencies where Perot ran well. In the South, Republicans won significant proportions of previously Democratic seats even without the help of the Texas billionaire, although they did realize some additional gain in districts where Perot ran most strongly in 1992. Thus, in Southern and non-Southern formerly Democratic districts where Perot did well in 1992, Republicans continued to retain their seats in the following three elections.

Thus far, we have concentrated on House elections because these races tend to reflect enduring partisan predispositions in American politics. The impact of the Perot vote on the Republican gains in 1994 produced a sea change in the two-party system. What effect did Perot's

---

1992 and if his vote losses had been distributed proportionately across all House districts, the number of his supporters in each district would have been smaller, and therefore there would have been fewer of them for Republican candidates to woo.

TABLE 8.1.   Percentage of Seats Held by Democrats in 1992 That Went to Republicans in 1994–2000

	Nonsouthern Districts Where			Southern Districts Where		
	<20% Voted for Perot in 1992	20% or More Voted for Perot in 1992	Difference	<20% Voted for Perot in 1992	20% or More Voted for Perot in 1992	Difference
1994	9.2	33.0	23.8	21.4	23.5	2.1
1996	10.3	35.1	24.8	28.6	41.2	12.6
1998	10.3	34.0	23.7	28.6	35.3	6.7
2000	11.5	33.0	21.5	30.4	35.3	4.9
Number of districts	87	97		56	17	

strong showing in 1992 have on the two ensuing presidential elections? Figure 8.6 shows how 1992 state votes for Perot relate to the share of the vote received by Republican candidates Robert Dole in 1996 and George W. Bush in 2000.[14] Other things being equal in 1996, and controlling for 1988 vote and 1992 Republican vote, a state's 1992 Perot vote increased Dole's vote share from about 32 percent in a state where Perot received 5 percent of the 1992 vote to about 46 percent in states where Perot attracted 30 percent of the 1992 vote. This effect is remarkable because Perot remained on the presidential ballot as a candidate in 1996, albeit with diminished support. In 2000, the impact of the 1992 Perot vote on Bush's vote share, eight years after Perot's first campaign, was even stronger than it was on Dole's vote. In states where Perot attracted 5 percent of the 1992 vote, Bush's 2000 vote share was about 36 percent, compared with 57 percent for Bush in an otherwise identical state where Perot attracted 30 percent of the 1992 presidential vote share.[15]

The 2000 election served as a dramatic reminder that the important outcome in presidential elections is not the popular-vote percentage but which candidate wins a plurality in each state and receives its electoral

---

14. The analysis controls for each state's 1988 and 1992 vote for Bush and includes dummy variables for the South and, because it is a significant outlier, Washington, D.C. See appendix B for the full results.

15. Using the same statistical model, we get very similar results predicting the 2004 presidential vote shares in the states. This reflects the continuity between Bush's vote share in 2000 and 2004, rather than an effect of Perot on the 2004 election independent of his impact in 2000. Indeed, there is no evidence Perot had an impact on 2004 independent of 2000.

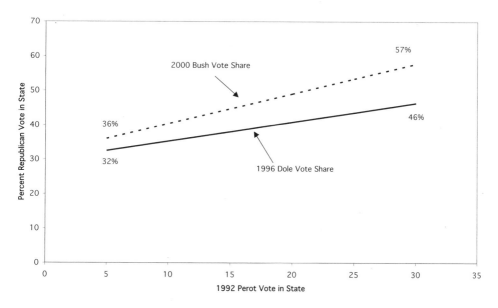

Fig. 8.6.   Effects of 1992 Perot vote on 1996 and 2000 presidential election results, controlling for other factors

votes. Figure 8.7 shows that the likelihood that Bob Dole in 1996 or George W. Bush in 2000 would carry a non-Southern state increased dramatically as the state's 1992 vote for Perot increased.[16] The results show that, at the margin, the 1992 Perot vote had strong effects on electoral college outcomes four and eight years later. At the same time, the differences between 2000 and 1996 are apparent: whereas the chances that either Bob Dole or George W. Bush would carry a state with a 5 percent or even a 10 percent Perot vote in 1992 were close to zero, prospects for the Republican nominees diverged significantly in states where Perot's vote was at the average for all states. The chance that Dole would carry a state with an average level of support for Perot in 1992 stood at only 0.04, but the chance that Bush would carry such a state in 2000 was 0.43. Needless to say, in an election as exquisitely close as the 2000 presidential contest, anything that had reduced Perot's 1992 vote by even a small amount might well have made the difference in the outcome of the election eight years

16. The logistic regression slopes in figure 8.7 are estimated using the same control variables used for figure 8.6 (see n. 13). We set the popular votes Bush received in 1988 and 1992 to their means, and we set the values of "South" and "D.C." to zero.

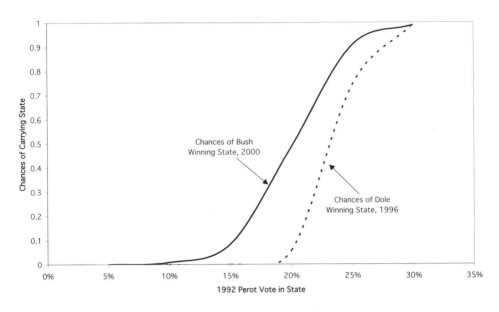

Fig. 8.7.   Effects of 1992 Perot vote on probability of Republican win in non-southern states, 1996 and 2000, controlling for other factors

later, one of the closest presidential elections in history. Without Perot's third-party candidacy in 1992, the Bush–Gore contest would have produced a Gore victory on November 7, 2000.

CONCLUSION

Although support for Perot declined between 1992 and 1996 and although the vote for the Reform Party all but disappeared in 2000, the third-party movement Ross Perot started had a lasting impact on the electoral fortunes of the major parties. The first evidence of an impact came in the 1994 midterm elections, in the form of the Republicans' surprising victory in the House. Effects on presidential politics were also significant, if less immediate: Republican success in carrying a given state in 1996 and 2000 was strongly related to Perot's 1992 support in the state. In 1996, Clinton ran as a successful incumbent, and Perot ran again as the Reform Party's nominee, so the Perot effect on the two-party vote, while present, was not sufficient to make the race competitive. But in 2000, with Perot no longer on the ballot and Gore struggling to assume the positive side of Clinton's heritage, Perot's legacy was to make the election more competitive than it otherwise would have been. Indeed, given how close the election was, it is no stretch to say that Ross Perot was more directly responsible for the victory of the second President Bush than he was for the defeat of the first.

The electoral data in this chapter link the Republican resurgence in U.S. national elections at the close of the twentieth century to the Perot movement. The results do not support the argument that Perot supporters temporarily left the Republican Party in 1992, only to return in subsequent elections. Our analysis takes full account of the partisan predispositions in congressional districts and states and finds strong and significant effects of the Perot vote up to eight years after the 1992 election. These results fit our expectation that the Republican surge in 1994 was a direct consequence of that party's bid for the Perot constituency after the 1992 election. That bid was manifest in organized efforts by party leaders, such as the Contract with America, and it was evident in experienced Republican candidates' individual decisions to run for office, whether in races for House districts previously off-limits to strong Republican challengers or, in the case of John McCain, in the presidential nomination campaign of 2000.

We recognize that tying the Republican victory in 1994 (and its subsequent successes in the remaining elections in the decade) to the Perot movement is at odds with the prevailing views of the reasons for the Republican successes.[17] While we regard the evidence here as compelling, both in supporting our thesis and in taking full account of other plausible explanations, we recognize the need for additional evidence and analysis to make our case. We have alluded to the absence of mass survey data that might, if adequate samples and appropriate measures had been taken, address the implications of the dynamic of third parties. While we do not have such data on ordinary voters (the best data we have on ordinary voters are in the form of the election returns analyzed in this chapter), we have the next best thing in our panel of potential Perot activists. We turn now to these data, to learn how the dynamic of third parties affected Perot activists in the years following their initial engagement in his 1992 campaign.

---

17. We are unaware of any other scholarly analyses of electoral outcomes after 1994 that tie Republican victories in any way to the lingering effects of the 1992 Perot movement.

IX

The Mobilization Effects of Perot Activity

E LECTORAL RETURNS SINCE 1994 demonstrate a link between the 1992 Perot vote and the subsequent strength and success of Republican candidates. Our argument is that in response to a bid made by the Republican Party, significant numbers of Perot supporters switched their votes to Republican candidates in 1994 and in the ensuing elections. Furthermore, to account for the gain in Republican fortunes, the movement of 1992 Perot supporters in subsequent elections cannot simply be a matter of coming home to the Republican Party after defecting to Perot in 1992. While the evidence in chapter 8 supports our claim that the Republicans captured former Perot backers' support, it does not address directly what individual Perot supporters did after the 1992 election. The connections we have shown between Perot support and Republican fortunes probably resulted from individual Perot voters changing their behavior after the 1992 election, but because we have so far not tracked individuals' behaviors after 1992, we cannot be absolutely certain that the changes resulted from the processes we describe. Linking the aggregate patterns of the previous chapter to individual behavior is the topic of this chapter.

Unfortunately, no survey of the American electorate gives us sufficiently large numbers of Perot voters over an extended period of time to enable us to follow them through the elections after 1992. Accordingly, we turn to our sample of potential Perot activists, both because the data are available in appropriate detail and over a sufficiently long period of time to test our expectations and because we expect that changes among activists stimulate change among less active supporters in the electorate as a whole. Certainly our analysis in chapter 8 shows that significant change occurred in the electorate after the 1992 election; in this chapter, we demonstrate that individual Perot supporters changed their behavior consistent with the dynamic of third parties.

SPILLOVER EFFECTS OF
CAMPAIGN ACTIVISM

In chapter 2, we summarized research on activism in the presidential nomination process and found spillover effects from the nomination to the general election stage of the process. These effects demonstrate that mobilization by one campaign can stimulate enhanced involvement in a subsequent campaign. This occurs between the nomination and the general election stages of presidential campaigns, when nomination activists are disproportionately mobilized into a fall general election campaign by their participation in a nomination candidate's effort in the previous spring. In this way, the nomination campaign stimulates future activity, most remarkably among supporters of losing candidates in nomination contests (McCann et al. 1996; Stone, Atkeson, and Rapoport 1992).

We expect similar spillover effects between Perot's 1992 campaign and subsequent major-party campaigns if the major-party bid for Perot activists was successful. We saw in chapter 7 that the more engaged activists were in Perot's 1992 campaign, the more likely they were to be contacted directly by Republican campaigns in 1994. This heightened level of contact reflects the bid the Republicans made for Perot activists' support in 1994. Campaign involvement for Perot in 1992 sensitized activists to the stake they had in political outcomes and increased their awareness of political stimuli, including the Republican bid made on the basis of the core issues that attracted them to Ross Perot in the first place. Thus, we expect to find that mobilization into Perot's 1992 campaign produced spillover into Republican campaigns in 1994 and beyond.

Because we have a panel survey of potential Perot activists that follows the same individuals after the 1992 election, we can test for spillover effects. We can also test for the conditional nature of these effects, consistent with our argument. In particular, based on the bid the Republican Party made for the Perot constituency, we expect to find spillover into Republican campaigns. Moreover, in 1994, which was the critical election for establishing the Republican Party's parity with the Democratic Party, we anticipate that spillover effects were conditioned on direct contact from Republican campaigns.

Spillover effects into Republican campaigns among Perot activists would strengthen our claims about how the dynamic of third parties applies to the aftermath of Perot's 1992 campaign, since such effects would indicate that core members of Perot's constituency moved into the Republican Party. Indeed, if the spillover hypothesis holds, those most involved for Perot should have become most engaged in Republican campaigns. It also provides a plausible mechanism for the much larger numbers of ordinary voters who moved in the same direction. We know that activists are more attentive to politics and better informed than the typical voter. But the process of Republican mobilization to which core activists were subject was certainly present for ordinary Perot voters as well. As we showed in chapter 7, Perot voters, along with activists, were targeted by Republican congressional candidates for campaign mailings and other contacts. Activists, however, are a particularly important target group, since they are themselves agents of change in the mass public. From studies of the effects of activism on voters, we know that the contacting, persuading, and mobilizing efforts of activists have substantial ripple effects in the electorate as a whole (Rosenstone and Hansen 1993; Verba, Schlozman, and Brady 1995). Thus, when activists migrate from one campaign to another, they take many ordinary voters with them. They are not only the leading edge of change; they are a significant reason the change occurs at all.

MAJOR-PARTY ACTIVISM, 1988–2000

We begin the present analysis by looking at levels of activism in Democratic and Republican campaigns from 1988 through 2000. Figure 9.1 presents the ratios of Republican to Democratic activism in our panel

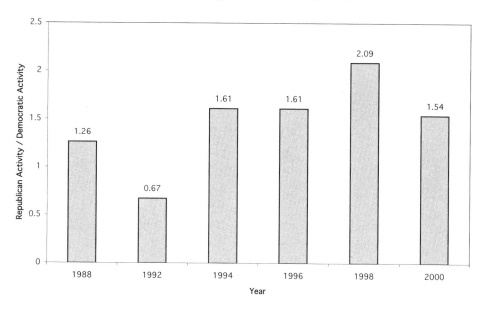

Fig. 9.1.   Ratio of Republican to Democratic campaign activity, 1988–2000

for election years between 1988 and 2000.[1] The pattern is consistent with voter recall data described in chapter 8, in that relative Republican activity in 1992 shows a substantial decline from 1988. These results therefore, render 1992 suspect as a baseline year for comparison with Perot activists' subsequent Republican support. However, even if we use 1988 as a base year, which makes allowances for Republicans "coming home" after 1992, the GOP still enjoyed substantial increases in activism after 1992, relative to the Democrats. Relative Republican activism went up in 1994 by 28 percent above the 1988 baseline. Thus, Republican activity increased not only relative to its nadir in 1992 but also over what it was before Perot initiated his campaign, and the Republican advantage

1.   We report the ratios of activity because comparisons of the simple rates of activism in each party from one year to the next are problematic, owing to differences in the contexts that affect how active individuals are in campaigns. By focusing on relative activity (the mean number of Republican campaign activities divided by the mean number of Democratic activities) in each year, we can make comparisons between presidential and off-year elections, where the rates of involvement are very different. The ratio of Republican to Democratic activism tells us whether the average level of activism among our Perot sample favors the Republican Party (in which case the ratio is greater than 1) or the Democratic Party (in which case the ratio is less than 1). The 1988 and 1998 measures are based on recall questions; all other measures are from waves of the eight-year Perot panel.

was large throughout the remaining elections in the decade, both in off-year and in presidential elections. Regardless of the accuracy of Republican complaints about Perot's campaign drawing supporters away from them disproportionately in 1992, the Republican advantage among core Perot supporters in 1994 had easily surpassed what it was in 1988.

Spillover Effects in 1994

The 1994 elections were critical to the dynamic of third parties in the aftermath of the 1992 Perot candidacy, because of the Republican Party's concerted bids for the Perot constituency in the form of the Contract with America and the emergence of strong House candidates. Thus, we begin with the 1994 elections.

Although the data in figure 9.1 indicate that the Republican Party attracted higher relative levels of activism in 1994 than it had in 1988 or 1992, it remains to be seen whether the Republican surge in activity can be tied to mobilization by the Perot campaign. As a test, we look to find that the more activists did for Perot, the more they responded to the bid from the Republican Party by becoming active in 1994 Republican House campaigns. In order to show that Republican involvement among Perot activists after 1992 entailed more than "coming home," we control for levels of Republican campaign activity in both 1992 and 1988. Because party identification may also predispose individuals to participate in Republican campaigns apart from their previous levels of engagement for Perot, it, too, must be taken into account. Finally, because we want to be sure that any apparent spillover relationship we observe is not merely a reflection of the quality of the candidates who happen to be running, we control for comparative evaluation of the major-party candidates in 1994.[2]

---

2. Including respondents' evaluations of the major-party candidates in the 1994 House election controls for the possibility that respondents were mobilized by the choice offered in the current campaign. This is a conservative strategy from the perspective of our overall framework, because it is possible that Perot participation stimulated respondents to favor Republican candidates over Democratic candidates in subsequent partisan elections. In addition, we have already seen that the size of the Perot vote in a district affected the probability that a high-quality Republican candidate would run, and such candidates are more likely to attract a following. While we acknowledge the possibility that the quality of 1994 candidates reflects a Perot effect, we preferred to control for attraction to the 1994 candidates, even though that may reduce our estimate of spillover effects.

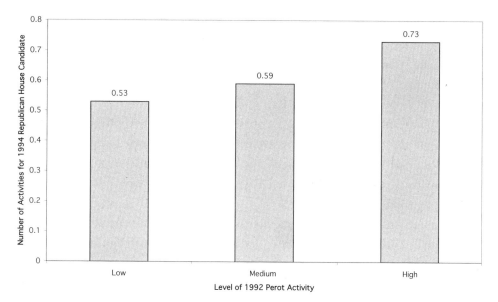

Fig. 9.2.   Spillover effect of 1992 Perot activity on 1994 Republican House activity, controlling for other factors

Figure 9.2 presents the impact of activism in the 1992 Perot campaign on activity level in 1994 Republican campaigns, independent of respondents' predispositions toward Republican campaign activism and evaluations of the House candidates.[3] The more active respondents were for Perot, the more engaged they subsequently became in 1994 Republican House campaigns, independent of the other factors that stimulated campaign involvement in 1994. There was a direct translation from Perot activity to Republican campaign involvement on the part of core members of the Perot constituency. Indeed, the more "core" (i.e., active in 1992) activists were, the more likely they were to transfer their participation to Republican campaigns in 1994, above what would be expected from their previous Republican activism and their predispositions toward the Republican Party. Those most active for Perot in 1992 were about half again as involved for Republicans in 1994 as those low in 1992 Perot activity, despite the fact that Perot ran against the established po-

---

3.   We divided the sample into three equal groups by their mean level of activity for Perot in 1992: for the bottom third, the mean was 0.38 activities; for the middle third, 2.1 activities; and for the top third, 5.36 activities. We assume that respondents are at the average for the sample on all control variables, including 1988 and 1992 Republican activity.

litical parties in 1992 and despite the fact that negative attitudes toward the parties helped explain participation for Perot in the first place. The spillover effect from Perot to Republican activism supports our understanding of the dynamics that produced the surge in Republican electoral support and the 1994 Republican victory, because it ties the shift by individual activists to the Republican Party directly to their involvement in the Perot movement. Moreover, it is consistent with other work that places activists at the center of explanations of party and electoral change (Carmines and Stimson 1989; Miller and Schofield 2003; Pastor, Stone, and Rapoport 1999).

Our theory asserts that a credible bid from the major party to the third party's constituency is necessary for mobilization by a major party. The Republicans made such a bid, and one explanation for spillover is that the Perot activists who were more involved in the Perot campaign were more aware of and susceptible to the Republican bid. Because concern with the core issues of Perot's campaign stimulated Perot activism in 1992, it stands to reason that a Republican bid concentrating on these issues would be especially effective among the most active Perot supporters. If this is true, then in the absence of contact by Republicans, the effect of 1992 activism for Perot would have little or no impact on 1994 Republican activism, whereas those who were most aggressively contacted by the Republicans in 1994 should show the strongest spillover to Republican involvement.

Figure 9.3 addresses the conditional nature of the spillover phenomenon by showing that spillover was dependent on the amount and type of contact by Republican House campaigns. We should expect to find that among those not contacted, there was no increase in 1994 Republican activity corresponding to greater 1992 Perot activism, while among those with the greatest contact from Republican campaigns, the effect of Perot activity on Republican activism was strongest. Among Perot activists who were not contacted by the Republican campaign in their district, there was no spillover effect.[4] Among those who were contacted by mail only, the positive spillover effect emerges cleanly; among those con-

---

4. The apparently negative relationship is not statistically significant, so it is safer to conclude that there is no relationship. However, a negative relationship in the absence of a bid might be expected, since those more active in Perot's campaign were more committed to his cause and thus may have had greater difficulty migrating to a major-party campaign.

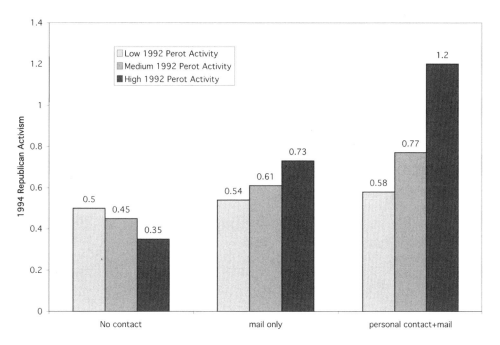

Fig. 9.3. Spillover effect of 1992 Perot activism on activity in 1994 Republican House campaigns by contact from Republican campaign, controlling for other factors

tacted both personally and by mail, the spillover effect was stronger still.[5] Thus, contact by Republican House campaigns produced the spillover effect we observed, consistent with our expectation that spillover was conditioned on an aggressive bid for the Perot constituency's support.

The presence of spillover effects conditioned on contact by the Republican Party cements the connection between the Republican victory in 1994 and the Perot movement. In previous chapters, we showed that districts where Perot ran strongest were most likely to flip to the Republican side and that these same districts were ones where experienced Republican candidates emerged to appeal to the Perot constituency in that year. In this chapter, we see that contact from Republican campaigns paid off by stimulating those who were most involved in the 1992 Perot

5. Almost all respondents who reported being contacted personally by their representative's or a candidate's staff also remembered receiving mail. In constructing the contact measure, we assumed that all who were contacted in person by staff were also contacted by mail.

campaign to move into the Republican camp. It is likely that the same sorts of processes were at work in the electorate as a whole. Moreover, the movement of the most active elements of the Perot constituency to Republican campaigns surely brought many ordinary citizens with them, as activists' convictions and behavior permeated their social, work, and political networks. The evidence, in other words, provides confirmation of individual change consistent with the shift to the Republican Party after the 1992 election.

Spillover Effects in House Campaigns after 1994

The electoral data indicate a relatively steady state of affairs after the sharp movement to the Republican Party in 1994. What does this imply for our expectations about the spillover hypothesis in the elections of 1996–2000? While we do not necessarily expect additional mobilization into Republican House campaigns after the 1994 elections, we do anticipate that the spillover tied to 1994 had staying power beyond that particular election. In other words, we expect that activism by former Perot supporters continued through the remaining elections of the decade, sustaining the gains the Republican Party made in 1994. The Perot constituency, in short, was pivotal in producing the Republicans' victory in 1994 and in their continued electoral success through the 2000 elections.

Figure 9.4 reports the spillover results from 1994 for purposes of comparison with results for each successive election.[6] A remarkable consistency in spillover to Republican House campaigns is evident, with continuing strong effects four, six, and eight years after the initial Perot campaign in 1992. Our analyses (see appendix B for the results) also show strong continuing effects of 1992 predispositions toward Republican activism, including party identification and previous Republican campaign involvement. But the effect of the Perot campaign is apparent even with these factors taken into account.

The spillover from 1992 Perot activism to Republican campaign participation in elections from 1994 through 2000 may result from the lingering impact of the mobilization the Republicans effected in 1994. In-

---

6. Once again we control for past activity (1988 and 1992), partisanship, and relative evaluation of the major party-candidates.

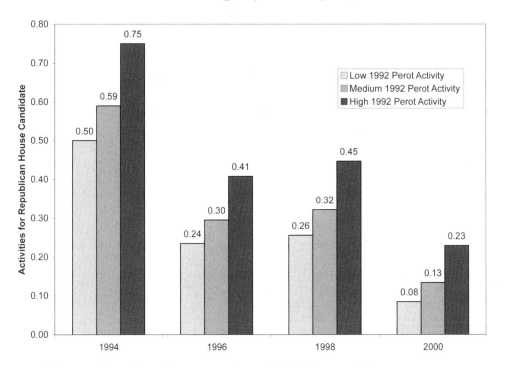

Fig. 9.4.   Republican House campaign activity by Perot activism, 1994–2000

deed, we strongly suspect that most of the continued activity by former Perot activists in Republican campaigns resulted from the bid and mobilization that occurred between the 1992 and 1994 elections. Nonetheless, it is worth asking whether there is "value added" beyond 1994, in the form of a spillover effect on post–1994 Republican House campaign involvement.

We anticipate the possibility of additional spillover for two reasons. First, Perot ran a second time, in 1996, under the banner of his newly created Reform Party. This may have given his activists a reason not to migrate to the Republican Party in 1996, although we have seen that they did not return in large numbers to support his cause that year. Thus, it was not until after 1996 that Perot was truly off the scene, and with his departure, the Reform Party all but disappeared in 2000. A second and related reason for an additional mobilization effect is that the Republican Party may have continued its bid for the Perot constituency's support, especially with Perot gone. We have already suggested that the GOP nomination bids of Buchanan in 1996 and McCain in 2000 targeted Perot supporters, and it is easy to imagine that Republican House candidates in 1998 and 2000 were alert to the possibilities created by large numbers of former Perot voters in their districts. Although there is no evidence of an orchestrated strategy at the national level to contact Perot supporters after 1994,[7] their shift to the Republican Party made contact by Republicans more likely.

Figure 9.5 shows the results of our test for "value-added" spillover from 1992 activism for Perot to the 2000 Republican House campaigns. The results are from a statistical model that controls for partisanship and the history of Republican activism in 1992 and before, plus the level of activism in 1994 Republican House campaigns. Thus, the effects of the initial mobilization into Republican House campaigns in 1994 is taken into account, and any further impact of 1992 Perot activism is "value added."

The results in figure 9.5 demonstrate an impact of Perot activism eight years after he first ran in 1992. The continuity effects from 1994 are not shown in the figure, but they are strong and highly significant. Thus, as we would expect, once individuals were mobilized by the Republicans in 1994, they had a tendency to remain engaged. However, taking into account the continuing effects of their 1994 Republican activism, additional spillover occurred, animated once again by contact from Republican House campaigns. In the absence of contact from a 2000 Republican House campaign, there is no additional impact of Perot activism. However, among those who received mail from Republican House candidates in 2000, Perot activity translates into significantly higher Republican activity, and among those contacted in person from a Republican House campaign and its supporters, the effect of Perot activity is substantially stronger. Even eight years after the Perot movement appeared, additional Republican mobilization occurred beyond the engagement stimulated by the pivotal Republican campaign in 1994. As with the original mobilization, it was tied directly to participation in the

---

7. Authors' interviews with Bill Paxon, October 29, 2003, and Dave Sackett, July 31, 2003.

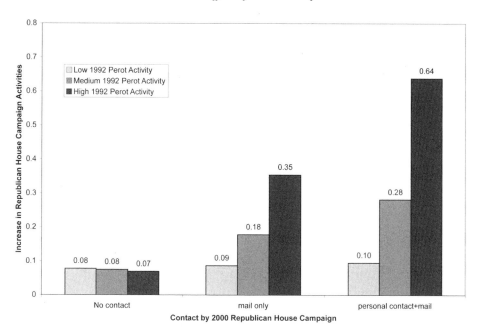

Fig. 9.5. "Value-added" spillover from 1992 Perot activism to 2000 Republican House campaign activism, by contact from 2000 Republican campaigns, controlling for other factors

Perot movement in the first place, firmly linking Republican fortunes to Perot's campaign.[8]

Addendum on Spillover to Democratic House Campaigns

We do not expect to find spillover into Democratic House campaigns, because the Democrats did not make a serious or sustained bid for the Perot constituency beyond President Clinton's early efforts to balance the budget. In the absence of a bid, including direct contact by the major party's campaigns, spillover should not occur. Figure 9.6 reports the relationship between 1992 Perot activity and subsequent activism in Democratic House campaigns, controlling for the usual predispositions toward House campaign activism. Even the apparently positive effects in 1994 and 2000 do not approach statistical significance, which means that there is no indication of spillover from the Perot campaign to Democratic House campaigns after 1992.

---

8. No such effects are present on the Democratic side.

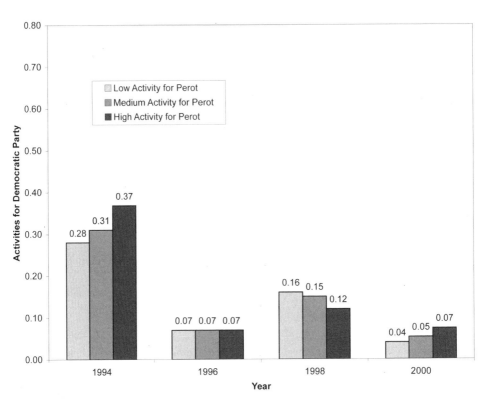

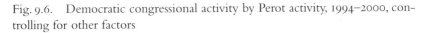

Fig. 9.6.   Democratic congressional activity by Perot activity, 1994–2000, controlling for other factors

Spillover in Presidential Nomination Campaigns

We have shown that the Republican Party's bid came from a coordinated effort by national party leaders (the Contract with America) as well as from individual decisions by experienced House candidates deciding whether to run. Political parties are amorphous organizations that provide opportunities for individuals to pursue their political careers, sometimes in coordinated ways, sometimes in ways that reflect individual interests that may compete with or undermine larger party purposes. The key is that Perot identified and mobilized a large constituency that could then be mobilized to deliver support to Republican candidates, both those in general elections and those competing for their party's nomination.

Two candidates ran against "establishment" Republicans in GOP presidential nomination races after 1992. As we pointed out in chapter 7, Pat Buchanan and John McCain overtly made appeals for support based

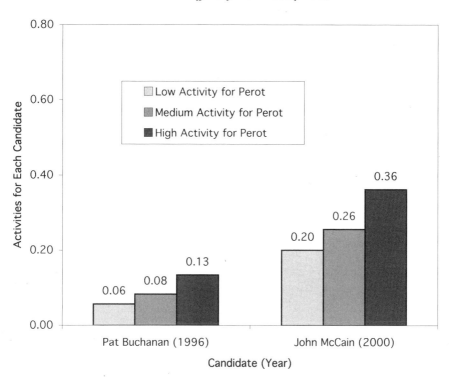

Fig. 9.7. Spillover from 1992 Perot activity to participation in Buchanan and McCain presidential nomination campaigns, controlling for other factors

on some of the same issues that Ross Perot used in 1992. In 1996, Pat Buchanan won the Republican primary in New Hampshire and gave Bob Dole anxious moments by stressing economic nationalism issues of the sort that Perot emphasized in 1992. In 2000, John McCain rode a reform agenda on his campaign bus—the "Straight Talk Express"—to win both New Hampshire and Michigan in a challenge to George W. Bush that echoed both the style and substance of Perot's 1992 campaign.

The question is whether we can tie the bids made by Buchanan and McCain to Perot activists' responses in the two nomination campaigns. Figure 9.7 shows that indeed there was spillover from activism in Perot's 1992 campaign to the nomination challenges of both Buchanan in 1996 and McCain in 2000.[9] The effect of 1992 Perot activity was more than

9. We do not have measures of contact by the nomination campaigns. The statistical models include controls for previous Republican activism, party identification, and affect toward Buchanan and McCain.

twice as strong on participation for McCain as for Buchanan, even though the time lag for McCain's nomination bid was four years further removed from the first Perot campaign. Even those not active for Perot participated more for McCain in 2000 than the most active Perot supporters had for Buchanan in 1996. This result is not too surprising, given that part of Buchanan's conservative agenda conflicted sharply with most Perot supporters' positions on social issues, such as abortion.[10] In contrast, McCain's campaign was built on a reform agenda, and his maverick, straight-talk image comported with the style and substance of Perot's 1992 campaign. Even so, Buchanan's emphasis on economic nationalism issues bore fruit in attracting modest spillover among former Perot activists. However, Mc-Cain's ability to invigorate the Perot constituency was one of the secrets of his success in 2000 and may have helped draw former Perot activists further into the Republican fold after his nomination bid fell short.

CONCLUSION

Our task in this chapter has been to demonstrate a link among individual supporters between the 1992 Perot campaign and subsequent Republican campaigns. Spillover effects provide that link by demonstrating that those engaged in the Perot campaign were most likely to shift their energies in response to Republican mobilization efforts. Such a shift would scarcely be expected if one examined only the rhetoric of Perot's third-party campaign. As is typical of an insurgent challenge, both major parties came under vitriolic attack by Ross Perot. An attack is necessary to mobilize new supporters and to retain potential backers, who may be tempted, during the campaign, by major-party appeals and the strategic imperatives of the two-party system. Despite the fact that the most active third-party backers were convinced by the attacks on the major parties, those most active for Perot were also most susceptible to appeals by the Republican Party after 1992.

In addition to supporting the dynamic of third parties, our results confirm the importance of third parties in American electoral politics.

---

10. Buchanan's social conservatism may help explain his dismal showing as the Reform nominee in 2000.

Some scholars contend that third parties do not have an independent effect on major-party change, that the two parties would respond to the discontent the third party taps into even without the third party (Beck 1997). The spillover results in this chapter help support our view that third-party movements have an independent impact on subsequent major-party behavior. While it is possible that the individuals who would have been most active for Perot in 1992 if he had not run still would have been most sensitive to Republican Party overtures, it seems more likely that they would have been less visible to the GOP and less susceptible to any appeals the Republicans might have mounted for their support. Spillover effects suggest that the dynamic of third parties works first because of the mobilization efforts of the third party. Indeed, the effects we observe depend on both the mobilization of the third party and major party bids for their support.

Thus, despite their alienation, Perot supporters did not disengage from "politics as usual" after their participation in his 1992 campaign. Their shift to the Republican Party was responsible for that party's historic successes in 1994, just two years after Perot's first campaign. Moreover, their shift to the Republicans persisted through the remainder of the decade; it was not limited to congressional races but also touched presidential politics in 1996 and especially in 2000. The impact of the Perot movement was dramatic, broadly felt in the two-party system, and of lasting duration.

X

The Impact of Perot on the Republican Party's Issue Positions

✍

So far, we have linked major-party change to the Perot movement by showing that Republican electoral fortunes improved because of the party's successful bid for the Perot constituency. However, there is more to party change than increased vote share and winning elections. The dynamic of third parties implies change in the composition of the bidding party's supporting coalition. By attracting former third-party supporters, the bidding party changes its own coalitional makeup and the policies supported by its adherents. The reason is simple. Third-party supporters back their insurgent candidate partly for issue reasons. The bidding major party appeals to them based on these issues, and those who migrate to the major party do so because of the same issue positions that motivated their original support for the third party. If the major party's bid is successful, as we have seen the Republicans' was, the party includes in its ranks new adherents who advocate the third party's positions, back candidates who reflect these issue preferences and priorities, and oppose candidates who disagree with them. In a nutshell, party change means winning votes *and* shifting policy commitments. In fact, it means winning votes *by* shifting policy commitments. Without both dimensions of party change, the dynamic of third parties would be incomplete.

Assessing change in the issue preferences of a major party is not as straightforward a task as it may seem. In fact, the concept of "issue preference of a major party" is itself murky. A national political party is an amorphous collection of officeholders, candidates and potential candidates, activists, and voters. Thus, it is important to assess the impact of Perot party change in several arenas of the Republican Party. We turn first to our activist surveys and then to data on the makeup of the Republican Party in Congress. Our analysis of the activist data enables us to understand the potential for a significant impact of the movement of Perot activists into the Republican Party, especially by comparing core Republican activists with those who were mobilized into Republican campaigns after 1992. Likewise, focusing on House members who were newly elected in 1994 and who owed their seats to Perot voters gives us a parallel look at the impact of Perot on the party in Congress.[1]

In assessing the impact of the Perot movement on the Republican Party, it is important to keep in mind what our argument is and what we are not arguing—especially in light of developments in the party since 1992. We do not suggest that the Republican Party as a whole will inevitably continue to move in the direction of Perot's supporters. Rather, our argument is that the party was closer to Perot's position than it would have been without the post-1992 influx of Perot supporters.

American political parties are not static organizations. Groups and factions within the parties continually vie for influence. Perot supporters were not the only newcomers to the Republican Party after 1992, nor were they the only ones who had a significant influence on the party. It is possible, for example, that the increased size and influence of the Christian Right in the Republican Party since 1994 surpassed the impact of the Perot movement, in which case the party's overall shift to the right might disguise or swamp the Perot effect in the aggregate. Nonetheless, the Perot movement would still have an impact if it altered this shift relative to the magnitude and direction it would have taken without the influx of Perot supporters after 1992.

---

1. Examples of analyses of change in the activist ranks of the parties are provided by Miller and Jennings (1986) and Rapoport and Stone (1994). Both studies use panel data of defined activist populations that allowed them to identify the proportions of newcomers. Miller and Jennings studied national convention delegates, and Rapoport and Stone studied caucus attendees in Iowa. Studies of change in Congress include Asher and Weisberg 1978 and Grenzke 1989.

THE POTENTIAL FOR CHANGE AMONG REPUBLICAN ACTIVISTS

The spillover process we described in chapter 9 had the potential to change the Republican Party if Republican activists newly mobilized from the Perot campaign differed from core Republican activists and if they were sufficiently numerous to alter the center of gravity in the Republican Party. Our approach in the present analysis is to compare former Perot activists mobilized into Republican campaigns since 1992 with contributors to the Republican National Committee, who represent core Republican activists. We compare both groups in the 2000 wave of our study, because by 2000, Perot was completely off the scene, and former Perot activists had the opportunity to be mobilized into a Republican campaign. Newly mobilized Republicans are those who were active in Perot's 1992 campaign, who had not been active for a Republican campaign in the 1988 election, and who subsequently became active in at least one Republican campaign between 1994 and 2000.[2] These individuals fit the profile of those who produced the spillover effects we analyzed in the previous chapter. These newly mobilized Republicans are former Perot activists who could alter the issue preferences of the Republican activist base, in part because there were a significant number of them—they constituted about 20 percent of our panel of potential Perot activists.

Figure 10.1, which is concerned with the 2000 election, compares former Perot and core Republican activists' preferences on the individual issues that had been at the center of the 1992 Perot movement. The figure also includes a measure that combines all Perot issues into a single index, as well as a measure of opinion on liberal-conservative issues.[3] With the

---

2. We exclude from our definition of newly mobilized Republicans anyone who was active in a Democratic campaign between 1994 and 2000.

3. The reform measure includes public financing of congressional elections, banning soft-money contributions to the political parties, and term limits; economic nationalism includes limiting U.S. involvement overseas, limiting immigration, and limiting foreign imports; the budget measure is represented by a single item on using the federal surplus to reduce debt; the liberal-conservative measure includes affirmative action, abortion, protecting the environment by regulating pollution, gun control, taxpayer-funded vouchers to pay for private schooling, and a government-sponsored national health insurance plan.

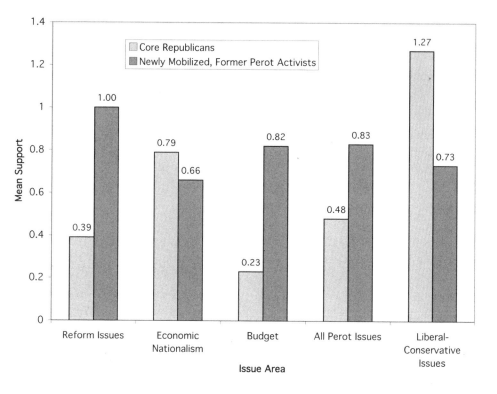

Fig. 10.1. Newly mobilized and core Republicans' preferences on Perot and liberal-conservative issues, 2000

exception of the economic nationalism issues, newly mobilized Republican activists from the Perot movement were significantly more supportive of the Perot agenda than were core Republican activists. Likewise, on traditional liberal-conservative issues, former Perot activists who had moved into the GOP were significantly more moderate in their positions than were core Republican activists.

Our tentative conclusion based on issue preferences, then, is that as former Perot activists moved into the Republican Party, they carried with them the potential to shift the GOP toward a more pro-reform stance and to moderate its positions on issues that sharply divide Republicans from Democrats. The differences that created this potential were detectable eight years after the initial Perot campaign. Figure 10.2 shows the priority former Perot and core Republican activists gave to the issues,

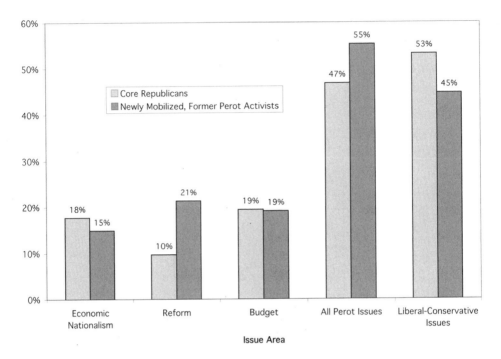

Fig. 10.2.   Percentage of newly mobilized and core Republican activists' most important issues, 2000

demonstrating again that former Perot activists differed from core Republicans, principally because of the priority they gave to reform issues. There was a corresponding tendency for core Republicans to give higher priority to traditional liberal-conservative issues.

In sum, the spillover of Perot activists into the Republican Party did more than merely enhance Republican electoral prospects. It also carried the potential for significant change in the overall issue preferences and priorities of the Republican Party. The influx of Perot supporters in response to the Republican bid for their support brought into the party activists who by and large were more committed than core Republican activists to the issues that motivated Perot's campaigns. These voters and activists provided opportunity for such presidential nomination candidates as Buchanan in 1996 and McCain in 2000 and increased the electoral prospects of House candidates prepared to appeal to the Perot constituency after 1992.

THE IMPACT OF PEROT IN CONGRESS

If the Perot movement had an impact on the issue positions of the Republican Party, that impact ought to be evident in the U.S. House of Representatives. We have seen a dramatic electoral impact in the House, with substantial numbers of districts that voted heavily for Perot in 1992 flipping from the Democratic Party to the Republican Party in the 1994 elections. We also found that experienced Republican challengers emerged to run for the House in districts where Perot had done well. Indeed, our simulation in chapter 8 shows that had Perot not run in 1992, Republicans would have picked up only fourteen seats, and the Democrats would have maintained their majority in the House. By this analysis, we can identify thirty-eight seats that were won by the Republicans in 1994 because of the Perot movement and the Republican Party's response to it. Following this logic, it is reasonable to expect these thirty-eight newly elected Republican representatives to be especially sensitive to the Perot agenda, because they were elected in districts where the Perot vote made the difference for them and because they probably targeted the pivotal Perot constituency in their campaigns.

Looking at members of Congress gives us a more complete way of assessing the impact of the Perot movement on the Republican Party than was possible from our comparison of former Perot volunteers with core Republican activists. While we know that about one-fifth of former Perot activists were mobilized into the Republican Party for the first time after the 1992 election, there is no bounded population of Republican activists that would allow us to determine the aggregate impact of the influx of former Perot activists into the party. As a result, we do not know what proportion of all Republican activists after 1994 were mobilized into the party by the Perot movement.

In the House of Representatives, in contrast, we can assess the aggregate impact of the Perot movement by comparing "Perot Republicans" with "core Republicans." Perot Republicans are those newly elected in 1994 who, according to our simulation, would not have won election without the Perot voters. Core Republican House members include those who had been in Congress since before the 1994 election and those who were first elected in 1994 but, by our simulation, would have been elected whether or not Perot had run. We know that the thirty-eight members elected because of Perot constituted almost 9 percent of the total House membership in 1994 and that they made up 16.5 percent of the Republican membership. Therefore, in addition to assessing how different they were from core Republican House members in the policies they supported in the House, by knowing their proportion among all Republican House members, we can estimate the impact of Perot movement on the Republican Party's issue positions in the House.

We do not have survey data from members of Congress, so in order to measure the issue impact of the Perot movement, we utilize roll-call votes taken on issues related to the Perot agenda. The issues include reform questions (e.g., term limits for members of Congress and campaign finance reform), the federal budget, U.S. intervention in Bosnia, and support for the United Nations.[4] To collect a number of roll-call votes on a range of Perot issues, we pooled votes from the 104th through the 106th Congresses (1995–2000).

Our approach entails a significant limitation because we restrict ourselves to districts that remained in Republican hands after the 1994 elections. However, as table 10.1 shows, districts held by Perot Republicans after the 1994 elections were about four times more likely to change back to the Democrats than were districts held by core Republicans after 1994. Despite the stable aggregate partisan division in Congress that prevailed with the Republican majority after 1994, there was significant change among individual districts, with a shade under 10 percent of core Republican districts and just over 10 percent of Democratic districts changing partisan hands. Meanwhile, however, more than three times the proportion of districts held by Perot Republicans switched back to the Democrats in 1996 or 1998.

We will return to the question of why districts held by Perot Republicans after 1994 experienced relatively high turnover after we consider the issue impact of the Perot Republicans on the Republican Party in the House.[5] Table 10.2 compares Perot Republicans, core Republicans, and Democrats over the three congresses in question. On all three mea-

---

4. Details on the roll-call votes are provided in appendix A.

5. We exclude from the analysis districts in which there was partisan turnover at any point after 1994, since we use roll-call votes from three congresses.

TABLE 10.1.   **Party Turnover among Districts won by Perot Republicans, Core Republicans, and Democrats in the 1994 Election (in percentages)**

	Perot Republicans	Core Republicans	Democrats
District remained in same party, 1996–2000	63.2	91.1	88.2
District changed party hands after the 1996 or 1998 election	36.8	8.9	11.8
Total	100	100	100
Number of districts	38	192	204

Note: Vermont, represented by an independent representative, was omitted from analysis.

TABLE 10.2.   **Roll-Call Issue Positions of Perot Republicans, Core Republicans, and Democrats, 1994–2000**

	Perot Republicans	Core Republicans	Democrats
Reform issues[a]	0.62	0.44	0.14
Foreign involvement issues[a]	0.66	0.50	0.05
All Perot issues[a]	0.63	0.47	0.11
Liberal-conservative issues[b]	0.44	0.36	−0.30
Smallest N of representatives	(23)	(169)	(178)

[a]Mean proportion of roll-call votes supporting Perot position.
[b]Mean D-Nominate score, 104th Congress, first dimension (Poole and Rosenthal 1997, 2001).

sures of support of Perot's issue positions, Perot Republicans supported the Perot position significantly more than did core Republicans.[6] On reform votes (concerning term limits and campaign finance reform), Perot Republicans supported the reform position 62 percent of the time, compared with core Republicans, who supported the Perot position only 44 percent of the time. Perot Republicans were also significantly more likely to oppose foreign involvement than were core Republicans, and on our index of all Perot issues, they voted an average of 63 percent of the time in favor of the Perot position, whereas core Republicans supported Perot's positions less than half of the time.[7]

6. The reform and overall Perot issue index comparisons are highly significant ($p <$ .001); the foreign involvement comparison also meets the standard level of significance ($p < .05$).

7. The differences between Perot and core Republicans persists even when we control for whether the district was in the South, whether the district was marginal, the liberal-conservative position of the representative, and the size of the Perot and Bush vote shares in the 1992 presidential election.

It appears that Republicans who owed their election in 1994 to former Perot supporters had the potential to produce change in the Republican Party on the issues of greatest importance to the Perot movement. Note, however, that on the traditional liberal-conservative issues, Perot Republicans were slightly more conservative in their roll-call voting than were core Republicans.[8] In contrast to activist Perot Republicans, therefore, Perot Republicans in the House were not more moderate than core House Republicans. However, recall that liberal-conservative issues were of lower salience for activist Perot Republicans than they were for core Republicans (see fig. 10.2). It is possible that the Perot constituency and the Republican House members they helped elect shared only a weak connection on liberal-conservative issues. We return to this point later in this chapter.

AGGREGATE ISSUE IMPACT
IN CONGRESS

Figure 10.3a shows the aggregate impact of the Perot movement by comparing core and Perot Republicans on support for Perot's agenda. The placement of the core Republicans (from table 10.2) represents what the Republican Party's position would have been without the election of Perot Republicans; that is, since core Republicans are GOP representatives who either were already in office before the 1994 elections or were identified by the simulation as winners in 1994 without Perot's help, core Republicans represent where the party would have been without Perot's intervention. The line representing the "Republican Party after 1994" is the Republican average attained by combining core and Perot Republicans' positions. Perot Republicans constituted 16.5 percent of the Republican House membership immediately after the 1994 elections. As a result, their preferences, while significantly different from the core Republicans' position, do not dominate.

Figure 10.3a shows that the Perot Republicans made the preferences of the Republican Party as a whole about 2 percent more supportive of

---

8. The difference is not statistically significant ($p = .266$).

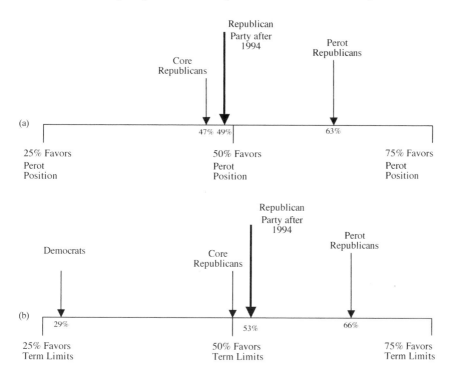

Fig. 10.3. Impact of the Perot movement on issue position of Republican Party on all Perot issues, 104th through 106th Congress (a) and term limits, 104th Congress only (b).

the Perot agenda than it would have been otherwise.[9] Figure 10.3b shows the impact of the Perot Republicans in the 104th Congress only, limiting the roll-call votes in the sample to those related to term limits. Looking only at the 104th Congress gives us the maximum impact of the Perot Republicans on the position of the party, because that is the Congress immediately after the 1994 elections, before Republican representatives were subject to reelection challenges that reduced their numbers in the next two elections. Here, the Perot Republicans shifted the GOP in the House about 3 percent toward favoring term limits.

---

9. The overall preference of the party reflects the preferences of the two factions discounted by their proportion of the total: $(.121 \times 63) + (.879 \times 47) = 49$. When roll calls from the three congresses are pooled, the proportion of Perot Republicans in the Republican Party drops to 12.1 percent, which is the proportion we use in this calculation. We address the implications of this drop in figure 10.3b.

As much as these results indicate a difference between Perot and core Republicans, what are we to make of the overall impact of the Perot movement on the issue preferences of the Republican Party? Is a 2 percent difference on all Perot issues or a 3 percent difference on term limits really noteworthy? We see the impact of Perot as important for several reasons. In the first place, a 2 or 3 percent shift on an issue may be enough to make a difference in the overall action of the House, especially in a closely divided Congress. On the Perot issues, the Republican Party itself was closely divided.[10] In addition, a narrowly divided party that shifts its majority position to favor that issue has agenda-setting consequences for the institution as a whole if it is the majority party. Thus, not only did the Republican Party change its position to become more favorable to term limits and the other Perot issues, but the addition of thirty-eight Republicans who owed their election to the Perot movement catapulted the GOP to majority control.

The fact that the Perot movement produced a shift in partisan control gave Republicans almost total control over the House rules. It is reasonable to suppose that had the Democrats maintained control of Congress after 1994, term limits (not to mention impeachment and many other initiatives) would not have been put on the agenda for a vote at all.[11] Although limits on congressional terms did not pass, forcing members to declare their positions publicly was an important success for the movement.

We have already shown that the Contract with America was a major part of this bid and that it bound the entire party, not merely those

---

10. Our analysis of the term limits issue in the 104th Congress includes House Joint Resolution 73, which proposed a constitutional amendment limiting the number of terms members of the House and Senate could serve. This was supported by 80 percent of core Republicans and 92 percent of Perot Republicans but failed to reach the two-thirds vote necessary for a constitutional amendment, because it was supported by only 19 percent of Democrats. The second roll-call vote on term limits involved the Peterson Amendment to HJR 73. This amendment, which proposed making term limits retroactive in order to take into account the prior service of members of Congress, failed to receive a majority vote from either party; it was supported by 43 percent of Perot Republicans but by only 20 percent of core Republicans.

11. In fact, the Democrats had kept reform of term limits off the agenda of the 103rd Congress. See Holly Idelson, "Republican Agenda: Despite Popular Appeal, Term Limits Are No Shoo-In," *Congressional Quarterly Weekly Report,* November 19, 1994, 3346.

elected in districts where Perot supporters were pivotal to the Republicans' success. This illustrates the cautious nature of our analysis of Perot's effect. Core Republicans, no less than Perot Republicans, signed the Contract with America and shared in the benefits of majority status rooted in the success of the Perot movement. Thus, the analysis in figure 10.3 arrives at a conservative estimate of the impact of Perot on Republican preferences in the House, because it ignores effects not tied directly to district election outcomes.

As noted, moving a party from minority to majority status in the House allows it to set the rules and agenda for the entire body. As one directly relevant example, the strong commitment of Perot Republicans to term limits produced significant reform within the House in the form of term limits for committee chairs and the House Speaker. Without the need to attract Perot voters and the success of these voters in electing Perot Republicans, such reforms would have been unlikely even if the Republicans had managed to take over the House by other means.

Despite the limited nature of our analysis of the Republican Party's issue preferences in the House, we do find an effect, albeit one that amounts to only a 2 or 3 percent increase in support on the Perot issues. Within the logic of the present analysis, the magnitude of the impact might have been made larger only by increasing the size of the class of Perot Republicans from the 16.5 percent they made up of the party as a whole after 1994 or by increasing the difference between Perot and core Republicans on the issues—or by increasing both factors. However, historical perspective suggests that on both the size of the Perot cohort and the difference between the two factions in the Republican Party, the impact was substantial. The thirty-eight new Republican House members who owed their election to Perot's 1992 campaign considerably exceeds the average loss experienced by the president's party in midterm elections since 1946 (twenty-six seats). Thus, although it is theoretically possible for a third party to produce an even larger swing in favor of a party that successfully bids for its supporters, the swing enjoyed by the Republicans in the 1994 elections was, by any standard, large.

Another way to assess the gap between Perot and core Republicans is to compare its magnitude with the difference between core Republicans and Democrats. In fact, in the 104th Congress, the difference between

Perot and core Republicans on the issue of term limits was fully 76 percent of the difference between core Republicans and the Democratic Party. On Perot issues generally, the difference between Perot and core Republicans from the 104th through the 106th Congresses was 44 percent of the gap between the Democrats and core Republicans. In light of the major-party differences, then, the class of Perot Republicans was truly distinct from their partisan colleagues. Therefore, while the overall impact was only a 2 or 3 percent shift, the components that produced the net effect on the Republican Party were substantial. Once we add to these effects the change to majority status by the Republicans, the case for a lasting and substantial impact of the Perot movement on the American two-party system is compelling.

PARTY LOSSES AMONG PEROT REPUBLICANS

Why were seats held by Perot Republicans so much more likely to flip back to the Democratic Party in 1996 or 1998 than were districts represented by core Republicans? We might conclude that these seats returned to Democratic hands because the Democrats held them before 1994. However, not only were formerly Democratic districts that were won by core Republicans in 1994 less likely to flip back to the Democrats, but their turnover after 1994 was actually about half the rate of the turnover by their fellow core Republicans elected before 1994. Among the seats won in 1994 by newly elected core Republicans, only one of eighteen (5.6 percent) flipped back to the Democrats, compared with 9.2 percent for core Republicans who held their seats before 1994 and 36.8 percent for Perot Republicans. What was it about Perot Republicans after 1994 that made them unusually vulnerable to party change?

If Perot issues and Perot supporters were the key to the Republican takeover of these districts, we should find that these newly elected members were held accountable on these issues. If, for example, newly elected members did not support term limits, they should have lost the votes of Perot supporters, with the consequent risk of losing their House seat. To test this idea, we constructed a statistical model to explain which districts

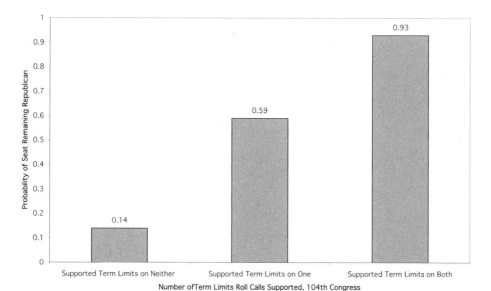

Fig. 10.4.   Probability of 1994 Perot Republican seats remaining Republican by term-limits support, 1996–2000

held by Perot Republicans after 1994 reverted to Democratic control in either 1996 or 1998. We surmised that districts with larger numbers of Democratic voters would be more likely to return to Democratic hands, as would districts that Republicans won by relatively narrow margins. Controlling for these factors, however, we also wanted to see if votes on term limits would have an effect beyond these background factors. As figure 10.4 demonstrates, the strength of Perot Republicans' support for term limits in the 104th Congress was indeed strongly related to holding the seat. Representatives who most strongly supported term limits were most likely to hold the seats they won from the Democrats in 1994, while newly elected Republican representatives who were less supportive of term limits were significantly more vulnerable. Controlling for all other factors, Perot Republicans who voted against term limits had only a 15 percent chance of holding their seats, while those consistently supporting term limits were virtually certain to win reelection. Apparently, a big reason that Perot Republicans lost their seats at higher than average rates was because some of them were insufficiently committed to the Perot agenda to satisfy their constituents.

We expected that Perot Republicans who were more extreme in their voting on traditional liberal-conservative roll calls would also be less likely to hold their seat, because Perot supporters in their districts would tend to be more moderate on these issues and because these districts had been in the hands of Democratic representatives before 1994. However, we found that the more conservative Perot Republicans were on these issues, the *more* likely they were to hold their seats. This finding is not quite as statistically secure as the effect based on the issue of term limits,[12] but it is strong enough to be suggestive.

Any conclusions reconciling these results are necessarily speculative, but the results do suggest that Perot Republicans faced conflicting constituency pressures, at least from the perspective of Perot supporters in these districts. We know that Perot activists who migrated into the Republican Party were more moderate on liberal-conservative issues than were core Republican activists, yet House Perot Republicans whose votes were relatively centrist risked electoral defeat almost as certainly as those whose support for term limits was insufficiently strong. The effects of roll-call votes concerning term limits and of votes concerning liberal-conservative issues are independent of the other variables in the model, which suggests that significant numbers of Perot Republicans in the House faced powerful conflicting pressures from their home districts. Many of these districts had been held by Democrats for the simple reason that they had large numbers of Democratic voters in them.[13] Thus, Perot Republicans had three groups in their districts: Democrats, former Perot supporters, and core Republican voters. Balancing among these was difficult, but since the Perot issues were most salient to former Perot supporters and since liberal-conservative issues were most important to core Republicans, balancing between these two groups may have been manageable by simultaneously supporting Perot issues and adopting relatively conservative positions on traditional left-right issues. Newly elected members of Congress who were unable to satisfy

---

12. The effect of votes concerning term limits on the chances of defeat is significant at the .05 level ($p = .03$), whereas there is only a marginal significant effect of votes concerning liberalism (i.e., D-Nominate scores) in the 104th Congress ($p < .07$).

13. The average Democratic vote for the House in 1992 among districts held by Perot Republicans after 1994 was 56.4 percent.

both groups on the issues of greatest saliency to each were vulnerable to electoral defeat.

CONCLUSION

A full assessment of the impact of the Perot movement on the Republican Party must combine its influence on the electoral fortunes of the party with the change it produced within the ranks of the GOP. We have presented extensive evidence in this book to support our claim that the 1992 Perot movement provided the Republican Party with a golden opportunity to enhance its electoral fortunes. Republican leaders and candidates recognized this opportunity and took full advantage, especially in the 1994 elections and in John McCain's 2000 nomination campaign. In the 1994 elections, of course, Republicans won control of the House of Representatives because of their ability to attract Perot supporters and activists. John McCain did not win the GOP nomination in 2000, but he did mount a campaign calculated to appeal to former Perot backers, a calculation that our data show was realized.

In this chapter, we have seen that the activists Perot mobilized into the Republican Party were different from core Republican activists and that on the key issues behind the Perot movement, these differences were also reflected in the roll-call voting of House members who owed their election in 1994 to former Perot supporters. These representatives produced the historic Republican majority in the House and shifted the position of their party on Perot issues. A shift of this sort can have momentous policy implications, as close students of the congressional policy process have shown (Brady and Volden 1998; Krehbiel 1998).

Although we have seen that the Perot Republicans had a significant impact on their new party, it would be a mistake to infer that former Perot supporters are locked into the GOP or that their continued support should be taken for granted. The fact that Perot Republicans elected to the House in 1994 but insufficiently devoted to the Perot agenda were vulnerable to defeat in subsequent elections is ample evidence that the Perot constituency remains committed to the issues that drove the movement in the first place. In this sense, the bid the Republicans made for their support may be the party's undoing if it is seen as going back on its commitments, especially on reform issues that continue to have traction in American politics. If the party moves away from the Perot agenda, Perot supporters could defect, which in turn would cause the party to shift even further from these issues and priorities.

The analysis in this chapter brings the discussion in this book full circle, to the importance of issues in how the dynamic of third parties plays out in the American two-party system. Issues are important in defining the coalitions of the two major parties, and they were important in defining Perot's insurgent electoral movement. Issue commitments and the resulting coalitions evolve over time in ways that can be quite dramatic, provoking major change in U.S. politics (Carmines and Stimson 1989; Miller and Schofield 2003). The part Perot supporters played in defining and redefining the issue coalitions of the major parties reshaped the political party landscape at the close of the twentieth century, with consequences that continued to play out in the first decade of the new millennium.

XI

Conclusion

THIRD PARTIES AND POLITICAL
CHANGE IN AMERICA

ॐ

THE AMERICAN POLITY, IMPLICITLY or explicitly, has chosen a two-party over a multiparty system. Apart from the wisdom of that choice, one consequence is that "successful" third parties in presidential politics are rare. Throughout the twentieth century, the number of third-party presidential candidates has been small—Theodore Roosevelt and Eugene Debs in 1912, Robert LaFollette in 1924, George Wallace in 1968, John Anderson in 1980, and H. Ross Perot in 1992 and 1996. Although such candidates are rare, they are hardly irrelevant, and their importance in the life and history of our politics means we must try to understand them. Comprehension, however, is made difficult by the fact that they are unusual. Regular patterns may be missed, and it is easy to mistake unique events and patterns for general ones. It may also be tempting to dismiss one or more of the third-party campaigns, as many observers have of Ross Perot's 1992 campaign, as idiosyncratic or irrelevant to the long-run shape of national politics.

Throughout this book, we have advanced the claim that independent and third-party electoral movements, such as Perot's, are fundamental to understanding subsequent change in the major-party system. Successful third parties emerge out of the two-party system principally because of some broadly recognized failure by the major parties to address an important public policy problem and/or because there is a substantial constituency dissatisfied with the policy positions and priorities of the major parties. Thus, a third-party movement is a creature of the two-party system that produces the conditions ripe for its emergence and electoral support, and its primary impact is typically on the two-party system after it dies.

The thesis that third parties matter, summarized as the dynamic of third parties, constitutes broad—even sweeping—claims about the importance of third-party movements to our politics. We have shown that the Perot movement and its aftermath fit this broad pattern: it was animated by issues and coherent policy concerns; the Republican Party bid for the constituency after the 1992 election appealed to that agenda; Perot voters and activists responded by moving into the Republican Party, beginning with the 1994 congressional elections, and were pivotal to the Republican resurgence. We also saw that Perot Republicans elected to the House of Representatives had a significant impact on the GOP in the House, not least by making the Republicans the majority party for the first time in four decades.

The "choice" Americans have made in favor of a two-party political system is knitted deeply into the institutional, legal, and cultural fabric of our politics (Bibby and Maisel 2003; Mazmanian 1974; Riker 1976, 1982). One of the major barriers to third-party formation, ballot-access restrictions, actually provided an opportunity for Perot to challenge his volunteers to rise to the grand purpose of getting his name on the ballot in all fifty states. But another impediment to third parties, the unit rule in the electoral college, left Perot with zero electoral votes after the election, despite his impressive popular-vote showing. The winner-take-all character of our institutions not only creates disincentives to potentially strong third-party candidates; it deters activists and voters from "wasting" their efforts on a hopeless cause in a system that recognizes only plurality winners. Again, whatever their merits, these institutional barriers to third parties reduce the instance of successful insurgent candidacies, such as Perot's, and make all the more remarkable and important those few that succeed in overcoming these impediments to attract significant support.

Later in this chapter, we will consider the place of third parties, such as Perot's, in contemporary U.S. politics. But first we will speculate about two questions that flow from our analysis of the Perot movement in 1992 and its aftermath: How real is the dynamic of third parties in explaining the impact of Perot and other similar movements in U.S. political history? And beyond the 2000 elections, what consequences for the U.S. two-party system are likely to follow from the continued presence of the Perot constituency?

REASSESSING THE DYNAMIC OF THIRD PARTIES

To our argument about how the Perot movement affected the two-party system, a skeptic might respond by asking how we can be sure the Republican resurgence would not have happened at the same time in pretty much the same way if Ross Perot's 1992 insurgent candidacy had never occurred. Skepticism about the impact of third parties was articulated by Paul Beck (1997, 49) in his textbook on American political parties.

> The evidence suggests . . . that the major parties grasp new programs and proposals in their "time of ripeness" when large numbers of Americans have done so and when such a course is therefore politically useful to the parties. In their earlier, maturing time, new issues need not depend on minor parties for their advocacy. Interest groups, the mass media, influential individuals, and factions within the major parties may perform the propagandizing role, often more effectively than a minor party.

Among other things, Beck argues that policy entrepreneurs exist throughout the political system and that if an issue's time is "ripe," someone will latch onto it to make political hay. Moreover, such political entrepreneurs exist within the two major parties as members of Congress, presidential nomination candidates, members of interest groups, and others who seek to advance their cause within the party. Indeed, it might even be fair to say that Ross Perot was one such policy entrepreneur, who might well have chosen to pursue his ambitions through one of the parties—perhaps by challenging President Bush for the Republican nomination—instead of running an independent campaign outside the parties.

Our position is to agree with Beck to a point, while admitting that we cannot absolutely defeat the skeptic's argument. We do not contend that third parties are the only or even necessarily the major way to effect change in the two-party system. We agree that the major parties are remarkably porous organizations, subject to influence from within by freelancing candidates and other entrepreneurs seeking to advance their own agenda and interests and from without by interest groups and others who see the parties as instruments to further their purposes. The major parties, in short, are both affected by and instigators of change, the mechanisms of which need not include a third-party or independent candidate's electoral movement.

If Perot had run as a Republican nomination candidate, he might have been even more effective as an agent of political change. Nomination candidates, even when they lose—it would have been virtually impossible for Ross Perot to wrest the Republican nomination from incumbent President Bush—mobilize activists and voters who may remain in the party by the same spillover mechanism we saw at work in the aftermath of 1992 (Pastor, Stone, and Rapoport 1999). Nonetheless, as a candidate for a major-party nomination, Perot would have been denied one of his bedrock strategies—attacking the two major parties. This could have undermined his effectiveness. He would have been unable to convert the barriers to third parties in the system into opportunities to mobilize and showcase his support. As a nomination candidate who lost, he would not have led in trial-heat polls in the early summer, nor would he have had standing to appear in the fall presidential debates or conduct his campaign of infomercials. Perot stood out and was effective because he was so different.

Our second response to Beck's claim that third parties do not have an independent effect on major-party change is to point to the conditions that seem necessary for the third-party dynamic to work: a large vote in the election in which the third party emerges, a reasonably well-defined issue constituency, and a bid targeting the supporters of the third-party movement. The spillover results we reported in chapter 9 suggest that without third-party mobilization, contact by the bidding major party would have no effect. We saw in figure 9.3 that in the absence of contact by the Republican Party in 1994, there was no spillover effect from

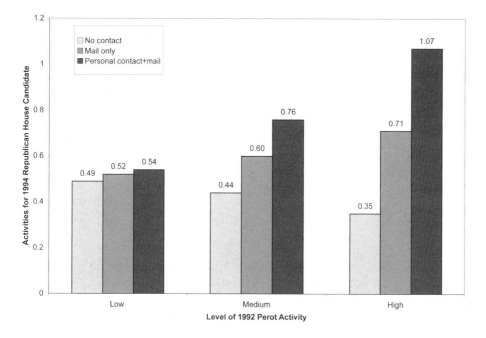

Fig. 11.1.   Effect of 1994 contact from Republican campaigns by level of 1992 Perot campaign activism

activism for Perot in 1992 to involvement in Republican House campaigns in 1994. As contact from the GOP increased, the strength of the spillover effect also increased. Figure 11.1 reorganizes those same spillover findings to show that as activism in the Perot movement increased, the mobilization effects of 1994 Republican contact had greater effect. In the absence of active participation for Perot in 1992, contact by the Republicans had only a weak (and statistically insignificant) effect; as activism for Perot increased, so did the efficacy of Republican contact. These results support our view that if there had been no Perot campaign in 1992, there would have been nothing to engage the energies of volunteers, stimulate their commitment to the cause, and sensitize them to the stakes in future political conflicts. In short, with no Perot campaign, there would have been little or no mobilization into the Republican Party in 1994.

What evidence can we provide that the dynamic of third parties is not unique to the case of Ross Perot? One indication that it is not unique certainly is that central insights summarized by the dynamic have been applied in the literature on party change and third parties to virtually every instance of a major third party except Perot's.[1] Apart from Perot's, the two most prominent examples of successful third-party movements in the last century are the Progressive movement that crystallized into third-party electoral movements, especially in the 1912 and 1924 presidential elections, and the George Wallace candidacy in 1968 under the American Independent Party (AIP) banner. Both movements and their aftermaths have been extensively analyzed, and we do not here engage the literature or an extensive analysis of the record on either case.[2] Instead, we briefly consider the case of George Wallace in the 1968 election, to show that a broadly similar pattern of third-party emergence and major-party response occurred in his case.

George Wallace was a Democratic segregationist governor of Alabama who bolted from his party in 1968 to run under the banner of his newly formed American Independent Party. The primary impetus for his campaign was his opposition to the civil rights positions of the national Democratic Party, which had animated an aborted Wallace run for the presidency in 1964. The Democratic Party had flirted with a commitment on African American civil rights since its 1948 convention, but under Lyndon Johnson, it had finally taken unambiguous stands against the Jim Crow laws propping up racial segregation in the South. In addition, the major parties' nominees in 1968—Richard Nixon for the Republicans and Hubert Humphrey for the Democrats—equivocated on the Vietnam War, at least as compared with Wallace's hawkish perspective (Page and Brody 1972). As the AIP candidate, therefore, Wallace took strong stands against the civil rights acts of the 1960s, and he took hardline positions against urban unrest. He also favored strong military action in Vietnam, opposing those who would withdraw or moderate American commitment to the South Vietnamese.

The historical case for applying the dynamic to George Wallace seems

---

1. An exception is John Anderson's candidacy in 1980. To our knowledge, no one has applied the logic of the third-party dynamic to his independent candidacy.

2. Mazmanian provides summary analyses of the Progressive movement, its agenda of anticorruption and institutional reform, and major-party responses after the elections of 1912 and 1924. In 1912, Theodore Roosevelt came in second in the popular vote, temporarily relegating the Republican Party to "third-party status"; in 1924, Robert M. LaFollette, as the Progressive nominee, won just under 17 percent of the popular vote.

strong, especially as it applies to the presidential politics of race. Richard Nixon won a narrow victory in 1968, deeply concerned that the Wallace candidacy would rob him of emerging Republican support among white Southerners opposed to the Democrats' commitment on civil rights. Four years before, the Republicans had nominated conservative Senator Barry Goldwater, whose opposition to the Civil Rights Act of 1964 had enabled him to make significant inroads in the formerly Democratic South. Nixon, for his part, developed a "Southern strategy" in his 1968 campaign, reassuring the South that he would appoint one of its own to the Supreme Court, a justice who would be a "strict constructionist" on matters related to civil rights, busing, and states' rights. This amounted to a bid for the Wallace constituency simultaneous to Wallace's third-party candidacy, though it is certainly true that Nixon never advocated overtly segregationist policies in the campaign or during his presidency (Carter 1991; Mazmanian 1974).

It is no secret that the states in the Old South moved sharply into the Republican camp in presidential elections after 1968. Analysis (not shown) shows that statewide Republican vote shares in the 1972 presidential election were associated with the size of George Wallace's vote share as the AIP candidate in 1968.[3] It is apparent from the historical record that the Southern realignment toward the Republicans occurred most abruptly in presidential voting, while a long-term gradual trend toward the Republicans in congressional voting began before Wallace's candidacy and continued through the remainder of the twentieth century (see fig. 8.2).[4]

There can be no doubt of the complexity of political change as it is registered in the two-party system, and we do not mean to suggest that the dynamic of third parties accounts for all of the change as the South

---

3. In an analysis that controls for states' Republican vote share in 1964 and 1968 and whether the state is in South, the effect of George Wallace's vote share on the Republican presidential vote in 1972 is substantively strong and statistically significant ($p = .009$). These findings are comparable to those presented in figure 8.6, which shows an independent effect of states' 1992 Perot vote on the 1996 and 2000 presidential elections.

4. We do not find an independent effect of Wallace's vote on Republican fortunes in the 1970 elections. Thus, the impact of the Wallace movement did not have the impact in the immediately following midterm U.S. House elections that we found for Perot in the 1994 elections.

moved into the Republican column. Indeed, given the magnitude and visibility of the social and political forces that swept through the South and the nation on racial matters in the post–World War II period, we can imagine that much or most of the realignment to the Republicans in the South would have taken place without the Wallace candidacy, much as Beck (1997) might argue. Unfortunately, we lack detailed survey data for Wallace activists (from the beginning of his movement through the ensuing years) comparable to what we have on Perot activists,[5] so we are unable to track for Wallace's movement the kind of microlevel processes and mechanisms of change that we have been able to observe in the Perot case.

RALPH NADER IN 2000 & 2004

Former consumer advocate Ralph Nader mounted a third-party candidacy that attracted a significant amount of attention, especially in the 2000 presidential campaign. Nader ran as the Green Party's nominee on a liberal-leftist platform that emphasized protecting the environment and workers' rights and interests, including keeping jobs in the United States, increasing wages, and attacking "corporate welfare" and the two major parties for selling out to corporate interests in domestic and foreign policy. For much of the campaign, Nader was expected to surpass the 5 percent of the vote required for federal funding in subsequent campaigns. In the end, however, he received less than 3 percent of the vote. Nonetheless, he was widely seen as having had a pivotal impact on the outcome of the election. Indeed, had Nader not run, it is easy to believe that enough of his ninety-seven thousand voters in Florida would have supported the Democratic nominee, Vice President Al Gore, to overcome the razor-thin margin of 537 votes (out of six million total votes cast) by which George W. Bush carried that state.[6] In the 2004 election, Nader ran again as an independent (and, ironically, the Reform Party's nominee), but

---

5. James Canfield (1984) conducted a study of Wallace activists in Michigan, but he did not extend his study to follow them in subsequent elections, nor did he test ideas related to the dynamic of third parties.

6. The election-return data are from the Federal Elections Commission Web site, http://www.fec.gov/pubrec/2000presgeresults.htm.

his vote share dropped below 1 percent, and the election was not close enough for his candidacy to have plausibly affected the outcome.

While Nader's 2000 candidacy may have been pivotal in that election, by winning only 2.7 percent of the vote nationwide, his candidacy did not attract a constituency large enough to divert major party effort to his supporters. This may seem a strange point to make about a third-party candidacy that arguably had the greatest impact on an election since 1968 or 1912. Given the importance of the election in hindsight, many observers have rightfully sought to understand the Nader candidacy and its significance for national politics. What does the dynamic of third parties and our understanding of the Perot movement imply for how we interpret the Nader candidacies? Why did the major parties fail to make any significant bid for the Nader constituency?

Given a close enough election (as in 2000), any number of candidates could claim to have influenced the outcome. For instance, Pat Buchanan, who got on the Florida ballot at the last moment, appears, because of the confusing ballot configuration, to have gained enough intended Gore votes to have shifted the election outcome. But he, like Nader, did not attract sufficient support to get the issue attention of the major parties. Nader's influence on the outcome largely resulted from how close the election was, which had little or nothing to do with Ralph Nader. In fact, we have shown that the competitive national balance between the Democratic and Republican parties in 2000 resulted from the Republican resurgence following the party's successful bid for the Perot constituency.

For the dynamic of third parties to work, a relatively large third-party vote share is important, because the third party's constituency must be large enough to be both identifiable and worth targeting by the major parties in subsequent elections. To be sure, the traditional 5 percent threshold is arbitrary, but it probably constitutes the lower level at which the major parties have an incentive to appeal to a third party's constituency and thus to set in motion the dynamic of third parties.

It is true that Ralph Nader's vote declined substantially in 2004, but we think this was due not primarily to an active bid by the major parties (in this case, it would have been a bid by the Democrats) but, rather, to his rejection as candidate by the Green Party, coupled with his disappointing showing in 2000 and his adverse influence (for many of his supporters) on the 2000 outcome. John Kerry and the Democratic Party worried about Nader in 2004, but their primary response was not an issue-based bid for the Nader constituency. Instead, they put most of their energy into keeping Nader off the ballot in as many states—especially battleground states—as possible. Thus, we do not think the dynamic of third parties is the best explanation for the decline in Nader's vote between 2000 and 2004. Moreover, a serious bid for the Nader constituency by the Democrats would have meant risking support in the center, because Nader's constituency, unlike Perot's in 1992, was relatively extreme on the liberal-conservative scale. Thus, bidding for 2000 Nader voters' support might have cost John Kerry more votes (in this case, centrist votes) than he could hope to win from those who had voted for the Green Party's nominee.

While we do not think the dynamic of third parties per se explains the decline in Ralph Nader's vote share between 2000 and 2004, the push-pull model of third-party vote does provide an explanation. Ralph Nader, like all third-party candidates before him, tried to emphasize the similarity between the Democratic and Republican parties in the 2000 election, because doing so increased the "push" that could drive potential supporters away from the closer of the two major parties (which for most was the Democratic Party). He could make this case plausibly to his potential constituency largely because Bush, running as a moderate "compassionate conservative," blurred many distinctions with Gore. Thus, voters and activists tempted by the Nader option could reasonably look upon the major-party nominees as relatively similar and not feel especially attracted to Gore or repelled by Bush. After Bush's first term, in which he aggressively pursued a conservative agenda both domestically and in Iraq, Nader's attempts to argue that it did not matter whether the nation elected a Democrat or a Republican rang hollow to many on the left. Thus, the perceived choice between Democratic and Republican candidates was certainly greater for most potential Nader voters in 2004 than it had been in 2000. Indeed, national polls repeatedly indicated that defeating George Bush was of paramount importance to a large percentage of Kerry voters. If this explanation is correct, the decline in Nader's vote was due more to change in the structure of major-party competition between the two elections than to the dynamic of third parties.

Finally, it is worth noting the possibility of a link between the Perot and Nader movements. Ralph Nader was advised to make an overt appeal to the Perot constituency in his 2000 campaign, but he chose largely to ignore that advice (Sifry 2002). Nonetheless, there were some issues common to the two campaigns, especially those related to economic nationalism and reform. In addition, we have seen that Perot attracted support because of general disaffection from politics as usual, a basis of appeal undoubtedly common to all third parties. Our panel survey of potential Perot activists reveals that whereas only 3.6 percent of those who voted for Perot in 1992 voted for one of the two Reform nominees (Pat Buchanan or John Hagelin) in 2000, 14.4 percent voted for Ralph Nader. Thus, Ralph Nader attracted a much larger share of former Perot activists than either of the pretenders to Perot's legacy who sought the Reform Party's nomination in 2000. This suggests that at least a portion of the Perot constituency remains available to insurgent third-party appeals in future elections.

THE FUTURE OF THE PEROT CONSTITUENCY

We have seen the pivotal effect of the Perot constituency on the balance of power between the major parties in American electoral politics after 1992. What does the future hold for this constituency, and what do former Perot supporters hold for the future of American politics? Is the Perot constituency locked into the Republican Party for the foreseeable future, or might it move back and forth between the two parties or follow some other path?

It seems fair to conclude that the administration of President George W. Bush reneged in significant ways on Republican commitments made when the party bid for Perot supporters in 1994. The Bush administration produced dramatic increases in the federal government's deficit; it backed away from its own opposition to nation-building, to undertake in Iraq the most dramatic nation-building effort in fifty years; and its commitment to reform was put seriously into question by its opposition to and foot-dragging over significant campaign finance reform. Moreover, it aggressively advanced the traditional Republican commitment to free trade. On all of these fronts, then, the George W. Bush presidency adopted policy positions that should have given pause to former Perot supporters' newfound support of the GOP.

Another potential strike against the Republicans from the perspective of the Perot constituency was that the GOP was no longer the party out of power, as it had been following the 1992 elections. Instead, the Republican Party controlled the presidency, Senate, and House following the 2002 midterm elections, when it recaptured majority control of the Senate. In the 2004 elections, the Republicans successfully reelected a sitting president at the same time that they defended their majority status in both the House and Senate, for the first time since 1900. Thus, to the extent that the Perot constituency was animated by dissatisfaction with politics as usual, its discontent might potentially be marshaled against the GOP.

All of this opens up an opportunity for a Democratic bid, but none has been forthcoming. Democrats were critical of the Iraq War, but their main argument that the administration should have involved the United Nations more fully is not a position calculated to enamor former Perot supporters.[7] It is true that several 2004 Democratic primary candidates made overtures to those opposing free-trade policies, especially since, as the economy faltered, many American jobs were once again seen as migrating oversees. However, reform issues played little role in the Democratic campaign, and the budget-deficit problem was similarly only a small part of the campaign.

Although we have no crystal ball, we can surmise that the place of the Perot constituency in national electoral politics might follow one of several general patterns. Without a strong bid from the Democrats, Perot supporters may stay on an inertial course, continuing to benefit the Republicans. Or if neither major party takes up their issues, we may see increasing rates of dropout from support of either party. Or dropouts might remain on the sidelines or, under proper circumstances and leadership, fuel another third-party effort. Either the dropout or the third-party scenario would disproportionately affect the Republican Party,

---

7. At this writing, we lack information about the Perot constituency's opinion on the Iraq War, so we cannot be certain of its opposition to the American invasion and occupation of Iraq.

which has become home to the majority of Perot supporters. Finally, one of the parties might decide to make an overt appeal. The Democrats, seeing a need to expand their constituency in the direction of reformist Perot supporters, might make a successful bid around Perot issues of reform, trade, and the deficit, as part of a larger attack on the record of George W. Bush's presidency. Alternatively, in 2008, the Republican Party might nominate a reform candidate, such as Senator John McCain, who could reenergize the Perot constituency's commitment to the Republican Party by reprising the appeals that defined his 2000 nomination campaign.

Strategic considerations and the skills and proclivities of leaders within the two major parties will determine whether the Perot constituency is the specific target of a Democratic bid to mobilize them, a Republican effort to retain them, or a new third-party movement. Whatever the two major parties do, our long-term panel shows that former Perot activists have maintained their commitment to the issues that animated Perot's 1992 campaign, a commitment that motivated their campaign activism through the 2000 election. The Perot constituency continues to be distinct and intact and, as a consequence, may affect our national politics for the foreseeable future.

CANDIDATE-CENTERED POLITICS & PARTY CHANGE

In the opening to this chapter, we alluded to the "choice" Americans have apparently made for a two-party system. Winner-take-all electoral rules, such as the unit rule in the electoral college and single-member districts, are prime examples of institutional mechanisms that reinforce the two-party system by making it difficult for third parties to form and attract support (Riker 1976, 1982; Bibby and Maisel 2003). This institutional bias against third parties combines with legal and policy limits on ballot access and campaign financing to compound the difficulties and barriers to would-be third-party movements. These barriers, however, do not preclude a third-party or independent candidate from succeeding to attract significant support and effecting change in the two-party system. Indeed, as we have seen in the case of Perot, the barriers to ballot access can provide a proving ground for a third-party candidate, giving him a way of demonstrating committed support and building an activist base, much as the primary process provides to nomination contenders in the major parties.

The literature on American electoral politics has emphasized a change in recent decades from "party-centered" to "candidate-centered" politics (Hershey 2005; Lowi 1985; Maisel 1999; Wattenberg 1991). The focus of our campaigns is less on the parties as enduring coalitions and institutions and more on the strategies and positions of individual candidates. Candidates run as individuals in direct-primary elections, where they develop their own organizations, their own base of funding, their own political identity, and their own loyal following in the electorate. A negative consequence of this development is that officeholders have not forged strong links with others in government, nor are they conditioned to practice the coalitional politics that is essential to policymaking and governance. Because they came into office as individuals, today's office-holders continue to depend on personal constituencies and reputations. As a result, the argument goes, the political parties are weakened in their ability to organize broad electoral coalitions, in their capacity to recruit and assist candidates who can further their cause, and in their ability to make programmatic commitments in government. Collective responsibility, as a result, is undermined, and the ability of citizens to direct the course of government is impaired (Fiorina 1980).

Ross Perot's 1992 candidacy epitomizes this development toward candidate-centered politics. After all, what could be more "candidate-centered" than a self-nominated, largely self-funded independent presidential candidate? Yet one of the ironies of the Perot movement was that it contributed to one of the greatest upsurges in partisan politics in American history. If presidential nominations are routinely pointed to as "Exhibit A" in the case for candidate-centered politics (Wattenberg 1991), "Exhibit B" is comprised of U.S. House elections, with candidates who declare themselves, rather than being recruited by the parties, and who run campaigns that are relentlessly local in their orientation (Herrnson 1998; Jacobson 2004). Nonetheless, two years after Ross Perot's stunning appearance on the national scene, Republican Party leaders nationalized their House campaigns under a set of programmatic commitments that would have made the most committed responsible-party theorist proud. The Republicans won in 1994 as much because of the individual strategic decisions made by potential candidates seeking to advance their own personal careers as because of their coordinated national campaign under the banner of the Contract with America. Both the coordinated and the candidate-centered components of 1994 House campaigns, however, had a common cause: an effort by ambitious Republican politicians to convert Perot supporters into Republican voters and activists. As a result of the 1994 elections, the Republicans won majorities in a narrowly divided Congress and touched off an extended period of intensive partisanship with still unfolding political and policy implications.

The partisan impact of the Perot movement did not stop with the 1994 congressional elections. Candidates for presidential nominations, especially insurgent candidates challenging a front-runner in their party, must mobilize new constituencies into the nomination process to have a chance. Prior nomination candidates from Barry Goldwater to Pat Robertson, from George McGovern to Jesse Jackson, some of whom won and some of whom lost, used this process to boost their own political ambitions. In doing so, they effected significant long-term change in their parties.

As we have seen, Pat Buchanan and especially John McCain followed this strategy in appealing to the Perot constituency in their nomination campaigns. As we have also seen, their campaigns, like those of House candidates in 1994, were conduits for former Perot supporters into the Republican Party. Thus, nomination candidates pursuing their own interests in expanding their pool of supporters for their campaigns sought and found backers among former third-party participants. Likewise, individual House candidates identified among former Perot voters and activists potential supporters whom they attracted to their cause in 1994. In all of these instances, candidate-centered campaigns produced a resurgence of the Republican Party. Candidate-centered campaigns in tandem with centrally coordinated party-centered leadership produced the bid for the Perot constituency in 1994 and after, in keeping with the dynamic of third parties.

There is, in short, no necessary conflict between candidate-centered campaigns and a healthy party system, just as there is no necessary conflict between vigorous nomination campaigns and a healthy party coalition in the fall campaign or in years following. The conflict among nomination contenders is a healthy mechanism for resolving intraparty conflict, identifying successful candidates and testing their skills, and mobilizing interests into the party. Nomination contests also assure that the party is responsive to change in society, since, in order to build their base of support, candidates have powerful incentives to identify underrepresented potential constituencies and the issues they espouse.

The same process occurs when a third-party or independent candidate has the political opportunity, skill, and resources to build a large popular following. Such candidates act first and foremost as politically ambitious individuals (whether or not they eschew "politics as usual"), by articulating and stimulating discontent with the major parties based on policy problems, oversights, and issues. The opportunity they exploit is most likely to be created because of perceived or real failures of the two major parties. Once underway, a third-party or independent candidacy can be counted on to attack the two major parties as failures, emphasizing the lack of substantive and meaningful choice between them, especially on the core issues driving the campaign.

As the dynamic of third parties describes, such an effort sends a powerful signal to the two major parties. If support for the insurgent candidacy is strong, the incentive among candidates and leaders in one or both major parties may be irresistible. The result, again, is not a conflict between "candidate-" and "party-centered" politics as much as it is a process that involves both candidates and parties, recognizing that candidates, potential candidates, activists, and other entrepreneurs close to the electoral process are critical players who participate directly in defining and shaping the interests and behavior of the party. John Aldrich (1995) has persuasively argued that the political parties are creatures of candidates and others whose purposes they serve. Likewise, Joseph Schlesinger (1991) points out that candidates define the party, rather than competing with it or undermining its essential purposes.

The logic of third parties compels us to recognize that they, too, are an integral part of the American two-party system. They arise from its failures, and they help shape its future. Three may be a crowd in the American party system, but because of the successes of such candidates as Ross Perot, the future of American politics will include successful third-party movements and independent candidates. Despite the barriers that limit and frustrate third-party movements, there will be another Ross Perot. On balance, the sting administered by the candidacy of Ross Perot transcends the death of his movement. Contrary to what many analysts have observed, movements such as his can have an enduring impact on the two-party system, compelling it to respond to interests and forces to which it might otherwise be inattentive. These are positive effects, lost to view in the hurly-burly of presidential politics and the bluster of spin and rhetoric that follow. Understanding the effects—positive and negative—of such movements enables us to comprehend larger forces at work in the evolution of the party system.

XII

Afterword

THE DYNAMIC OF THIRD PARTIES AND THE
FUTURE OF THE PEROT CONSTITUENCY

ᗕᑊ₽

THROUGHOUT THIS BOOK, WE have argued that the Perot constituency played a pivotal role in U.S. national politics in the elections after Perot first ran for president in 1992. The "dynamic of third parties" describes the process whereby Perot's or any third-party movement might have a lasting impact on the electoral system: the third-party candidate emerges to attract a significant electoral constituency animated by distinct issue concerns; one or both of the major parties subsequently bids for the third party's constituency based on the issues that motivated the movement in the first place; and members of the third party disproportionately shift their support to the major party that makes the stronger bid. As a result of this shift in support, the third-party movement itself loses steam and disappears, and the party making the successful bid is changed to the extent that the bid entails policy commitments that are different from its long-standing issue and policy positions.

In the years following the emergence of the 1992 Perot movement, the Republicans made a successful bid with two important consequences. First, the Republican Party increased its vote share by adding a significant portion of the Perot constituency that had not supported the Republicans prior to 1992. As a result of attracting former Perot supporters as newcomers to its ranks, the Republican Party was able to win and hold control of Congress for the first time since the 1952 elections and to win the presidency in 2000. In short, the Republican bid helped produce a "resurgence" in that party's fortunes. The second consequence of the party's bid was that it drew into the GOP a cohort of activists and voters committed to the Perot issue agenda, especially issues related to reform, balancing the federal budget, and "economic nationalism."

What might these developments imply for the years since we completed the first edition of *Three's a Crowd*? In this afterword, we examine the extent to which the Perot constituency remained intact through the 2004 election, and we speculate about how changes in the Republican Party since the election of President George W. Bush in 2000 might affect the continued involvement of Perot supporters in Republican campaigns. We argue that by 2004 the Bush record was at considerable odds with the Perot agenda, effectively amounting to a Republican disavowal of its bid for the Perot constituency in the Contract with America and elsewhere during the 1990s. Therefore, to the extent that Perot supporters remained committed to the issues that originally motivated them to commit to Perot and to switch their support to Republican candidates in the elections after 1992, two questions arise: Did former Perot supporters respond by withdrawing their backing for Republicans, and what might their response suggest for the future? To address these questions, we rely on a continuing survey of former Perot backers that we conducted immediately after the 2004 election.[1]

CONTINUITY IN THE PEROT CONSTITUENCY

A third-party constituency, such as Perot's, can remain pivotal in American national elections if its former supporters continue to hold the issue positions that originally motivated them. In the case of Perot's backers, these issue commitments were the basis of the Republican bid and explained their willingness to move to the GOP (see chap. 7). An implication, however, is that the third-party supporters can remain pivotal even

---

1. The data we report are based on samples of Reform and major-party contributors begun in 1996 (see app. A).

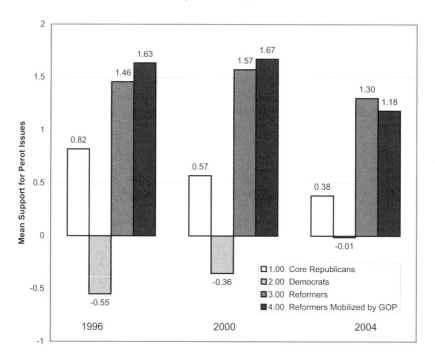

Fig. 12.1. Mean position on Perot issues for core Republicans, Democrats, Reformers, and Reformers mobilized by the Republican Party, 1996–2004

after they have responded to the bid of one of the major parties, if they are also willing to withdraw their support if the bid is renounced.

To assess their reaction to Bush's disavowal of the Perot agenda, the first step is to determine whether the Perot constituency maintained its commitment to the issues that defined it in 1992. Figure 12.1 presents data from our surveys of major-party and Reform contributors, comparing the commitment to the Perot agenda of each of four groups: core Republicans, by which we mean Republican contributors who were never active in the Perot movement; Democratic contributors; Reform contributors as a whole; and Reform contributors who were mobilized into Republican Party campaigns between 1994 and 2000 in response to the Republican bid.[2] Comparing Reform contributors with Republicans

---

2. In the 2004 survey, the items composing the Perot index were limiting immigration, limiting imports, limiting foreign involvement, support for term limits, eliminating soft-money contributions to parties, and raising taxes to reduce the deficit.

and Democrats gives an idea of how distinctive the Perot constituency was compared with each of the major parties' core supporters, and comparing Reform contributors with those who were mobilized into the Republican Party provides an indication of whether Perot's backers who migrated into the Republican Party maintained their commitment to the Perot issues.

Figure 12.1 demonstrates that the Perot constituency remained intact and distinct through the 2004 elections. In 1996, Reform contributors who had been active in Republican campaigns, as well as Reformers who had remained outside the Republican Party, were strongly committed to the Perot issues. In the same year, Republicans were modestly supportive of Perot issues, and Democrats were moderately opposed. The same basic pattern holds through the two following elections, except that Democrats' opposition to the Perot agenda softened such that they were, on average, indifferent by 2004. Notice, however, that Republican support for Perot issues dropped approximately in half between 1996 and 2004 (from 0.82 to 0.38). Although there was some decline in support for the Perot agenda among former Reform Party contributors by 2004, Reform contributors were more distinctive from Republicans in 2004 than they had been in 1996.

Figure 12.1 provides evidence of continuity and distinctiveness in the Perot constituency, up to twelve years after Perot's initial campaign. While it may not be surprising that Perot activists remained strongly committed to the Perot agenda, it is also notable that there is little difference between those who were drawn into active support for GOP candidates and those who remained outside the Republican Party. Moreover, when we break the Perot issue index into individual issue items (data not shown), Reformers were consistently distinct from core Republicans.

THE REPUBLICAN AGENDA UNDER
PRESIDENT GEORGE W. BUSH

The persistence of the Perot constituency through 2004 is potentially of great political significance. The Republican Party, under the leadership of President George W. Bush, retreated spectacularly from the positions it took in the 1990s when it bid for Perot supporters. Indeed, across the three issue dimensions that define the Perot agenda, the Republicans adopted positions and policies between 2000 and 2004 that were opposed to those advocated by Ross Perot and consistently held by his constituency since 1992.

Under President Bush, the United States committed to its most important military venture since Vietnam, when it invaded Iraq in 2003. More troubling than that invasion, from the perspective of Perot supporters' long-term policy interests, was the decision to undertake the most extensive nation-building projects—in Afghanistan and Iraq—since the Marshall Plan after World War II. This commitment was contrary to Perot's emphasis on domestic priorities and limited foreign involvements.[3]

Bush's renunciation of the economic nationalism part of the Perot agenda extended to trade and immigration as well. In contrast to Perot activists' persistent support of limiting immigration, Bush offered strong support for an agreement between the United States and Mexico, which would "pave the way for many illegal Mexican immigrants—up to 3 million—to remain in the United States and would serve as a precedent for other nationalities."[4] Although the 9/11 attacks prevented immediate follow-up on this initiative, the administration maintained its guest-worker program, especially for farmworkers, even in the face of strong opposition from a large number of Republican lawmakers. Bush's support for NAFTA and the Central America–Dominican Republic Free Trade Agreement (CAFTA) remained a linchpin of Republican trade policy, despite the opposition of Perot and his supporters. Bush even backed down on his only trade policy meant to appeal to Perot's supporters: his promise to impose tariffs on steel imports for up to three years to help domestic producers.[5]

Finally, Bush's performance in the areas of the federal budget and

---

3. Our 2004 survey shows that Reform contributors were much more strongly opposed to the Bush administration's Iraq policy than were Republicans, though the former were not quite as strongly opposed as Democratic contributors.

4. Frank Davies, "Relief for Mexican Workers a Top Priority," *San Diego Union-Tribune*, August 4, 2001, A2.

5. Richard W. Stevenson and Elizabeth Becker, "After 21 Months, Bush Lifts Tariff on Steel Imports," *New York Times*, December 5, 2003, A1.

reform was less in keeping with GOP commitments to Perot and his supporters than his performance on other Perot issues. Under Bush and Republican majorities in Congress, the deficit ballooned from a surplus of $236 billion under Clinton in fiscal year 2000 to a deficit of $412 billion by fiscal year 2004. As tax revenues declined and spending increased, the prospects for ever-increasing deficits became a prominent aspect of President Bush's legacy. The most significant reform initiative during Bush's first term dealt with campaign finance through the vehicles of the McCain-Feingold proposal in the Senate and the Shays-Meehan proposal in the House. These proposals sought to eliminate soft money in campaigns, a policy with overwhelming support from Perot activists. But this was far from a priority for the Bush administration. Although President Bush did not threaten a veto, he did not endorse the bill, saying he would "reserve judgment" until he saw "the final product."[6] Without Bush's support, only thirty-nine Republicans voted for the House version, and it passed on a close vote. Bush further signaled his ambivalence by failing to arrange a high-profile signing of the legislation. To add insult to injury, President Bush did not invite Senator McCain, the leading Republican proponent of reform in Congress, to attend the signing.

In sum, the Bush administration and the Republican Party effectively reneged on the bid the GOP made for the Perot constituency after the 1992 election. Since the issue commitments behind the Perot constituency remained largely intact through the 2004 election, what are the possible implications from the perspective of the dynamic of third parties? In our analysis of the Perot response to the Republican bid between 1994 and 2000, we showed that Perot activists were more involved in Republican than in Democratic campaigns from 1994 through 2000 (see fig. 9.1). The question is whether there was a change in activism between 2000 and 2004 in response to the Bush administration's policies. Our measure of Republican campaign activity is a simple count of the number of activities that respondents did for Republicans in presidential and House campaigns, as well as for the Republican ticket as a whole. We create identical counts of Democratic

---

6. Greg Gordon and Lawrence M. O'Rourke, "Senate Bars 'Soft Money': Campaign-Finance Battle Moves Next to House," *Minneapolis Star Tribune*, April 3, 2001, 1.

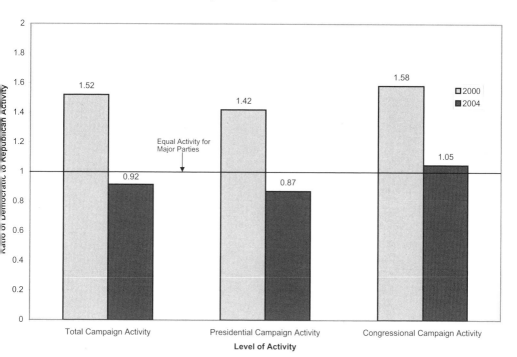

Fig. 12.2.   Relative major party campaign activity for Reform contributor sample, 2000 and 2004

campaign activity in both years and compare them by taking the ratio of Republican to Democratic activity.[7]

Figure 12.2 reports the ratio of Republican to Democratic activities for 2000 and 2004. A score above 1.0 indicates a Republican advantage in activity; a score below 1.0 indicates greater Democratic than Republican activism. Consistent with our results reported in figure 9.1, there was substantially more Republican activism than Democratic activism in all campaigns in the 2000 election. In fact, Reformers were about half again as active in Republican campaigns as they were for Democratic candidates. However, by 2004, there was a noticeable shift in overall activity. Not only did the Republican advantage disappear in 2004, but there was slightly more activity in Democratic than in Republican campaigns (indicated by the total activity ratio of less than 1.0). In the presidential campaign, there

---

7. The advantage of using a ratio is that it controls for different levels of mobilization and activism that occur in both parties in different election years.

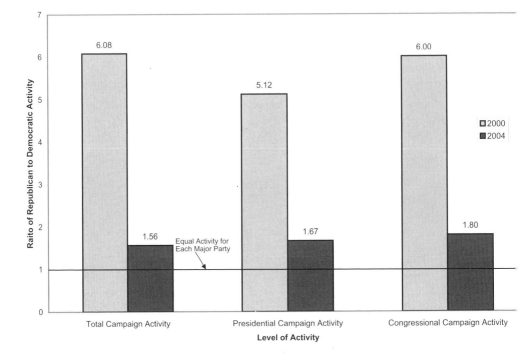

Fig. 12.3.   Relative major party activity for Perot Republicans, 2000 and 2004

was only 87 percent as much Republican as Democratic activity, a decline in the ratio between 2000 and 2004 of almost 40 percent. Although Republican House candidates retained a slim advantage over their Democratic counterparts, this was probably due to the larger number of Republican incumbents running for reelection. But even in House races, the GOP advantage over the Democrats declined to virtual parity.

A decline in relative activity for the Republican Party is also evident when we restrict the analysis to Reformers who were mobilized into Republican campaigns (see fig. 12.3). In 2000, Perot Republicans were between five and six times more active for Republican candidates than they were for Democrats. High levels of Republican activism are not surprising, because we define "Perot Republicans" as Reformers who were mobilized into Republican campaigns. However, their level of participation in 2004 plummeted to the point where they were less than twice as active in Republican campaigns relative to their activism for

Democrats. In 2000, only about 15 percent of Perot Republicans' total activity was on behalf of Democratic candidates; in 2004, 40 percent of it was. The commitment to the Republican Party of both Reform Party contributors in general and Perot Republicans in particular clearly dropped in the first four years of the Bush administration. We attribute this decline to the Republican shift in priorities, actions, and commitments away from those of the Perot movement.

SPILLOVER FROM PEROT TO THE MAJOR PARTIES

Chapter 9 reports on mobilization effects from the Perot movement into the Republican Party. We showed that the more active former Perot supporters were in Perot's 1992 presidential campaign, the more responsive they were to the bid from the Republicans. Thus, the spillover effect reflects the dynamic of third parties at work on individual third-party activists: the more engaged they were in Perot's insurgent campaign, the more subject they subsequently were to mobilization by the bidding major party. These spillover effects from Perot's campaign into Republican races were evident in every election year between 1994 and 2000 (see fig. 9.4). In contrast to what occurred in Republican campaigns, these years show no evidence of spillover from the 1992 Perot campaign into Democratic campaigns. The question, then, is whether the Republican renunciation of the Perot program resulted in spillover into Democratic campaigns in 2004. Spillover into Democratic campaigns would provide additional evidence that the Perot constituency reacted against the Republican policy shifts under President George W. Bush.

Figure 12.4 presents the results of analyzing the effects of activism for Perot in 1992 on relative major-party activity in 2004. We show the prevalence of Democratic activity over Republican activity for those engaging in zero, two, four, and six activities for Perot. A bar with a negative value (extending below the zero line) indicates that respondents engaging in that number of activities for Perot in 1992 were, on average, more active for Republican candidates in 2004 than for Democrats. A positive bar (extending above the zero line) indicates that respondents

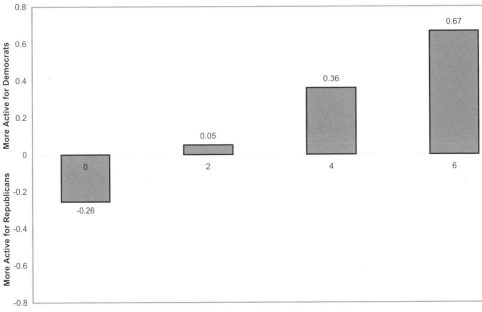

Fig. 12.4.   Democratic/Republican advantage in 2004 campaign activity by 1992 Perot activity, controlling for 2000 activity, party ID, and party contact

were more active for Democratic candidates than for Republicans.[8] The pattern is clear: Reform Party respondents who were most active for Perot in 1992 shifted their 2004 involvement, to the greatest extent, away from Republican candidates toward the Democrats. We see this as further evidence of the potential of third-party movements to have an enduring impact on the two major parties. Whereas the initial reaction of the Perot constituency was to fuel a "Republican resurgence" during the 1990s, the turnabout that President George W. Bush and the Republican leadership in Congress engineered in the GOP's commitment to the Perot agenda prompted a shift toward the Democrats for the first time by the same former Perot activists who contributed to Republican successes between 1994 and 2000.

---

8. Figure 12.4 presents the partial effect from an analysis that controls for the effect of 2000 major-party activity, party identification, and contact from each of the major parties.

SPECULATIONS AND CONCLUSIONS

Unfortunately, our surveys ended with the 2004 elections, so we are unable to continue the analysis of the Perot constituency through the 2006 elections, when the Democrats won back control of both houses of Congress for the first time since the historic Republican victory in 1994. We think that the Perot constituency probably helped deliver the Democratic victory in 2006. However, because of the inevitable erosions that occur over a long period of time and because the Democrats did not mount an aggressive bid for the Perot constituency in 2006, we doubt that it was as strong a factor in that year as it was twelve years before, in 1994. While we are reluctant to conclude that the Perot constituency was as pivotal in producing the 2006 Democratic triumph as it was in delivering victory to the Republicans in 1994, there does seem to be sufficient evidence of an effect to conclude that the Perot constituency retains its potential to have important effects in the competition between the two major parties in 2008 and beyond.

Because the Perot constituency maintained its commitment to the issues that defined and motivated it during the 1992–2000 period and because it demonstrated its openness to persuasion from either party, there is every reason to suggest that it could be pivotal in future national elections. It also seems that the Democrats could make a much more aggressive appeal to Perot voters. Results (not shown) of the statistical model for figure 12.4 indicate that Democratic contact with Reformers was more efficacious than was Republican contact in 2004, but our survey also reveals that there were lower levels of Democratic than Republican contact among Reformers in that election. The failure of Democrats to bid for the Perot constituency led two top Democratic strategists, Stan Greenberg and James Carville, to call on their party in 2006 to "revisit the Perot voters and their concerns, even if Perot has faded from view."[9] They picked up on the same dynamic we have shown by saying that the Perot constituency "brought the Republicans back" and that it has the potential to do the same for Democrats.

Democratic strategists were not alone in suggesting the potential

---

9. Stan Greenberg and James Carville, "Re: Defining the Choice," October 17, 2005, http://www.gqrr.com/articles/1634/1435_DefiningtheChoice.pdf.

importance of Perot's backers in 2006. Republican pollster and strategist Frank Luntz argued that in 2006, "the Perot voters, who were the key to the Republican takeover in 1994, deserted the GOP in droves and turned control of Congress back to the Democrats [when] . . . red ink budgets, earmarked appropriations for bridges to nowhere, endless ethics scandals and a debacle of a war made them mad once again."[10] Luntz saw the continuing need for his party to appeal to this group rather than take their support for granted. He went on to endorse a strategy for the future that, as he put it, had "both the early front-runners for the GOP presidential nomination in 2008 . . . appeal[ing] beyond the party's base of conservative supporters." Luntz continued, "Arizona Sen. John McCain tapped into the old Perot constituency in his bid for the nomination in 2000, and former New York mayor Rudolph W. Giuliani is doing that now."[11]

That the Perot constituency remained committed to its issues does not mean that former Perot backers thought of themselves as remaining in his political movement or that they retained their loyalty to him as a leader. Indeed, we found that by the 1996 election, when he ran for the second time, a large percentage of those who had been supportive in 1992 dropped out and evaluated him much less positively than they had in 1992. By 2000, his support had evaporated, even as the issues he stressed retained their appeal and priority. Thus, the issues defined the Perot constituency in the years after his initial candidacy, and those same issues give it the potential to play a pivotal role in American politics.

That the Perot constituency was largely intact twelve years after 1992 is a lesson of enduring importance for the American two-party system. Two different scenarios seem possible for the Perot constituency in 2008 and beyond. One possibility is the emergence of a new third-party movement. Perot demonstrated in 1992 that a candidate with the necessary skills and resources can exploit discontent with the major parties to attract significant support. At this writing, New York Mayor Michael Bloomberg is frequently mentioned as a possible "centrist" candidate who might lead an independent campaign to tap into discontent with the polarization between the major parties. Bloomberg himself has so far

---

10. Frank Luntz, "Stuck in the Mud: How Can the GOP Get Moving Again? Drop the Dirty Politics and Get Real," *Washington Post,* February 25, 2007, B01.

11. Ibid.

denied an interest in running, but if discontent with the two parties and their nominees is substantial, an opening for a third-party movement may occur. If so, the Perot constituency would be an obvious starting point for an independent candidate looking for a base of support.

A second scenario following the Bush renunciation of the Perot agenda is based on the opportunity it provides the Democrats, as hinted by Greenberg and Carville. An entrepreneurial Democratic candidate or leader might articulate a program that could appeal to Perot supporters and, much as the Republicans did in 1994, target former Perot backers with direct campaign appeals. A strategy of this sort could tip the national electoral balance in the Democrats' favor. Such a leader might point to the balanced federal budget and surplus during the Clinton years, to a more measured form of internationalism built on dissatisfaction with the Iraq experience, and to domestic economic insecurities stemming from a global economy. If so, our study suggests that there may be more than a remnant of the Perot movement available for mobilization, waiting in the wings to stimulate a new direction in major-party politics.

Whatever occurs in 2008, third-party movements will remain important to understanding major-party change years after their initial appearance. Make no mistake: there will be another Ross Perot. The future will see third-party and independent candidacies arise when the major parties fail to address important issue and policy concerns and when entrepreneurial politicians seek major elective office by running against, rather than within, the two-party system. Especially when such candidacies succeed in identifying novel and significant issue constituencies, the signals they send to the major parties will prompt response, adjustment, and change. Comprehending the forces energized by these movements enriches our understanding of the larger processes of change at work in the American two-party system.

APPENDIX A

Design & Data Sources

≈

THE SAMPLE OF PEROT CALLERS

Our analysis of the Perot effect relies primarily on a sample of callers to the Perot headquarters' toll-free number in 1992. As discussed in chapter 3, the campaign began getting calls from individuals almost immediately after Perot's appearance on *Larry King Live* on February 20, 1992. As the campaign went on, callers were often referred to their state organizations, and many called their state or local Perot organizations directly. Our sample was drawn from a database of approximately five hundred thousand names and addresses, held by the national Perot campaign headquarters in Dallas.[1] Individuals in the database from which we sampled called between February and June of 1992.

As table A.1 shows, we began our study with a sample of 1,905 names for which we had complete address information. We conducted the first wave of the survey in August 1992 (1992a) and followed up with a postelection wave (1992b) in which we recontacted respondents to the 1992a wave. Following the 1992 waves, we recontacted our panel respondents for a third wave immediately after the 1994 elections; and then again in February 1996, during the Republican nomination campaign (1996a); immediately following the 1996 general election (1996b); and following the 2000 election. In each post-1992 wave, our strategy was to recontact all respondents to the immediately preceding wave, plus those who had responded to two of the three preceding waves. Not surprisingly, we received reduced response rates from respondents who skipped a wave, but the strategy netted a higher overall retention rate, which is important in a long-term panel study. Table A.1 presents the numbers of former respondents contacted in each wave and the return rate of questionnaires mailed. The breakdown of preceding and penultimate wave respondents for each mailing from 1994 on is also given.

For each mailing, we followed the same procedures. In the 1992a wave, we sent a letter introducing the study. In all subsequent years, the initial letter

---

1. Authors' telephone communication with Clay Mulford, August 1995.

TABLE A.1.   Response Rates for Toll-Free Perot Caller Panel

Wave	Surveys Sent Out	Surveys Returned	Response Rate (%)	Response Rate as Percentage of Original Number of Surveys Sent Out (Response rate as percentage of original number of respondents appears in parentheses.)
1992a (August 1992)	1,905	1,321	69.3	69.3 (100)
1992b (postelection)	1,321	937	70.9	49.2 (70.9)
1994 (postelection)	1,321	774	58.6	40.6 (58.6)
Respondents to 1992b	937	655	69.9	
Those who responded to 1992a but not to 1992b	384	119	31.0	
1996a (during Republican nomination campaign, February 1996)	984	573	58.2	30.1 (43.4)
Respondents to 1994	749	523	69.8	
Those who responded but not to 1994	235	50	21.3	
1996b (postelection)	739	461	62.0	24.2 (34.5)
Respondents to 1996a	573	412	71.9	
Those who responded to 1994 but not to 1996a	166	49	29.5	
2000 (postelection)	572	334	58.4	17.5 (25.3)
Respondents to 1996b	444	272	61.3	
Those who responded to 1996a but not to 1996b	128	62	48.4	

Note: Preapproach mailings were sent "address correction requested" to respondents eligible to receive a survey. Some of these were returned indicating that individuals had moved with no forwarding address or that individuals were deceased. We did not send these individuals our surveys.

included a brief summary of our results from a previous phase of the study. Following the initial letter, we sent the questionnaire packet, followed one week later by a postcard reminder. Within approximately a month to six weeks after the initial mailing, we sent a second questionnaire to individuals who had not responded to the first mailing.

ASSESSING PANEL-RESPONSE BIAS

Although selective mortality is always a problem in long-term panels, succeeding samples are surprisingly unbiased in this case, as tables A.2–3 show. Our method of assessing panel-response bias is to compare respondents who remained with the study through the final wave of the panel (2000) with those who dropped out of the panel at an earlier point (in 1992b, 1994, or 1996).[2] Comparing the re-

2. Most comparisons are from the 1992a wave, but comparisons involving campaign activism in the 1992 election use the 1992b wave as the basis of comparison and have a smaller base sample, because of nonresponse in the 1992b wave, which we used to create the campaign activism scale.

spondents who dropped out by the end of the panel with those who remained in the sample provides the most rigorous test of selective mortality problems. We have performed similar analyses of mortality and potential bias for each interme-diate wave (comparing, e.g., those who dropped out between 1992 and 1996 with those still in the 1996b wave of the survey), and in the vast majority of cases, the differences are smaller than when we use the full panel.

Table A.2 compares respondents and nonrespondents on the means of vari-ous campaign activism measures, while table A.3 compares respondents with nonrespondents on selected key attitudinal and demographic measures. The correlations reported in table A.3 (using the Somer's *d* statistical test) are be-tween the response variable (coded 0 for those who dropped out of the panel before the 2000 wave and 1 for those who remained in the panel through 2000) and the variable in question. A correlation of .0 indicates no bias, since there is no difference between respondents and nonrespondents. A positive correlation indicates that respondents were higher than nonrespondents on the attribute, while a negative correlation means that respondents were lower than nonre-spondents. In both tables, we report levels of statistical significance to indicate bias that is sufficiently strong so that it is probably not due simply to chance.

TABLE A.2.   Difference of Means for Respondents and Nonrespondents to the 2000 Wave on 1988 and 1992 Activity Variables

Activity Variable	Response Group	N	Mean	Standard Deviation
Republican House activity, 1988★	2000 nonrespondent	1,000	0.119	0.448
	2000 respondent	313	0.230	0.649
Activity for Bush-Quayle, 1988★★	2000 nonrespondent	1,000	0.306	0.662
	2000 respondent	313	0.406	0.887
Activity for GOP nomination candidates, 1992	2000 nonrespondent	1,000	0.218	0.606
	2000 respondent	313	0.198	0.554
Republican House activity, 1992	2000 nonrespondent	643	0.126	0.494
	2000 respondent	286	0.147	0.542
Activity for Bush-Quayle, 1992	2000 nonrespondent	643	0.151	0.474
	2000 respondent	286	0.178	0.542
Democratic House activity, 1988	2000 nonrespondent	1,000	0.134	0.490
	2000 respondent	313	0.179	0.555
Activity for Dukakis-Bentsen, 1988	2000 nonrespondent	1,000	0.185	0.521
	2000 respondent	313	0.211	0.594
Activity for Democratic nomination candidates, 1992	2000 nonrespondent	1,000	0.447	0.885
	2000 respondent	313	0.495	0.920
Democratic House activity, 1992	2000 nonrespondent	643	0.128	0.449
	2000 respondent	286	0.168	0.586
Activity for Clinton-Gore, 1992	2000 nonrespondent	643	0.328	0.740
	2000 respondent	286	0.308	0.765
Perot activity preparty conventions, 1992a	2000 nonrespondent	1,000	1.480	1.410
	2000 respondent	313	1.498	1.417
Perot-Stockdale activity, fall campaign, 1992	2000 nonrespondent	643	1.031	1.191
	2000 respondent	286	1.014	1.262

★*p* < .05   ★★*p* < .10

TABLE A.3. Correlations between Response to 2000 Survey and
Demographic and Attitudinal Factors

Demographic or Attitudinal Factor	Correlation with Response/Nonresponse
Political interest, 1992	−0.005
Party identification, 1992	−0.052
Liberal-conservative political ideology, 1992	0.016
Level of education	0.106★
Family income	0.117★
Sex	−0.007
Age	0.217★

★$p < .01$

While there is no significant relationship between remaining in the panel through the 2000 wave and political interest, party identification, liberalism, and sex, there is a weak tendency for those with higher levels of education and income to remain in the panel. Age has the strongest correlation, with older respondents continuing to participate to a higher degree. All three effects are modest but significant and probably reflect our inability to track respondents who were more mobile during the period of the eight-year panel.

Although demographic bias is potentially problematic, a more serious difficulty would be presented by mortality related to involvement with the Perot campaign or with major-party campaigns. It is gratifying that there is almost a total lack of bias in partisan and Perot political activity, which is consistent with the lack of bias in partisan and ideological attitudes. Of twelve measures of political activity from 1988 and 1992—including House elections, presidential nomination campaigns, and presidential general election campaigns—only one shows a statistically significant difference of means at the .05 level (activity for Republican House candidates in 1988), and only one other is significant at the .10 level. These results are very close to what would be expected by chance alone. Most important, there are no differences on either the spring or fall Perot activity measures. Those people most active for Perot in 1992 did not drop out disproportionately (nor did they stay in the panel disproportionately). In addition to their similarity on behavior, respondents and nonrespondents are also indistinguishable on ideology, partisanship, and political interest (see table A.3).

THE CONTRIBUTOR SAMPLES

In 1996, we drew parallel samples of contributors to the Democratic, Republican, and Reform parties. Because we did not want to limit ourselves to those giving over $250 (whose names we could have gotten from the Federal Elections Commission), we went to the Democratic National Committee and the Republican National Committee. Each supplied us with samples of two thousand individuals who contributed to their party in response to direct-mail appeals between October 1994 and October 1995. The average contribution was less than fifty dollars. The Reform Party also supplied us with a sample of twenty-five hundred of its contributors from its inception in the fall of 1995 through 1996.

The Reform Party Sample

About 7 percent of the Reform Party sample had incomplete or incorrect addresses, leaving a sample of 2,321 Reform Party contributors. Because we received the sample after the election, we were not able to mail the surveys (1996b) out until February 1997. Nonetheless, we followed the same protocol as we had with the Perot caller sample (and with the Democratic and Republican contributor samples), sending an introductory letter, a survey packet, a follow-up postcard, and a second survey packet to nonrespondents. Overall, the response rate was 60.7 percent. For the year 2000 survey, we sent surveys to those responding to the 1996 survey and received responses from 58.5 percent.

Democratic Party Contributors

The Democratic sample consisted of two thousand names, of which two hundred lacked complete address information. Because the Democratic race was uncontested, we sent out February surveys to slightly over half of our sample, reserving the remainder for the postelection survey only. Of the Democrats receiving the February 1996 survey, slightly less than half (45.8 percent) responded. Of those who did respond, almost three-quarters of them responded to the postelection survey (while only 42.2 percent of those receiving only the postelection survey responded). In 2000, the response rate for the combined sample was 64.1 percent.

Republican Party Contributors

The Republican contributor sample consisted of two thousand names, of which virtually all (1,991) had complete addresses. Because there was a contested Republican nomination, we sent February surveys to the entire sample and postelection surveys to first-wave respondents. All those responding to the postelection wave in 1996 received 2000 postelection surveys. The response rate to the first wave (February 1996) was slightly over half (53.8 percent), and of this group, almost three-quarters responded to the postelection wave. Once again the four-year gap between surveys (i.e., between 1996 and 2000) reduced the response rate—to 63.3 percent in 2000.

CONTENT ANALYSIS

For party platforms of 1992, each section (or subsection) was coded according to its length in pages and issue focus, and topics were combined into general categories. The combined pages for each topic were then divided by the total number of pages in the document, to yield percentage distributions across categories. Platforms were coded independently by two coders, and where disagreements occurred (in about 5 percent of the cases), they were resolved by the coders.

For the Contract with America and the Perot checklist from *United We Stand America,* we counted the number of proposals that dealt with each issue focus

TABLE A.4.   Response Rates for Party Contributors

Wave	Surveys Sent Out	Surveys Returned	Response Rate (%)	Response Rate as Percentage of Original Number of Surveys Sent Out (Response rate as percentage of original number of respondents appears in parentheses.)
RNC 1996a (February 1996)	1,991	1,071	53.8	52.3 (100)
RNC 1996b (postelection)	1,071	789	73.7	39.6 (73.7)
RNC 2000 (postelection)	780	494	63.3	24.8 (46.2)
DNC 1996a (Feburary 1996)	950	435	45.8	45.8 (100.0)
DNC 1996b panel (postelection)	435	307	70.6	32.3 (70.6)
DNC 1996b new sample (those who received only the postelection survey)	850	359	42.2	
DNC 2000 (combined)	653	419	64.1	23.2 (53.9)
Reform Party contributors, 1996b (survey sent out in February 1997)	2,422	1,470	60.7	60.7 (100.0)
Reform Party contributors, 2000 (postelection)	1,220	714	58.5	35.5 (58.5)

Note: Preapproach mailings were sent "address correction requested" to respondents eligible to receive a survey. Some of these were returned indicating that individuals had moved with no forwarding address or that individuals were deceased. We did not send these individuals our surveys.

In 2000, we selected a subsample of 1,220 Reform Party contributors to receive our mailings.

and took these as a percentage of all proposals. Sections were coded independently by coders and were then reconciled in cases where there were differences.

The Buchanan brochures chosen to represent the 1992 and 1996 campaigns were selected by the Web site http://www.4President.org because "they represented a generic brochure that was probably the most common one used for the campaign."[3] Each proposal in these brochures was coded according to its policy area.

CONGRESSIONAL VOTE INDICES USED IN CHAPTER 10

The following votes were used to construct the indices in chapter 10 in the analysis of congressional voting. In the case of the complete Perot issue index (which included all of the following votes), we counted an affirmative vote as 1 and a negative vote as 0. We then took the mean for all representatives on Perot votes, provided that votes were cast on at least seven of the fourteen roll calls. We also created a separate term limits index for the 104th Congress. Once again we took the mean as previously described, but this time we required that a member vote on at least one of the two issues, although virtually no one was excluded by this procedure.

---

3. Authors' personal email correspondence with Mike Dec of 4President.org, June 25, 2004.

Term Limits Votes

HJR 73   104TH CONGRESS
Joint resolution proposing an amendment to the Constitution of the United States with respect to the number of terms of office of members of the Senate and the House of Representatives.

HJR 73A   104TH CONGRESS   PETERSON AMENDMENT
Substitute that sought to make term limits retroactive (in order to take into consideration service occurring before the amendment), to limit lifetime service of the members of the House to six terms (twelve years) and of members of the Senate to two terms (twelve years), and to protect state laws limiting congressional terms of service if the state laws are shorter.

HJR 2   105TH CONGRESS
Joint resolution proposing an amendment to the Constitution of the United States with respect to the number of terms of office of members of the Senate and the House of Representatives.

HJR 2A   105TH CONGRESS   SCOTT AMENDMENT
Amendment that sought to limit the election of House members to six two-year terms and of Senators to two six-year terms, to provide that no person who has served in the House for more than one year shall be eligible for election more than five times and that no person who has served in the Senate more than three years shall be eligible for election more than once, and to allow any state to enact shorter term limits.

HJR 2B   105TH CONGRESS   BLUNT AMENDMENT
Amendment that sought to limit service of House Members to three two-year terms and of Senators to two six-year terms, with the provision that upon ratification, incumbents and others who have served in the House are limited to two additional terms and those who have served in the Senate are limited to one additional term, and with the allowance that any state may enact longer and shorter term limits by state constitutional amendment. This amendment was identical to the ballot initiative approved by the voters of Missouri.

HJR 2C   105TH CONGRESS   FOWLER AMENDMENT
Amendment that sought to limit service of House members to four consecutive two-year terms and of senators to two consecutive six-year terms, not counting any term that began before the adoption of the amendment.

Balanced Budget Votes

HR 2003   105TH CONGRESS
Bill to reform the budget process and enforce the Bipartisan Balanced Budget Agreement of 1997.

HCR 84   105TH CONGRESS   DOOLITTLE AMENDMENT
Amendment in the nature of a substitute that sought to achieve a balanced budget and reduce nondefense discretionary spending, to provide additional tax

cuts, and to allow a point of order against any concurrent resolution on the budget or against any measure that would cause total outlays to exceed total receipts in fiscal year 2002 and beyond.

United Nations Votes

HR 1757   105TH CONGRESS   PAUL AMENDMENT
Amendment that sought to withdraw the United States from the United Nations upon enactment; to terminate peacekeeping operations and U.S. contributions to the United Nations; to withdraw UN presence in facilities of the U.S. government; and to repeal diplomatic immunity for UN employees. The amendment also sought to repeal the United Nations Participation Act; the United Nations Headquarters Agreement; the United Nations Educational, Scientific, and Cultural Organization; and the United Nations Environment Program Participation Act.

HR 2415   106TH CONGRESS   PAUL AMENDMENT
Amendment that sought to eliminate the authorization of funding for UN programs.

Bosnia Votes

HR 2770   104TH CONGRESS
Proposal to prohibit federal funds from being used for the deployment on the ground of U.S. armed forces in the Republic of Bosnia and Herzegovina as part of any peacekeeping operation or as part of any implementation force.

HCR 82   106TH CONGRESS
Resolution to direct the president, pursuant to Section 5(c) of the War Powers Resolution, to remove U.S. armed forces from their positions in connection with the present operations against the Federal Republic of Yugoslavia.

HR 1401   106TH CONGRESS   SKELTON AMENDMENT
Amendment to strike section 1006(a) of HR 1401, which would prohibit any funding for combat or peacekeeping operations in the Federal Republic of Yugoslavia.

APPENDIX B

Statistical Analysis

The multivariate analysis for this book has been presented almost exclusively in graphic form, representing the relationships of interest in figures, without the statistical details scholars and specialists may wish to see. This appendix provides those details for each figure in the text that is based on multivariate statistical analysis.

Almost all of the analysis is based on ordinary least squares (OLS) regression or on logistic regression, when the dependent variable is dichotomous. OLS assumptions are reasonably well satisfied in the analysis of the survey data when campaign activism is the dependent variable, because the activism measure is a count of a number of items and because it is a relative measure of major-party activism subtracted from Perot activism. The resulting variable is pseudocontinuous and approximately normally distributed, with a large number of categories. Comparison of OLS with ordered probit and logit analyses provides results consistent with those we obtain from OLS, which we favor because of ease of interpretation and presentation. We describe cases where OLS assumptions are especially problematic and where more appropriate techniques lead to modified substantive conclusions. Most of our OLS and logistic regression results are displayed in figures (although the statistical tables appear in this appendix). When we examine the impact of a particular independent variable on a dependent variable in the figures, we generally set each of the other independent variables at the mean (except in the case of dummy variables).

TABLE B.1. Regression for Candidate Evaluations Test of Push-Pull Model: Difference between Activity for Major-Party Candidates and Perot in 1992[a]

Independent Variable	b (standard errors in parentheses)
Evaluation of Perot	1.293***
	(0.111)
Evaluation of **M1**	−.738***
	(0.171)
Difference in evaluation of major-party candidates	−0.324**
	(0.150)
Democratic identifier	−1.538***
	(0.279)
Republican identifier	−0.384
	(0.266)
Constant	2.085***
	(0.315)
Adjusted R^2	0.308
Standard error of the estimate	2.596
F	66.592***
N	739

[a]This table provides the statistical model behind figure 5.5.

$*p < 0.10$ $**p < 0.05$ $***p < 0.01$

TABLE B.2. Regression for Issue Components of Push-Pull Model Components: Difference between Activity for Major-Party Candidate and Perot in 1992[a]

Independent Variable	b (standard errors in parentheses)	Standardized Coefficient
Perot issue most important	0.517**	0.083
	(0.214)	
Difference between major candidates on liberal-conservative issues	−0.129	−0.035
	(0.124)	
Difference between candidates (**M1** and **M2**) on Perot issues	−0.445**	−0.073
	(0.204)	
Strong issue commitment on liberal-conservative issues, 1992	−0.118	−0.059
	(0.072)	
Strong support for Perot issues, 1992	0.362***	0.175
	(0.076)	
Democratic identification dummy	−2.174**	−0.338
	(0.279)	
Republican identification dummy	−0.840**	−0.133
	(0.273)	
Constant	2.491**	
	(0.325)	
Adjusted R^2	0.134	
Standard error of the estimate	2.896	
F	19.701***	
N	850	

[a]This table provides the statistical model behind figure 5.6.

$*p < .10$ $**p < .05$ $***p < .01$

TABLE B.3. **Regression for Partial Effects of Push-Pull Model Components: Difference between Activity for Major-Party Candidate and Perot in 1992**[a]

Independent Variables	b (standard errors in parentheses)	Standardized Coefficient
Activity for major-party candidates, 1988	−0.159★★★	−0.096
	(0.055)	
Number of group memberships	0.289★★★	0.095
	(0.101)	
Contact with Perot campaign	2.603★★★	0.180
	(0.476)	
Alienation from politics as usual	0.247★★	0.080
	(0.106)	
Perot issue most important	0.580★★★	0.091
	(0.211)	
Expected percentage of vote Perot will get in November	0.034★★★	0.148
	(0.008)	
Evaluation of Perot minus evaluation of preferred major-party candidate	0.822★★★	0.322
	(0.105)	
Proximity to Perot minus proximity to preferred major-party candidate	0.202★	0.062
	(0.120)	
Evaluation of national economy over last 12 months	−0.005	−0.002
	(0.111)	
Democratic identification dummy	−1.049★★★	−0.160
	(0.299)	
Republican identification dummy	0.141	0.022
	(0.289)	
Constant	−0.063	
	(0.421)	
Adjusted R^2	0.373	
Standard error of the estimate	2.510	
F	34.314★★★	
N	617	

[a]This table provides the statistical model behind figure 5.8 (campaign activism dependent).

★$p < .10$ ★★$p < .05$ ★★★$p < .01$

TABLE B.4. Regression of Expected Perot Vote on Predictors[a]

Independent Variable	b (standard errors in parentheses)	Standardized Coefficient
Activity for major-party candidates, 1988	0.001 (0.273)	0.000
Number of group memberships	−0.674 (0.500)	−0.050
Contact with Perot campaign	0.942 (2.368)	0.015
Alienation from politics as usual	1.560★★★ (0.525)	0.115
Perot issue most important	−1.534 (1.048)	−0.055
Evaluation of Perot minus evaluation of preferred major-party candidate	4.465★★★ (0.493)	0.400
Proximity to Perot minus proximity to preferred major-party candidate	−0.366 (0.596)	−0.026
Evaluation of the economy	−0.859 (0.554)	−0.062
Democratic identification dummy	−1.855 (1.486)	−0.064
Republican identification dummy	−2.937★★ (1.432)	−0.105
Constant	16.138★★★ (2.813)	
Adjusted R^2	0.189	
Standard error of the estimate	12.499	
F	15.317★★★	
N	617	

[a]This table provides the statistical model behind figure 5.8 (Perot's electoral prospects dependent).
★$p < .10$ ★★$p < .05$ ★★★$p < .01$

TABLE B.5. **Regression for Difference in Evaluation of Perot versus Preferred Major-Party Candidate (M1)**[a]

Independent Variable	b (standard errors in parentheses)	Standardized Coefficient
Activity for major-party candidates, 1988	−0.023	−0.035
	(0.022)	
Number of group memberships	0.005	0.004
	(0.041)	
Contact with Perot campaign	0.864***	0.152
	(0.192)	
Alienation from politics as usual	0.138***	0.113
	(0.043)	
Perot issue most important	0.167*	0.067
	(0.086)	
Proximity to Perot minus proximity to preferred major-party candidate	0.458***	0.359
	(0.045)	
Evaluation of economy over last year	0.189***	0.152
	(0.045)	
Democratic identification dummy	−0.604**	−0.235
	(0.120)	
Republican identification dummy	−0.359***	−0.143
	(0.117)	
Constant	−0.146	
	(0.232)	
Adjusted R^2	0.313	
Standard error of the estimate	1.030	
F	32.146***	
N	617	

[a]This table provides the statistical model behind figure 5.8 (candidate evaluation dependent).

*$p < .10$ **$p < .05$ ***$p < .01$

TABLE B.6. Regression for Difference in Proximity to Perot versus Preferred Major-Party Candidate (M1)[a]

Independent Variable	b (standard errors in parentheses)	Standardized Coefficient
Activity for major-party candidates, 1988	−0.038* (0.020)	−0.074
Number of group memberships	0.014 (0.037)	0.015
Contact with Perot campaign	−0.185 (0.171)	−0.041
Alienation from politics as usual	0.132*** (0.038)	0.139
Perot issue most important	0.168 (0.077)	0.086
Evaluation of economy over last year	0.118*** (0.040)	0.121
Democratic identification dummy	−0.574*** (0.105)	−0.284
Republican identification dummy	−0.249** (0.104)	−0.126
Constant	−0.303 (0.206)	
Adjusted R^2	0.109	
Standard error of the estimate	0.920	
F	10.468***	
N	617	

[a]This table provides the statistical model behind figure 5.8 (issue preferences dependent).

*$p < .10$ **$p < .05$ ***$p < .01$

TABLE B.7. Regression for Testing Predisposition Explanation of Change in Perot Activity, 1992–96[a]

Independent Variable	b (standard errors in parentheses)	Standardized Coefficient
Democratic identification dummy	−0.095	−0.066
	(0.108)	
Republican identification dummy	−0.101	−0.071
	(0.102)	
Contact with Perot campaign, 1992	0.156	0.055
	(0.158)	
Activity for Perot-Stockdale, 1992	0.117★★★	0.220
	(0.041)	
Spring activity for Perot, 1992	0.023	0.047
	(0.636)	
Strong support for Perot issues, 1992	0.079★	0.101
	(0.046)	
Evaluation of Perot, 1992	0.063	0.087
	(0.042)	
Evaluation of preferred major-party candidate, 1992	−0.050	−0.071
	(0.042)	
Strong views on traditional liberal-conservative issues	−0.037	−0.060
	(0.036)	
Evaluation of economy over last 12 months, 1992	0.058	0.080
	(0.041)	
Constant	−0.062	
	(0.154)	
Adjusted R^2	0.110	
Standard error of the estimate	0.661	
F	4.936	
N	320	

[a]This table provides the statistical model behind the predispositions-only explanation for change, discussed in the context of figure 6.6.

★$p < .10$ ★★$p < .05$ ★★★$p < .01$

TABLE B.8. Regression for Testing the Candidate and Issue Change Explanation of Perot Activity Change, 1992–96[a]

Independent Variable	b (standard errors in parentheses)	Standardized Coefficient	Mean for Change Variable
Democratic identification dummy	0.109	0.076	
	(0.099)		
Republican identification dummy	0.035	0.024	
	(0.091)		
Contact with Perot campaign, 1992	0.189	0.067	
	(0.139)		
Activity for Perot-Stockdale, 1992	0.073**	0.138	
	(0.037)		
Spring activity for Perot, 1992	0.005	0.010	
	(0.032)		
Strong support for Perot issues, 1992	0.115*	0.148	
	(0.048)		
Evaluation of Perot, 1992	0.085**	0.117	
	(0.038)		
Evaluation of preferred major-party candidate, 1992	−0.081*	−0.115	
	(0.043)		
Strong views on traditional liberal-conservative issues	−0.020	−0.033	
	(0.037)		
Evaluation of economy over last 12 months, 1992	−0.034	−0.047	
	(0.056)		
Contact with Reform Party, 1996	0.379***	0.248	
	(0.076)		
Change in strong support for Perot issues, 1992–96	0.142***	0.170	−0.144
	(0.047)		
Change in level of evaluation for preferred major-party candidate, 1992–96	−0.118***	−0.148	0.245
	(0.043)		
Change in strong views on traditional liberal-conservative issues	0.016	0.028	0.169
	(0.032)		
Change in evaluation of the economy, 1992–96	−0.099**	−0.184	0.944
	(0.045)		
Change in evaluation of Perot, 1992–96	0.094***	0.246	−0.944
	(0.019)		
Constant	0.172		
	(0.197)		
Adjusted R^2	0.314		
Standard error of the estimate	0.580		
F	10.11***		
N	320		

[a]Because of the skewed dependent variable, which is a count of activities, we replicated this analysis employing negative binomial regression. The results are consistent with one exception: the effect of change in strong support for Perot issues, which is significant in the OLS results, is not significant in the same model using negative binomial regression. Further exploration indicates that there is an effect of change in commitment to Perot issues, but it is indirect through changed evaluations of Perot, rather than the direct effect in the OLS results. This table provides the analysis in support of figures 6.6 and 6.7.

*$p < .10$ **$p < .05$ ***$p < .01$

TABLE B.9. Level of Contact by Republican House Campaigns by 1992 Perot Activity[a]

Independent Variable	b (standard errors in parentheses)	Mean
Campaign activity for Perot, 1992	0.041★★★	2.623
	(0.011)	
Republican campaign activity, 1988	−0.004	0.908
	(0.019)	
Republican general election activity, 1992	0.044	0.565
	(0.028)	
Republican nomination campaign activity, 1992	0.060	0.276
	(0.050)	
Party identification, 1992	0.065★★★	0.210
	(0.019)	
Contact by Democratic House candidate, 1994	0.499★★★	0.710
	(0.042)	
Degree of preference for Democratic House candidate, 1994	−0.046★★	−0.444
	(0.018)	
Constant	0.278★★★	
	(0.052)	
Adjusted R^2	0.318	
Standard error of estimate	0.578	
F	29.90★★★	
N	435	

[a]This table provides the statistical model behind figure 7.3.

★$p < .10$ ★★$p < .05$ ★★★$p < .01$

TABLE B.10. Logistic Regression Predicting Probability That an Experienced Nonincumbent Candidate Ran in 1994 by 1992 Perot Vote in District[a]

Independent Variable	Emergence of Quality Republican Challenger in Districts with No Republican Incumbent		Emergence of Quality Democratic Challenger in Districts with No Democratic Incumbent	
	b (standard errors in parentheses)	Mean	b (standard errors in parentheses)	Mean
Percentage of two-party vote for Democratic candidate, 1992	0.0004 (0.020)	64.265	0.054* (0.031)	39.533
Perot percentage of three-party vote, 1992	0.080** (0.038)	17.549	−0.014 (0.052)	20.350
Bush percentage in 1992 (three-party vote)	0.029 (0.057)	33.890	0.037 (0.074)	42.233
Democratic open seat	0.965** (0.455)	0.114	0.642 (0.678)	0.150
Republican open seat	0.322 (0.733)	0.077	1.964*** (0.577)	0.102
Dukakis percentage of two-party vote, 1988	−0.034 (0.045)	51.177	0.126** (0.059)	39.602
Quality of party's candidate in previous election	0.946 (0.307)	1.348	0.475 (0.358)	1.592
Constant	−3.839 (4.935)		−11.061*** (6.222)	
−2 log likelihood	225.061		155.476	
Overall percentage correct	78.8%		82.0%	
N	273		206	

[a]This table provides the statistical model behind figure 7.4.

*$p < .10$ **$p < .05$ ***$p < .01$

TABLE B.11. Regression of 1994 Republican Party Expenditures in Districts Held by Democrats[a]

Independent Variable	b (standard errors in parentheses)	Mean
Perot percentage of three-party vote, 1992	906.079*** (344.722)	
Bush percentage in 1992 (three-party vote)	594.904** (261.452)	34.20
Open seat	14,320.343*** (5,843.395)	0.14
Marginal seat	22,290.211*** (5,700.042)	0.37
Percentage of two-party vote for Republican House candidate, 1992	488.083* (251.568)	34.67
Constant	−29,829.045*** (10,070.246)	
Adjusted R^2	0.350	
Standard error of the estimate	29,512.074	
F	25.415***	
N	228	

[a]This table provides the statistical model behind figure 7.5.

*$p < .10$ **$p < .05$ ***$p < .01$

TABLE B.12. OLS Regression of 1994 Republican District Vote on 1992 Perot Vote and Logistic Regression of Republicans' Chances of Winning Democratic-Held Marginal Seats[a]

Independent Variable	Republican Vote Share in Seat Held by Democrats before 1994 Election b (standard errors in parentheses)	Probability of Republican Winning Seat Held by Democrats before 1994 Election b (standard errors in parentheses)
Percentage of two-party vote for Democratic candidate, 1992	−0.052 (0.198)	−0.096 (0.138)
Bush percentage in 1992 (three-party vote)	0.270 (0.187)	0.285** (0.133)
Dukakis percentage of two-party vote, 1988	−0.192 (0.149)	0.023 (0.099)
Perot percentage of three-party vote (1992)	0.309** (0.123)	0.194** (0.091)
No Republican candidate in 1994	−31.111*** (4.186)	−12.077 (28,275.21)
Experienced Democratic House candidate	2.970 (2.978)	1.511 (1.830)
Experienced Republican House candidate	3.576*** (1.267)	0.465 (0.721)
Democratic incumbent ran, 1994	−73.044** (34.183)	−64.510* (39.197)
Natural log of nonincumbent Republican expenditures	2.625*** (0.580)	1.235** (0.530)
Natural log of nonincumbent Democratic expenditures	−3.385 (2.341)	−3.756 (2.921)
Natural log of incumbent Democratic expenditures	3.534 (2.761)	4.866 (3.041)
Combined congressional quarterly presidential support, 1993–94	−0.068 (0.090)	0.018 (0.064)
Presidential support × Democratic incumbent running	0.144 (0.102)	−0.005 (0.069)
South dummy	0.794 (1.412)	−0.035 (0.839)
Constant	66.760* (35.450)	20.052 (36.462)
Adjusted R^2	0.788	
Standard error of the estimate	4.672	
−2 log likelihood		71.893
Overall percentage correct		80.900
F	24.366***	
N	89	89

[a]This table provides the statistical model behind figure 8.4.
$*p < .10$ $**p < .05$ $***p < .01$

TABLE B.13.   Regression for Partial Effects of 1992 Perot Vote on 1996 and 2000 Presidential Election Vote Share[a]

Independent Variable	Effect on 1996 Dole Vote Share	Effect on 2000 Bush Vote Share
	b (standard errors in parentheses)	b (standard errors in parentheses)
Percentage voting for Bush in 1988	0.098	0.122
	(0.134)	(0.189)
Percentage voting for Bush in 1992	1.209★★★	1.369★★★
	(0.160)	(0.226)
South dummy	1.362	3.056
	(1.430)	(2.023)
Percentage voting for Perot 1992	0.555★★★	0.867★★★
	(0.122)	(0.173)
District of Columbia dummy	15.628★★★	17.453★★
	(5.303)	(7.503)
Constant	−21.079★★★	−26.380★★★
	(5.464)	(7.732)
Adjusted R^2	0.837	0.795
Standard error of the estimate	3.344	4.732
F	52.396★★★	39.799★★★
N	51	51

[a]This table provides the statistical model behind figure 8.6.

★$p < .10$ ★★$p < .05$ ★★★$p < .01$

TABLE B.14.   Logistic Regression of 1996 and 2000 Republican Presidential State Wins[a]

Independent Variable	Dole, 1996	Bush, 2000
	Coefficient (standard errors in parentheses)	Coefficient (standard errors in parentheses)
Bush percentage, 1988	−0.334	0.084
	(0.209)	(0.160)
Bush percentage, 1992 (three-party vote)	1.106★★★	0.745★★
	(0.385)	(0.362)
Perot percentage of three-party vote, 1992	0.772★★	0.466★
	(0.316)	(0.244)
South dummy	3.363	13.861
	(2.224)	(51.123)
District of Columbia dummy	25.229	20.744
	(61.378)	(271.075)
Constant	−42.043★★★	−41.969★★★
	(13.562)	(15.444)
−2 log likelihood	20.845	18.551
Percentage correctly predicted	90.200	96.100
N	51	51

[a]This table provides the statistical model behind figure 8.7.

★$p < .10$ ★★$p < .05$ ★★★$p < .01$

TABLE B.15. Regression of 1994 Republican House Activity on Activism for Perot, 1992[a]

Independent Variable	b (standard errors in parentheses)	Mean
1988 Republican campaign activity	0.043	0.908
	(0.026)	
1992 Republican general election activity	0.090**	0.566
	(0.039)	
1992 Republican nomination activity	0.107	0.276
	(0.072)	
Activity for Perot, 1992	0.049***	2.623
	(0.016)	
Party identification, 1992	0.067**	0.207
	(0.028)	
Degree of preference for Democratic House candidate	−0.156***	−0.444
	(0.025)	
Constant	0.282***	
	(0.061)	
Adjusted R^2	0.283	
Standard error of estimate	0.822	
F	29.51***	
N	435	

[a]This table provides the statistical model behind figure 9.2.

*$p < .10$ **$p < .05$ ***$p < .01$

TABLE B.16. Spillover Effect of 1992 Perot Activism on Activity in 1994 Republican House Campaigns by Contact from Republican Campaign[a]

Independent Variable	b (standard errors in parentheses)	Mean
1988 Republican campaign activity	0.041	0.908
	(0.026)	
1992 Republican general election activity	0.080**	0.566
	(0.039)	
1992 Republican nomination activity	0.099	0.276
	(0.070)	
Activity for Perot, 1992	−0.031	2.623
	(0.029)	
Party identification, 1992	0.062**	0.207
	(0.027)	
Level of Republican contact, 1994	0.012	0.811
	(0.085)	
Degree of preference for Democratic House candidate	−0.152***	−0.444
	(0.025)	
Interaction of Perot activity and Republican contact	0.070***	2.453
	(0.023)	
Constant	0.325***	
	(0.089)	
Adjusted R^2	0.312	
Standard error of estimate	0.8051	
F	25.65	
N	435	

[a]This table provides the statistical model behind figure 9.3.

*$p < .10$ **$p < .05$ ***$p < .01$

TABLE B.17.   Republican Party Congressional Campaign Activity by Perot Activity (1994–2000)[a]

Independent Variable	1996 Coefficient	1996 Mean	1998 Coefficient	1998 Mean	2000 Coefficient	2000 Mean
1988 Republican campaign activity	0.024 (0.030)	0.918	0.018 (0.025)	0.939	0.055 (0.018)	0.922
1992 Republican general election activity	0.071** (0.034)	0.679	0.015 (0.039)	0.532	0.038 (0.027)	0.517
1992 Republican nomination activity	−0.047 (0.071)	0.279	0.307*** (0.092)	0.183	0.037 (0.063)	0.187
Activity for Perot, 1992	0.035** (0.017)	2.564	0.038** (0.016)	2.525	0.029*** (0.011)	2.561
Party identification, 1992	0.038 (0.027)	0.136	0.073*** (0.024)	0.058	0.010 (0.017)	0.013
Preference for Democratic House candidate	0.088*** (0.018)	0.743	n.a.[b]	n.a.	−0.020 (0.008)	−0.617
Perot-Choate activity, 1996	−0.084 (0.047)	0.354	n.a.	n.a.	n.a.	n.a.
Constant	0.124** (0.062)		0.156*** (0.057)		−0.017 (0.040)	
Adjusted R^2	0.201		0.156		0.185	
Standard error of estimate	0.647		0.630		0.391	
F	11.019***		11.222***		9.659***	
N	280		278		230	

[a]This table provides the statistical model behind figure 9.4.

[b]The abbreviation n.a. indicates not applicable.

*$p < .10$ **$p < .05$ ***$p < .01$

TABLE B.18. "Value-Added" Spillover from 1992 Perot Activism to 2000 Republican House Campaign Activism by Contact from 2000 Republican Campaigns[a]

Independent Variable	b (standard errors in parentheses)	Mean
1988 Republican campaign activity	0.029* (0.017)	0.923
1992 Republican general election activity	0.045* (0.026)	0.520
1992 Republican nomination activity	0.054 (0.059)	0.188
Activity for Perot, 1992	−0.002 (0.012)	2.57
Party identification, 1992	−0.004 (0.016)	0.017
Level of Republican contact, 2000	−0.013 (0.046)	0.546
Degree of preference for Democratic House Candidate	−0.014* (0.008)	−0.620
Interaction of Perot activity and Republican contact	0.056*** (0.013)	1.463
Republican House activity 1994	0.060* (0.033)	0.489
Constant	−0.020 (0.045)	
Adjusted R^2	0.300	
Standard error of estimate	0.363	
F	11.833	
N	229	

[a]This table provides the statistical model behind figure 9.5.

*$p < .10$ **$p < .05$ ***$p < .01$

TABLE B.19. Democratic Party Congressional Campaign Activity by Perot Activity (1994–2000)[a]

Independent Variable	1994 Coefficient	1994 Mean	1996 Coefficient	1996 Mean	1998 Coefficient	1998 Mean
1988 Democratic campaign activity	0.095★★★ (0.024)	0.658	−0.013 (0.027)	0.689	0.038 (0.025)	0.662
1992 Democratic general election activity	0.079★★★ (0.024)	0.701	0.139★★★ (0.027)	0.714	0.098★★★ (0.025)	0.748
1992 Democratic nomination activity	0.139★★★ (0.040)	0.487	0.021 (0.040)	0.529	0.073★ (0.040)	0.511
Activity for Perot, 1992	0.018 (0.012)	2.623	−0.001 (0.017)	2.564	−0.008 (0.012)	2.525
Party identification, 1992	−0.048★★ (0.021)	0.207	0.012 (0.023)	0.136	−0.013 (0.019)	0.058
Preference for Democratic House candidate	0.079★★★ (0.019)	−0.444	0.079★★★ (0.015)	−0.743	n.a.	n.a.
Perot-Choate activity, 1996	n.a.[b]	n.a.	−0.084 (0.047)	0.354	n.a.	n.a.
Constant	0.132★★★ (0.049)		0.157★★★ (0.054)		0.030 (0.046)	
Adjusted R^2	0.349		0.261		0.200	
Standard error of estimate	0.608		0.540		0.493	
F	39.848		15.075★★★		14.882★★★	
N	435		280		278	

[a]This table provides the statistical model behind figure 9.6.
[b]The abbreviation n.a. indicates not applicable.
★$p < .10$ ★★$p < .05$ ★★★$p < .01$

TABLE B.20. Perot Activity Spillover into Major Party Presidential Nomination Campaigns: Pat Buchanan (1996) and John McCain (2000)[a]

Independent Variable	Pat Buchanan, 1996		John McCain, 2000	
	b (standard errors in parentheses)	Mean	b (standard errors in parentheses)	Mean
1988 Republican campaign activity	−0.007 (0.014)	0.872	−0.021 (0.026)	0.976
1992 Republican general election activity	−0.017 (0.019)	0.614	0.062 (0.039)	0.566
1992 Republican nomination activity	0.134★★★ (0.043)	0.234	0.052 (0.088)	0.195
Activity for Perot, 1992	0.016★ (0.008)	2.644	0.032★★ (0.015)	2.570
Party identification, 1992	−0.021 (0.013)	0.064	−0.014 (0.024)	0.092
Degree of preference for Democratic House candidate	0.063★★★ (0.011)	−0.587	−0.173★★★ (0.029)	2.845
Constant	0.074★★ (0.034)		0.655★★★ (0.102)	
Adjusted R^2	0.127		0.142	
Standard error of estimate	0.377		0.591	
F	8.933		7.881	
N	329		251	

[a]This table provides the statistical model behind figure 9.7. Most comparisons are from the 1992a wave, but comparisons involving campaign activism in the 1992 election use the 1992b wave as the basis of comparison and have a smaller base sample because of nonresponse in the 1992b wave that we used to create the campaign activism scale.
★$p < .10$ ★★$p < .05$ ★★★$p < .01$

References

ঞ৶

Abramowitz, Alan I. 1995. "The End of the Democratic Era? 1994 and the Future of Congressional Election Research." *Political Research Quarterly* 48 (4): 873–89.

Abramowitz, Alan I., and Kyle L. Saunders. 1998. "Ideological Realignment in the U.S. Electorate." *Journal of Politics* 60 (August): 634–52.

Abramson, Paul R., John H. Aldrich, Philip Paolino, and David W. Rohde. 1995. "Third-Party and Independent Candidates in American Politics: Wallace, Anderson, and Perot." *Political Science Quarterly* 110 (3): 349–67.

———. 2000. "Challenges to the American Two-Party System: Evidence from the 1968, 1980, 1992, and 1996 Presidential Elections." *Political Research Quarterly* 53 (3): 495–522.

Abramson, Paul R., John H. Aldrich, and David W. Rohde. 1998. *Change and Continuity in the 1996 Elections.* Washington, DC: Congressional Quarterly Press.

Aldrich, John H. 1995. *Why Parties? The Origin and Transformation of Political Parties in America.* Chicago: University of Chicago Press.

Alvarez, R. Michael, and Jonathan Nagler. 1995. "Economics, Issues, and the Perot Candidacy: Voter Choice in the 1992 Presidential Election." *American Journal of Political Science* 39 (August): 714–44.

Asher, Herbert B., and Herbert F. Weisberg. 1978. "Voting Change in Congress: Some Dynamic Perspectives on an Evolutionary Process." *American Journal of Political Science* 22 (May): 391–425.

Atkeson, Lonna Rae, James A. McCann, Ronald B. Rapoport, and Walter J. Stone. 1996. "Citizens for Perot: Activists and Voters in the 1992 Presidential Campaign." In *Broken Contract? Changing Relationships between Citizens and the Government in the United States,* ed. S. C. Craig. Boulder: Westview Press.

Balz, Dan, and Ronald Brownstein. 1996. *Storming the Gates: Protest Politics and Republican Revival.* Boston: Little, Brown.

Barnes, James A. 1992. "Exit Polling '92: On the Perot Factor, and 'Who Votes?'" *Public Perspective* 3 (4): 19.

Barta, Carolyn. 1993. *Perot and His People.* Fort Worth: Summit Group.

Beck, Paul Allen. 1974. "Environment and Party: The Impact of Political and Demographic County Characteristics on Party Behavior." *American Political Science Review* 68 (December): 1229–44.

———. 1997. *Party Politics in America.* New York: Longman.

Berry, William D., and Mitchell S. Sanders. 2000. *Understanding Multivariate Research: A Primer for Beginning Social Scientists.* Boulder: Westview Press.

Bibby, John, and L. Sandy Maisel. 2003. *Two Parties—or More? The American Party System.* Boulder: Westview Press.

Black, Gordon S. 1972. "A Theory of Political Ambition: Career Choices and the Role of Structural Incentives." *American Political Science Review* 66 (March): 144–59.

Black, Gordon S., and Benjamin D. Black. 1994. *The Politics of American Discontent: How a New Party Can Make Democracy Work Again.* New York: John Wiley and Sons.

Black, Jerome H. 1978. "The Multicandidate Calculus of Voting: Applications to Canadian Federal Elections." *American Journal of Political Science* 22 (August): 609–38.

Bond, Jon R., Cary Covington, and Richard Fleisher. 1985. "Explaining Challenger Quality in Congressional Elections." *Journal of Politics* 47 (August): 510–29.

Brady, David W., Hohn F. Cogan, Brian J. Gaines, and Douglas Rivers. 1996. "The Perils of Presidential Support: How the Republicans Took the House in the 1994 Midterm Elections." *Political Behavior* 18 (4): 345–67.

Brady, David W., and Craig Volden. 1998. *Revolving Gridlock: Politics and Policy from Carter to Clinton.* Boulder: Westview Press.

Budge, Ian, and Richard I. Hofferbert. 1990. "Mandates and Policy Outputs: U.S. Party Platforms and Federal Expenditures." *American Political Science Review* 84 (March): 111–31.

Burnham, Walter Dean. 1970. *Critical Elections and the Mainsprings of American Politics.* New York: Norton.

Bush, George. 1999. *All the Best, George Bush: My Life in Letters and Other Writings.* New York: Scribner's.

Cain, Bruce. 1978. "Strategic Voting in Britain." *American Journal of Political Science* 22 (August): 639–55.

Cain, Bruce, John Ferejohn, and Morris Fiorina. 1987. *The Personal Vote: Constituency Service and Electoral Independence.* Cambridge: Harvard University Press.

Canfield, James Lewis. 1984. *A Case of Third Party Activism: The George Wallace Campaign Worker and the American Independent Party.* Lanham, MD: University Press of America.

Carmines, Edward G., and James A. Stimson. 1989. *Issue Evolution: Race and the Transformation of American Politics.* Princeton: Princeton University Press.

Carter, Dan T. 1991. *George Wallace, Richard Nixon, and the Transformation of American Politics.* Waco: Markham Press Fund.

Ceaser, James W., and Andrew Busch. 1993. *Upside Down and Inside Out: The 1992 Elections and American Politics.* Lanham, MD: Rowman and Littlefield.

Cox, Gary W., and Jonathan N. Katz. 2002. *Elbridge Gerry's Salamander: The Electoral Consequences of the Reapportionment Revolution.* Cambridge: Cambridge University Press.

Cox, Gary W., and Mathew D. McCubbins. 1993. *Legislative Leviathan: Party Government in the House.* Berkeley: University of California Press.

Downs, Anthony. 1957. *An Economic Theory of Democracy.* New York: Harper.

Eldersveld, Samuel J. 1956. Experimental Propaganda Techniques and Voting Behavior. *American Political Science Review* 50 (March): 154–65.

———. 1964. *Political Parties: A Behavioral Analysis.* Chicago: Rand McNally.

Fenno, Richard F. 1978. *Home Style: House Members in Their Districts.* Boston: Little, Brown.

Fiorina, Morris. 1980. "The Decline of Collective Responsibility in American Politics." *Daedalus* 109 (1): 25–45.

———. 1981. *Retrospective Voting in American National Elections.* New Haven: Yale University Press.

Fishel, Jeff. 1985. *Presidents and Promises.* Washington, DC: Congressional Quarterly Press.

Fowler, Linda, and Robert McClure. 1989. *Political Ambition: Who Decides to Run for Congress.* New Haven: Yale University Press.

Frankovic, Kathleen. 1993. "Public Opinion in the 1992 Campaign." In *The Election of 1992,* ed. G. Pomper. Chatham, NJ: Chatham House.

Gaddie, Ronald Keith, and Charles S. Bullock. 2000. *Elections to Open Seats in the U.S. House: Where the Action Is.* Lanham, MD: Rowman and Littlefield.

Gerber, Alan S., and Donald P. Green. 2000. "The Effects of Canvassing, Telephone Calls, and Direct Mail on Voter Turnout: A Field Experiment." *American Political Science Review* 94 (September): 653–63.

Germond, Jack, and Jules Witcover. 1981. *Blue Smoke and Mirrors: How Reagan Won and Why Carter Lost the Election of 1980.* New York: Viking.

Germond, Jack, and Jules Witcover. 1993. *Mad as Hell: Revolt at the Ballot Box, 1992.* New York: Warner Books.

Gillespie, J. David. 1993. *Politics at the Periphery: Third Parties in Two-Party America.* Columbia: University of South Carolina Press.

Gimpel, James G. 1996. *Legislating the Revolution: The Contract with America in Its First 100 Days.* Boston: Allyn and Bacon.

Gold, Howard J. 1995. "Third Party Voting in Presidential Elections: A Study of Perot, Anderson, and Wallace." *Political Research Quarterly* 48 (4): 775–94.

Goldman, Peter Louis, Thomas M. DeFrank, Mark Miller, Andrew Murr, and Tom Matthews. 1994. *Quest for the Presidency, 1992.* College Station: Texas A&M University Press.

Greenberg, Edward S., Leon Grunberg, and Kelley Daniel. 1996. "Industrial Work and Political Participation: Beyond 'Simple Spillover.'" *Political Research Quarterly* 49 (2): 305–30.

Grenzke, Janet M. 1989. "PACs and the Congressional Supermarket: The Currency is Complex." *American Journal of Political Science* 33 (February): 1–24.

Herrnson, Paul S. 1998. *Congressional Elections: Campaigning at Home and in Washington.* 2nd ed. Washington, DC: Congressional Quarterly Press.

Hershey, Marjorie Randon. 2005. *Party Politics in America.* 11th ed. New York: Longman.

Hofstadter, Richard. 1955. *The Age of Reform: From Bryan to FDR.* New York: Vintage Books.

Huckfeldt, Robert, and John Sprague. 1995. *Citizens, Politics, and Social Communication: Information and Influence in an Election Campaign.* New York: Cambridge University Press.

Jacobson, Gary C. 1989. "Strategic Politicians and the Dynamics of U.S. House Elections, 1946–1986." *American Political Science Review* 83 (September): 773–93.

————. 1996. "The 1994 House Elections in Perspective." In *Midterm: Elections of 1994 in Context,* ed. P. A. Klinkner. Boulder: Westview Press.

————. 2000. "Party Polarization in National Politics: The Electoral Connection." In *Polarized Politics: Congress and the President in a Partisan Era,* ed. J. R. Bond and R. Fleisher. Washington, DC: Congressional Quarterly Press.

————. 2004. *The Politics of Congressional Elections.* 6th ed. New York: Longman.

Jacobson, Gary C., and Samuel Kernell. 1983. *Strategy and Choice in Congressional Elections.* 2nd ed. New Haven: Yale University Press.

Johnson, Donald B., and James R. Gibson. 1974. "The Divisive Primary Revisited: Activists in Iowa." *American Political Science Review* 68 (March): 67–77.

Katz, Daniel, and Samuel J. Eldersveld. 1961. "The Impact of Local Party Activity upon the Electorate." *Public Opinion Quarterly* 25 (spring): 1–24.

Kazee, Thomas A. 1994. *Who Runs for Congress? Ambition, Context, and Candidate Emergence.* Washington, DC: Congressional Quarterly Press.

Kelley, Stanley, Jr., and Thad W. Mirer. 1974. "The Simple Act of Voting." *American Political Science Review* 68 (June): 572–91.

Kenney, Patrick J., and Tom W. Rice. 1987. "The Relationship between Divisive Primaries and General Election Outcomes." *American Journal of Political Science* 31 (February): 31–44.

Key, V. O., Jr. 1966. *The Responsible Electorate.* Cambridge: Harvard University Press.

Kirkpatrick, Jeane. 1975. "Representation in the American National Conventions: The Case of 1972." *British Journal of Political Science* 5 (3): 265–322.

Klinkner, Philip A. 1996. "Court and Country in American Politics: The Democratic Party and the 1994 Election." In *Midterm: Elections of 1994 in Context,* ed. P. A. Klinkner. Boulder: Westview Press.

Koch, Jeffrey. 1998. "The Perot Candidacy and Attitudes toward Government and Politics." *Political Research Quarterly* 51 (): 141–54.

————. 2001. Attitudes toward Government, Partisan Dispositions, and the Rise of Ross Perot. In *Ross for Boss,* ed. T. G. Jelen. Albany: State University of New York Press.

Krasno, Jonathan S. 1997. *Challengers, Competition, and Reelection: Comparing Senate and House Elections.* New Haven: Yale University Press.

Krehbiel, Keith. 1998. *Pivotal Politics: A Theory of U.S. Lawmaking.* Chicago: University of Chicago Press.

Lacy, Dean, and Barry C. Burden. 1999. "The Vote-Stealing and Turnout Effects of Ross Perot in the 1992 U.S. Presidential Election." *American Journal of Political Science* 43 (January): 233–55.

Lewis-Beck, Michael S. 1980. *Applied Regression: An Introduction.* Vol. 22, *Quantitative Applications in the Social Sciences.* Beverly Hills: Sage Publications.

Lowi, Theodore J. 1985. *The Personal President.* Ithaca: Cornell University Press.

Maestas, Cherie D., L. Sandy Maisel, and Walter J. Stone. 2005. "National party Efforts to Recruit State Legislators to Run for the U.S. House." *Legislative Studies Quarterly* 30 (2): 277–300.

Maisel, L. Sandy. 1999. *Parties and Elections in America.* Lanham, MD: Rowman and Littlefield.

Maisel, L. Sandy, and Walter J. Stone. 1997. "Determinants of Candidate Emergence in U.S. House Elections: An Exploratory Study." *Legislative Studies Quarterly* 22 (February): 79–96.

Mann, Thomas E., and Raymond E. Wolfinger. 1980. "Candidates and Parties in Congressional Elections." *American Political Science Review* 74 (September): 617–32.

Markus, Gregory B. 1988. "The Impact of Personal and National Economic Conditions on the Presidential Vote: A Pooled Cross-Sectional Analysis." *American Journal of Political Science* 32 (February): 137–54.

Mayhew, David. 1974. *Congress: The Electoral Connection.* New Haven: Yale University Press.

Mazmanian, Daniel A. 1974. *Third Parties in Presidential Elections.* Washington, DC: Brookings Institution.

McCann, James A., Randall W. Partin, Ronald B. Rapoport, and Walter J. Stone. 1996. "Presidential Nomination Campaign Participation and Party Mobilization: An Assessment of Spillover Effects." *American Journal of Political Science* 40 (August): 756–67.

McCann, James A., Ronald B. Rapoport, and Walter J. Stone. 1999. "Heeding the Call: An Assessment of Mobilization into Ross Perot's 1992 Presidential Campaign." *American Journal of Political Science* 43 (January): 1–28.

McClosky, Herbert, Paul J. Hoffman, and Rosemary O'Hara. 1960. "Issue Conflict and Consensus among Party Leaders and Followers." *American Political Science Review* 54 (September): 406–27.

Merrill, Samuel, III, and Bernard Groffman. 1999. *A Unified Theory of Voting: Directional and Proximity Spatial Models.* New York: Cambridge University Press.

Miller, Arthur H., Martin P. Wattenberg, and Oksana Malunchuk. 1986. "Schematic Assessments of Presidential Candidates." *American Political Science Review* 80 (June): 521–40.

Miller, Gary, and Norman Schofield. 2003. "Activists and Partisan Realignment in the United States." *American Political Science Review* 97 (June): 245–60.

Miller, Warren E., and M. Kent Jennings. 1986. *Parties in Transition.* New York: Russell Sage.

Ornstein, Norman J., Thomas E. Mann, and Michael J. Malbin. 2002. *Vital Statistics on Congress, 2001–2002.* Washington, DC: American Enterprise Institute.

Page, Benjamin I., and Richard A. Brody. 1972. "Policy Voting and the Electoral Process: The Vietnam War Issue." *American Political Science Review* 66 (September): 979–95.

Pastor, Gregory S., Walter J. Stone, and Ronald B. Rapoport. 1999. "Candidate-Centered Sources of Party Change: The Case of Pat Robertson, 1968." *Journal of Politics* 61 (May): 423–44.

Perot, H. Ross. 1992. *United We Stand: How We Can Take Back Our Country.* 1st ed. New York: Hyperion.

Pitney, John J., Jr., and William F. Connelly Jr. 1996. "'Permanent Minority' No More: House Republicans in 1994." In *Midterm: Elections of 1994 in Context,* ed. P. A. Klinkner. Boulder: Westview Press.

Polsby, Nelson W. 1983. *The Consequences of Party Reform.* New York: Oxford University Press.

Pomper, Gerald M. 1973. *Elections in America.* New York: Dodd, Mead.

Poole, Keith T., and Howard Rosenthal. 1997. *Congress: A Political-Economic History of Roll Call Voting.* New York: Oxford University Press.

Poole, Keith T., and Howard Rosenthal. 2001. "D-Nominate after 10 Years: A Comparative Update to Congress: A Political-Economic History of Roll-Call Voting." *Legislative Studies Quarterly* 26 (1): 5–29.

Popkin, Samuel L. 1994. *The Reasoning Voter: Communication and Persuasion in Presidential Campaigns.* 2nd ed. Chicago: University of Chicago Press.

Posner, Gerald L. 1996. *Citizen Perot: His Life and Times.* New York: Random House.

Rabinowitz, George, and Stuart Elain Macdonald. 1989. "A Directional Theory of Issue Voting." *American Political Science Review* 83 (March): 93–121.

Rapoport, Ronald B., Alan Abramowitz, and John McGlennon, eds. 1986. *The Life of the Parties.* Lexington: University of Kentucky Press.

Rapoport, Ronald B., and Walter J. Stone. 1994. "A Model for Disaggregating Political Change." *Political Behavior* 16 (4): 505–32.

Riker, William H. 1976. "The Number of Political Parties: A Reexamination of Duverger's Law." *Comparative Politics* 9 (1): 93–106.

———. 1982. "The Two-Party System and Duverger's Law: An Essay on the History of Political Science." *American Political Science Review* 76 (December): 753–66.

Rohde, David W. 1991. *Parties and Leaders in the Post-Reform House.* Chicago: University of Chicago Press.

Rosenstone, Steven J., Roy L. Behr, and Edward H. Lazarus. 1996. *Third Parties in America: Citizen Response to Major Party Failure.* 2nd ed. Princeton: Princeton University Press.

Rosenstone, Steven J., and John Mark Hansen. 1993. *Mobilization, Participation, and Democracy in America.* New York: Macmillan.

Royer, Charles T. 1994. *Campaign for President: The Managers Look at '92.* Ed. C. T. Royer. Hollis, NH: Hollis Publishing.

Schattschneider, E. E. 1975. *The Semisovereign People: A Realist's View of Democracy in America.* Hinsdale, IL: Dryden Press.

Schlesinger, Joseph A. 1991. *Political Parties and the Winning of Office.* Ann Arbor: University of Michigan Press.

Sifry, Micah L. 2002. *Spoiling for a Fight: Third-Party Politics in America.* New York: Routledge.

Stanley, Harold W., Richard G. Niemi. 2001. *Vital Statistics on American Politics.* Washington, DC: Congressional Quarterly Press.

Stanley, Harold W., and Richard G. Niemi. 2004. *Vital Statistics on American Politics.* Washington, DC: Congressional Quarterly Press.

Stokes, Donald E. 1966. "Some Dynamic Elements of Contests for the Presidency." *American Political Science Review* 60 (March): 19–28.

Stone, Walter J. 1986. "The Carryover Effect in Presidential Elections." *American Political Science Review* 80 (March): 271–79.

Stone, Walter J., Lonna Rae Atkeson, and Ronald B. Rapoport. 1992. "Turning On or Turning Off? Mobilization and Demobilization Effects of Participation in Presidential Nomination Campaigns." *American Journal of Political Science* 36 (August): 665–91.

Stone, Walter J., L. Sandy Maisel, and Cherie D. Maestas. 2004. "Quality Counts: Extending the Strategic Politician Model of Incumbent Deterrence." *American Journal of Political Science* 48 (September): 479–95.

Stone, Walter J., and Ronald B. Rapoport. 1998. "A Candidate-Centered Perspective on Party Responsiveness: Nomination Activists and the Process of Party Change." In *The Parties Respond,* ed. L. S. Maisel. Boulder: Westview Press.

Stone, Walter J., Ronald B. Rapoport, and Lonna Rae Atkeson. 1995. "A Simulation Model of Presidential Nomination Choice." *American Journal of Political Science* 39 (1): 135–61.

Stone, Walter J., Ronald B. Rapoport, Patricia A. Jaramillo, and Lori M. Weber. 1999. "The Activist Base of the Reform Party in 1996: Problems and Prospects." In *The State of the Parties: The Changing Role of Contemporary American Parties,* ed. J. C. Green and D. M. Shea. Lanham, MD: Rowman and Littlefield.

Stone, Walter J., Ronald B. Rapoport, and Monique Schneider. 2004. "Party Members in a Three-Party Election: Major-Party and Reform Activism in the 1996 American Presidential Election." *Party Politics* 10 (4): 445–69.

Sundquist, James L. 1983. *Dynamics of the Party System.* Washington, DC: Brookings Institution.

Verba, Sidney, Kay Lehman Schlozman, and Henry E. Brady. 1995. *Voice and Equality: Civic Voluntarism in American Politics.* Cambridge: Harvard University Press.

Wattenberg, Martin P. 1991. *The Rise of Candidate-Centered Politics: Presidential Elections of the 1980s.* Cambridge: Harvard University Press.

———. 1996. *The Decline of American Political Parties, 1952–1994.* Cambridge: Harvard University Press.

Zaller, John, and Mark Hunt. 1994. "The Rise and Fall of Candidate Perot: Unmediated vs. Mediated Politics." Part 1. *Political Communication* 11 (October): 357–90.

———. 1995. "The Rise and Fall of Candidate Perot: Unmediated Vs. Mediated Politics." Part 2. *Political Communication* 12 (January): 97–123.

Index

Note: Page references to figures are indicated by italics.